D0836587

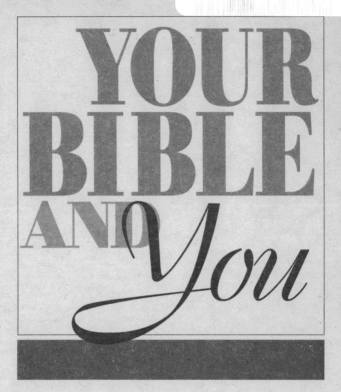

YOUR BIBLE AND *You*

Priceless Treasures in the
Holy Scriptures

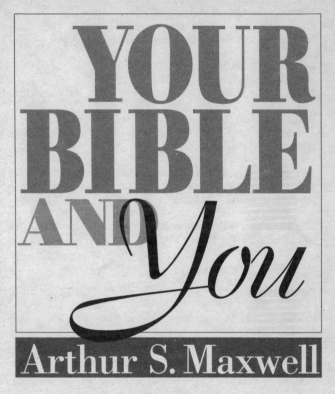

YOUR BIBLE AND *You*

Arthur S. Maxwell

Author
of *The Bible Story, Bedtime Stories,* and
How to Read the Bible.

REVIEW AND HERALD® PUBLISHING ASSOCIATION
HAGERSTOWN, MD 21740

Cover Design: Helcio Deslandes
Cover Photos by PhotoDisc
Typeset: 10.5/11.5 Garamond Book Condensed

The Bible texts in this book credited to Moffatt are from *The Bible: A New Translation,* by James Moffatt. Copyright 1954. Used by permission of Harper & Row, Publishers, Incorporated.

Bible texts credited to Phillips are from J. B. Phillips: *The New Testament in Modern English.* Revised Edition. © J. B. Phillips 1958, 1960, 1972. Used by permission of Macmillan Publishing Co., Inc.

Bible texts credited to RSV are from the Revised Standard Version of the Bible, copyrighted 1946, 1952 © 1971, 1973.

41st printing

OFFSET IN U.S.A.

ISBN 0-8280-1353-5

CONTENTS

PREFACE

Public-opinion polls have revealed that the average person's knowledge of the Bible is extremely limited. Few of those questioned could name a dozen of its leading characters. Fewer still could list its 66 books. Many had but the vaguest concept about its teachings. They could not distinguish between the books of the Old and the New Testaments and were completely at a loss to find a familiar text.

How is it with you and your Bible? Do you read it? Do you enjoy it?

Some people start out in earnest to read the Bible, only to give up after glancing at the first few chapters. Unable to find anything of gripping interest, or bored by some unfamiliar phraseology, they set it aside as if it were completely beyond their understanding.

There must be millions of Bibles lying around in Christian homes, unopened and unread, save possibly on special occasions such as weddings and funerals.

Yet, down through the centuries the Bible has proved itself to be a book of high spiritual potency. Many of the finest men and women known to history have drawn their inner strength from its pages. Time and again it has demonstrated a mysterious power to change lives, ennoble the spirit, enrich the mind, enlarge the vision, broaden the sympathies, and transform the desires. Great preachers have found it to be a treasure house of truth, while statesmen, teachers, and writers have never ceased to mine its literary riches.

Here, then, is a strange paradox. We have a book that everybody is willing to admit is the best, the greatest, and the most wonderful ever written; a book that has lasted longer than any other; a book that has done more good than any other; and yet one of the least read of all books published today.

What can be done to change this situation? How can people who possess this Book be lured, enticed, persuaded, to open and read it, and so discover for themselves the precious blessings stored within its pages?

To answer this question and meet this urgent need is the purpose of *Your Bible and You*. It is designed to help you realize what a priceless book your Bible really is, to show you how it is in many ways the most up-to-date book in your library, and to suggest how it may become an endless source of benefit and inspiration to you and your family.

It is, intentionally, a very personal volume, as a glance at the list of contents will reveal. Our aim has been to help you see what the Bible says about *our* God, *your* life, *your* home, *your* health, *your* problems, *your* future. We have followed this form of presentation so that you might see how much there is in the Bible for you.

Admittedly, this volume, despite its 256 pages, is but an introduction to the Bible. Many more pages would be needed to deal thoroughly with all the deep and wonderful themes the Holy Scriptures contain. But if it succeeds in leading you to explore further this fabulous mine of spiritual riches, it will not have been published in vain.

We would add that *Your Bible and You* has been designed as a friendly volume, warm with the love of God. It is not intended to be a profound theological treatise, weighed down with a multitude of quotations from ecclesiastical authorities. On the contrary, it is a simple setting forth of what the Bible has to say on certain vital subjects. It is not a series of arguments, but rather a fireside chat. It does not criticize or condemn anything or anybody, but seeks—very gently—to release the flood tide of divine wisdom and love forever pent up within the sacred pages of this Book of books.

ARTHUR S. MAXWELL

THE BOOK FOR
THE HOUR

BEYOND all question we are living in the most momentous period of history. It is a time of vast and rapid changes. Human thought and progress, which for millenniums advanced like some slow-moving glacier, have thawed into a thousand torrents of intense activity, plunging precipitously toward a frightening tomorrow.

"Great clocks of destiny are striking now," and with each thunderous clang some new epoch-making event occurs. Long pent-up hatreds burst forth in flaming revolt. Old empires totter and collapse. Science breaks through another barrier into the unknown.

This is *an age of revolution* in every phase of life. Everywhere there is ferment and turmoil as the 5.5 billion inhabitants of earth polarize around their self-appointed champions.

"The last half century has witnessed changes unprecedented both in their nature and their extent," says Cyril Garbett, formerly archbishop of York. "It is possible that within this brief period of time greater changes have taken place than in all the centuries between the coming of Christ and the middle of this last century"(*In an Age of Revolution*, p. 13).

It is also *an age of discovery and invention* without parallel. Swiftly we have moved from the steam age to the electric age; to the atomic age and the space age, the plastic age and the computer age.

Having conquered the last frontiers of earth, man is reaching for the stars. Already he has been to the moon. Spacecraft have probed Mars and Venus and peered closely at Neptune and Pluto. Night and day, at fantastic speeds, satellites circle the earth, by radio and television continuously reporting conditions in outer space.

The harnessing of the atom has put more power within man's reach than he has possessed since the dawn of time. So enormous are the sources of energy now available that they could turn the world into a paradise—or a shambles. Unfortunately, their primary use has been for the creation of weapons so destructive that a few dozen could destroy every major city in any country on which they might fall.

Computers have brought startling changes, and more are close at hand. Microchips have been developed that can perform almost 4 billion math problems per second, and the race is on to multiply that capacity several times! Insiders predict that laptops soon will do what mainframes used to!

In just the past few years, plastics have revolutionized the way we live. Even more astonishing has been the progress in health care. More than 3 million people in the United States live with artificial parts—pacemakers, heart valves, hips, knees, and finger joints. Within a decade, scientists predict, artificial livers and lungs will replace diseased tissue. Quickly following them will come prosthetic joints and bones that will function more smoothly than the ligaments and cartilage they replace. About all that won't be replaceable will be the brain *(U.S. News & World Report,* Nov. 12, 1990).

David Sarnoff, chairman of the Radio Corporation of America, has written, "Our laboratories are burgeoning with half-realized dreams that sound as fantastic as radio and television did when I was a boy. As Isaac Newton said, we are merely picking up pebbles on the beach while the great ocean of truth lies undiscovered before us" ("What I See Ahead," *Reader's Digest,* April 1957). His statement is even more true today than when he wrote it.

Tragically, despite these glowing prospects, we have entered also *an age of lawlessness* for which there is no precedent save the corruption that prevailed in the antediluvian world. It is seen not only in the mounting statistics of murder, rape, and robbery, but in the seemingly hopeless battle being waged by police and other public authorities against juvenile delinquency and illegal drugs. Crowded prisons and reformatories tell the same sad story, as do the daily reports of cruel, sadistic crimes that crowd the pages of our newspapers. Lying and perjury are so common that truth and honesty seem to have well-nigh vanished from the earth. In some lands contending factions have cast off all restraints and know no law but violence.

As a result we live in *an age of fear*. Never have people been so afraid of the future. Describing the "pall of fear which at present dims the hopes of mankind," Bertrand Russell said not long ago, "Never before . . . has there been valid reason for such fear. Never before has such a sense of futility blighted the visions of youth. Never before has there been reason to feel that the human race was traveling along a road ending only in a bottomless precipice."

The restructuring of Eastern Europe and the Soviet Union has brought some relief and a host of new worries. Who now controls the missiles in states no longer submissive to Moscow? And those nuclear weapons in the smaller nations — can they be kept out of the hands of determined terrorists?

Besides bombs, who is to protect the world from pollution, acid rain, global warming, ozone depletion, overpopulation, declining food production, the rapacity of nations greedy for their neighbors' wealth, and the swarms of other problems casting their black shadows like fearsome clouds over the future?

No wonder James T. Farrell, famous novelist, writing in *The Race for Space*, expresses the opinion that the awful fear now gripping many hearts has revived concern that the end of the world may be near. "We think of it as possible now and in our own lifetime," he says. "We even sometimes ask ourselves if we are to be the last generation."

In the United States Senate, Chaplain Frederick Brown Harris, D.D., uttered this prayer: "Our Father God, with whom a thousand years are as one day, in this volcanic hour of history save us, we beseech Thee, from panic and despair."

What an apt description of our time! This is indeed *a volcanic age*, with the whole world rumbling with age-old discontents and frustrations, throwing up the white-hot lava of hatred and fury with ever-increasing force and frequency. Fumes from the constant eruptions stifle all hopes of peace and prosperity, choke every worthy effort for human betterment, and fill every heart with fear that a final crowning catastrophe may be at hand.

The chaplain's prayer, "Save us, we beseech Thee, from panic and despair," could not be more timely. It expresses the innermost thoughts and longings of all hearts in these tremendous times.

Beyond question we all need help from some source outside ourselves. We need peace of mind. We need courage and hope. We need guidance and direction.

In the gathering storm we need a light that will not go out. Amid the increasing darkness and confusion we need a voice to say with certainty, "This is the way."

But where shall such help be found? In some local discussion group? At a political forum? On a psychiatrist's couch?

There is a better place. Your Bible!

If you will take the time to read this precious volume, you will discover that it is indeed the Book for this hour. It has a message for our day, for all mankind, for you.

So remarkably does it anticipate the present world situation that it seems to have been written especially for our generation. Though centuries old it is amazingly up to date. It deals with matters of universal interest today. It offers a solution for our current perplexities. It even draws back the curtain of the future, revealing things to come.

Open it now. See how marvelously it speaks the words of comfort and courage, inspiration and challenge, that the times demand and your own heart needs.

BURIED TREASURE

FROM ancient Greece comes the story of a rich farmer who on his deathbed said to his sons, "My treasure is buried in my fields. If you would be rich, dig for it."

Upon the old man's death the two sons, presuming that their father had hidden his money in an ironbound chest somewhere on his farm, set out eagerly to find it.

Equipped with spades and mattocks, they dug with great enthusiasm and perseverance, but seemingly without success. Carefully they turned over the soil in every field, digging to a depth no plow had ever reached. But no sign of a treasure chest did they discover.

When spring came, the search was abandoned in order that the land might be sown with corn. Then came summer and harvest. And what a harvest! The like had never been seen before. In digging the land so thoroughly the boys had won the riches they had sought. Their wise old father's plan had succeeded!

You too have inherited a precious heirloom that has come down to you through many generations. It too is buried. Not in a field, but in a book. And He who bequeathed it to you says, "If you would be rich in all the best and most beautiful things life has to offer, search this Book. Dig into it with all the spiritual tools at your command.

Read it. Study it. Meditate upon it. Pray over it. And within it you will find the richest of treasures."

This Book is, of course, the Bible. Your Bible. Admittedly, in some respects it is much like other books. From its appearance no one would suspect that it might be more valuable than the rest. But open it, begin to search, and the first glint of treasure will soon be seen. Indeed, all who turn its pages with earnest, reverent, loving hands will reap a harvest of spiritual blessings—peace, strength, courage, wisdom, inspiration—the very help for which you have longed but thought impossible to attain.

Here is a treasure worth digging for. And the more you dig, the more you will find. Every turn of the spade will reveal fresh gems. You will begin to understand the mysteries of life and death. You will find the reason for good and evil. You will glimpse the master plan that links the past, the present, and the future. You will see the meaning of history and glimpse events as yet in the womb of time. Above all, you will discover how earth is linked with heaven by ties that can never be broken.

This treasure is available to all. No one is debarred from searching for it on grounds of caste, color, or creed. This Book will speak to *anybody*, regardless of his religion, his nationality, the nature of his work, or the size of his bank account. It will speak to you. No matter what your past may have been, or your present state of mind, or your physical disabilities, it has a message for you today. To old or young, high or low, rich or poor, privileged or underprivileged, it will bring the same strong encouragement, the same helpful counsel, the same rich enlightenment.

Come to your Bible in the innocence of youth, wondering, dreaming, hoping, and you will find it radiant with glowing ideals and worthy ambition, and with power to make your most beautiful dreams come true.

Come to it in the prime of life, when burdens are heaviest and pressing duties crowd your every hour, and you will find in it the strength for the task and sustenance for the journey.

Come to it in advancing years, when energy is failing and

shadows are falling, and you will find in it light for your eventide, and a wondrous hope of a new and better life to come.

Come to it conscious of sin, burdened with a desire to be the kind of man or woman you know you should be, and you will find in it a way of escape from the shackles that hold you in bondage. Peace will come to your troubled conscience as you receive power for victory over evil.

Come to it depressed in spirit, crushed by the hardness of the way and the perplexities that confront you, and you will find in it the refreshing of spirit for which you yearn.

Come to it in sorrow because of some great loss or tragic bereavement, and you will find in it comfort such as nothing else can give and a promise of glad reunion beyond the grave.

Throughout your Bible runs a veritable river of life, flowing from heaven itself. Open it, read it, and this spiritually radioactive flood will begin to flow through the channels of your mind, healing, cleansing, restoring, invigorating, with a mysterious energy no other source can supply. It will clarify your vision, correct your judgment, purify your ambitions.

Given free course, the first tiny trickles of this wondrous stream will swell into a mighty torrent, sweeping away all that is unlovely and unholy from your nature and stimulating the development of every noble quality. Then, sooner than you think, it will overflow naturally and irresistibly into selfless service for others.

What a treasure is this! And what a pity to have it in your home and not look for it! To be poor when you might be rich! To be weak when you might be strong! To be sad and dejected when you might be radiant with joy!

Believe me when I say that this treasure is very close to you. You may even be touching it at this moment.

It is in *your* Bible.

WHAT IS
THE BIBLE?

PERHAPS you are looking at your Bible wondering why its content is so different from that of any other book you have read.

Granted, it is different. At first glance it doesn't seem to contain any semblance of a continued story. With its many short chapters and numbered verses its appearance isn't too inviting. Moreover, should your Bible happen to be a copy of the King James Version, you may feel that the language has a somewhat antique flavor, reminiscent of Milton and Shakespeare—very beautiful, but not the easiest to understand.

You may have other questions, such as why your Bible is divided into two sections, labeled "Old Testament" and "New Testament." Not long ago I met a prosperous businessman who was much troubled on this point. "Why," he wanted to know, "is part of the Bible marked 'Old' and part of it 'New,' when in fact it is all old?"

Perhaps you have wondered who wrote your Bible, and when, and where. Did one person write it all, or is it the work of several authors? Is it an original work or a copy?

But there is a more important question still. Most people look upon the Bible as a sacred book. They call it God's Book or the Word of God. Why? Is there a reason? And is it a good reason?

First of all, let us look at the Book as a whole. Actually, it isn't a single book, but a collection of books. It has often been called a library, and in a sense it is.

In most Bibles, and probably in yours, too, there is a list of all these books, usually on one of the opening pages. If you will glance at this, you will see that there are 39 books grouped under the section marked "Old Testament" and 27 under the "New Testament," making 66 in all.

Many of these "books" are not really books at all in the usual meaning of the word. Some are merely letters, while others are messages so short that they could be copied on two or three typewritten pages.

As to the differences between the Old Testament and the New Testament, the Old was written before Christ, and the New after Christ. Approximately 400 years elapsed between the writing of the last book of the Old Testament — Malachi — and the writing of Matthew, the first book in the New Testament. Then, too, the Old Testament was written in Hebrew (with a few passages in Aramaic) and the New Testament in Greek.

Your Bible was sixteen hundred years in preparation. The earliest book — Job — is believed to have been written by Moses about 1500 B.C., while John finished writing his contributions to the Scriptures in the last decade of the first century A.D.

The 66 books, pamphlets, letters, messages — whatever you wish to call them — were the work of some 35 authors, the two most prolific being Moses in the Old Testament and Paul in the New. Moses is credited with writing all the first 5 books, namely, Genesis, Exodus, Leviticus, Numbers, and Deuteronomy. Paul wrote all 13 Epistles, or letters, from Romans through to Philemon, and possibly also Hebrews.

Other prominent writers were David, who wrote many of the psalms; Solomon, to whom are credited Proverbs, Ecclesiastes, and the Song of Solomon; Luke, who wrote both the books of Luke and Acts; and John, who wrote the Gospel that bears his name, three Epistles, and the book of Revelation.

The many authors represent a wide variety of experience and background.

There was Moses, "learned in all the wisdom of the Egyptians," the grand old man who led one of the first freedom movements of all time.

There was Joshua, the valiant army captain who established Israel in the land of Palestine.

There was David, who rose from a sheepfold to a palace, enduring endless hardships and sorrows in the process, first from Saul and later from his own son Absalom.

There was Solomon, who brought Israel to its highest pinnacle of fame and wealth; Daniel, for many years prime minister of Babylon; Amos, the herdsman; Matthew, the tax gatherer; Luke, the doctor; Peter, the fisherman; Paul, the Pharisee; and many others.

What a company to write a book! And the great marvel is that the words they wrote blended together so perfectly that they have stayed together for more than 2000 years.

Consider now *where* your Bible was written. Little, if any, of it was produced in a warm, comfortable study such as a modern author might require for his work. Parts were written in the Wilderness of Sinai, others in Jerusalem, and some in Babylon while the Jews were in captivity there. A few books were composed in a prison cell in Rome and one was written on the island of Patmos in the Mediterranean.

Most of your Bible was written under very difficult conditions. The authors had no typewriters or word processors, no smooth white paper. They wrote with reed stalks on animal skins or papyrus, often with no light but that of a candle or a primitive oil lamp.

How remarkable that the work of so many diverse individuals, living in such widely scattered places, under such elementary conditions, and separated by hundreds of years of time, should, when gathered together, become the greatest, the best-known, and the best-loved book in the world!

Do any of the original writings exist today? No. Not one. All those priceless documents were lost ages ago. Probably they have long since moldered into dust.

Fortunately, in those far-off days when the original manuscript or "autographs" were still in existence, good men sensed their importance and copied them. Indeed, as centuries rolled by they were copied so often that today there are many of these early documents—whole or in part—in the great museums and libraries of the world.

Almost always the copying was done with such precise care that when the work is examined today the differences on account of faulty workmanship are found to be so slight as to have no essential effect upon the overall meaning.

It is interesting to recall that about the year A.D. 700 a group of Jewish scholars called Masoretes took upon themselves the task of ensuring the accurate transmission of the Old Testament to future generations. They established strict rules to be followed by all copyists. No word or letter could be written from memory. The scribe had to look attentively at each word and pronounce it before writing it down. Even the words and letters of each section were counted, and if these did not tally with the newly made copy, the work was discarded and the task begun again.

Because of the eagerness of scholars to find the perfect text—the one most nearly like the original autograph—every Biblical manuscript discovered today is studied with patient skill. Hence the extraordinary excitement in 1947 when it became known that a considerable number of very ancient manuscripts had come to light in a cave near the Dead Sea. This interest was enhanced a thousandfold when scholars declared that these scrolls of Isaiah and other Old Testament writers were hundreds of years older than any yet found, dating back to the first century before Christ.

More than 40 years of study by the greatest Hebrew authorities have revealed only slight differences between the Masoretic text and that of the Dead Sea scrolls, a marvelous tribute to the faithfulness of the copyists.

But the original Hebrew was not only copied; it was also

translated. One of the earliest and most important translations was into Greek. This is called the Septuagint, because of the 70 Jewish scholars who were supposed to have prepared it. The work was done in Alexandria, Egypt, during the second and third centuries B.C.

Because the Septuagint was in Greek, the early Christian church—which was for the most part a Greek-speaking church—adopted it as its Old Testament, even though it differed in some details from the Hebrew text.

The New Testament was written in a form of Greek known as Koine, which, far from being a dead language, was the common speech of the masses in apostolic times. Large numbers of recently discovered letters, business records, and public inscriptions prove this to be true.

It is probable that the apostles and Jesus Himself spoke in Aramaic, but when the time came for their words to be recorded it was done in the language of the people of that day.

As in the case of the Old Testament, not a single original document exists. The Gospel of John in John's own handwriting would be worth a king's ransom today, but no one knows where it is. Probably it was burned during one of the fierce persecutions the early church endured. But many copies of the New Testament books were made by devoted Christians, and of these some 4,500 are treasured in museums and libraries around the world.

The Codex Vaticanus is probably the oldest almost-complete copy of the Bible in existence. It derives its name from the fact that in 1481 it was already in the library of the Vatican in Rome, and is still a part of it. Little is known of its history before that date, but scholars have declared that it belongs to the first half of the fourth century. Its vellum sheets measure 10 by 10½ inches, with three columns of writing on each page.

Another priceless manuscript is the Codex Sinaiticus, discovered in 1844 by the German scholar Tischendorf at the monastery of St. Catherine near Mount Sinai. In 1859 he presented it to the czar of Russia at St. Petersburg, where, three years later, it was published by Tischendorf. It remained there until 1933, when for £100,000 sterling—raised by public subscription throughout Great Britain, and a government grant—it was purchased for the British Museum. This manuscript is also written on vellum sheets, 15 by 13½ inches, with usually four columns to each page. It is dated by scholars about the middle of the fourth century, probably somewhat later than the Codex Vaticanus.

A third important manuscript, known as the Codex Alexandrinus, also in the British Museum, dates back to the first half of the fifth century A.D. Originally it contained the entire Bible, but today it lacks almost all of Matthew and much of the Psalms and of 2 Corinthians.

Besides these three great volumes that have come down to us from the earlier centuries, hundreds of other smaller but vitally important fragments of the New Testament have also been preserved. Many have come to light in recent years. Each one when found is critically studied by New Testament scholars, whose prime objective is to prepare a Greek text that shall bear the closest possible resemblance to the true but lost original.

Consequently, although there does not exist today any of the actual writings of Moses, David, Isaiah, Matthew, Mark, Luke, John, or Paul, it can nevertheless be truthfully said that the present Hebrew text of the Old Testament and the Greek text of the New Testament are as accurate as men of the highest skill, integrity, and devotion can make them.

What has all this to do with you and your Bible?

Just this: You need entertain no doubt concerning the essential accuracy of the original text. In the words of the late Sir Frederic Kenyon, one-time director of the British Museum and an authority on biblical manuscripts: "The Christian can take the whole Bible in his hand and say without fear or hesitation that he holds in it the true Word of God, handed down without essential loss from generation to generation throughout the centuries" (*Our Bible and the Ancient Manuscripts* [Harpers, 1941], p. 23).

WHICH VERSION
IS BEST?

THIS is the most difficult question, like choosing the winner of a beauty contest or the best performer in a talent program. There will always be those who hold widely different opinions.

The problem of versions goes back a long, long way into a very distant and troubled period of history. As Christianity spread, the need arose for translation of the Holy Scriptures into various languages in addition to the Koine or common language of the day. One of the first such translations was into Syriac, about A.D. 200. Later, in the fifth century, this became the Peshitta or "simple" version.

Next the need was felt for a Latin Bible to bring the Word of God to the large numbers in the Roman Empire who used this language. About the middle of the second century A.D. the first Latin version appeared, followed by many others. Then came Jerome, who revised these Latin versions of the New Testament (A.D. 382-405) and translated the Old Testament from Hebrew into Latin. His version became known as the Vulgate, which throughout the Middle Ages was the standard Bible of the church. It was copied again and again, and there are said to be more than 8,000 copies of it in Europe today. Since the Council of Trent (1545-1563) the Vulgate has been the official Bible of the Roman Catholic Church.

Other translations were made into Armenian and Gothic (in the fourth century) and still another into Ethiopic around A.D. 600. There was no complete translation into English, however, until 1382, when John Wycliffe gave the people of England the first Bible in their own tongue. His translation was handwritten, being copied and distributed by his followers, the Lollards.

In 1525 William Tyndale published the first printed English New Testament, meeting fierce opposition and finally martyrdom for doing so. He worked from the Greek text of Erasmus, and his language was so beautiful that it exerted great influence on subsequent translations. Almost 90 percent of the King James Version is believed to be Tyndale's wording.

English versions now began to appear in rapid succession. The year 1535 saw the publication of the Coverdale Bible, with the Matthew's Bible appearing in 1537 and Taverner's Bible in 1539. In that same year Coverdale revised his translation, which was now published as the Great Bible, under license from King Henry VIII. This was the first authorized version.

In 1560 the Geneva Bible was printed in Switzerland—the first to be divided into verses. Eight years later the Great Bible was revised and reissued as the Bishops' Bible, which was the second authorized version.

The Catholic Douay-Reims Version was brought out over a period of years, from 1582 to 1610, being translated from the Latin Vulgate. Then, in 1611, the King James Version was published. This became known as *the* Authorized Version because the work of translation was encouraged and sponsored by King James I of England. However, as a matter of fact, it was never actually "authorized" by state or church, being only appointed to be read in churches in place of the Bishops' Bible.

Throughout this period of intense interest in Bible translation, which preceded and coincided with the great Reformation, versions appeared in many other languages besides English. Most notable of these was Martin Luther's German translation of 1522. However, in no other language have there been so many different translations and revisions of the Bible as in English. As archaeological research has brought to light more and more ancient manuscripts, both of biblical books and secular works throwing light on the life and customs of the people in Bible times, there has been constant effort on the part of scholars to prepare translations more nearly in harmony with the original text.

During the past century scores of new translations and revisions have been made, especially of the New Testament. More than 50 have appeared in just the past 40 years. Most notable have been the English Revised Version of 1881-1885, the American Standard Version of 1901, and the Revised Standard Version of 1946-1952, all direct descendants of the King James Version of 1611.

In 1961-1970 the *New English Bible* was translated in Great Britain, and in America the *Good News Bible* appeared in 1966-1976, followed by the New International Version in 1973-1978. The total list of English translations — Protestant, Catholic, and Jewish — is far too long to enumerate here.

And the work of translation and revision never stops. The 1901 American Standard Bible was revised again in 1973 to become the New American Standard Version. The 1952 Revised Standard Version has just been revised again to be known as the New Revised Standard Version. In England the *New English Bible* of 1970 was revised in 1989 as the *Revised English Bible*.

And there will be others after these, not only because of advancing knowledge of the Greek and Hebrew text, but because the English language itself is ever changing. Hundreds of words in common use in the seventeenth and eighteenth centuries are meaningless today, and hundreds more that we use today will be obsolete tomorrow.

So the work of translation and revision will go on — not only in English, but in all the languages of the world. Already the Bible societies have translated the whole or part of the Bible into more than 1,900 tongues, and every few weeks still another name is added to the long and imposing list of nations and tribes for whom the Book of books has been provided.

WHICH VERSION IS BEST?

As we look back across the centuries it is inspiring to reflect how many great and good men have felt impelled to devote their lives to the work of making the Bible available to the common people. Since Wycliffe's day there has always been someone, or some group of men, working to perfect the English translation and bring it up to date. The supreme ambition of the scholars is revealed in the prefaces to the Bibles they prepared.

Tyndale wrote in the quaint English of 1525 that he "perceaved by experyence how that it was impossible to stablysh the laye people in any truth, excepte the scripture were playnly layde before their eyes in their mother tongue."

The translators of the King James Version declared that it was their purpose to help forward the saving of souls. "Now what can be more available thereto," they asked, "than to deliver God's book unto God's people in a tongue which they understand?"

In the preface to the Revised Standard Version are found these words from the committee of scholars that prepared it: "It is our hope and our earnest prayer that this Revised Standard Version of the Bible may be used by God to speak to men in these momentous times, and to help them understand and believe and obey His Word."

Naturally some people are troubled by the great variety of versions. They think that it must be indicative of many mistakes in the text. They wish there were only one version so that they could have complete and implicit faith in every word and phrase. Perhaps you too are wondering whether the Book you hold in your hand is really the Bible.

You need not worry. No matter what version it may be, it is still the Word of God.

When the scholars who prepared the King James Version had completed their task they added these very wise words in the preface, now alas, no longer included in modern editions: "We do not deny, nay we affirm and avow, that the very meanest translation of the Bible in English set forth by men of our profession . . . containeth the word of God, nay, is the word of God: As the King's speech, which he uttered in Parliament, being translated into French, Dutch, Italian, and Latin, is still the King's speech, though it be not interpreted by every translator with the like grace, nor peradventure so fitly for phrase, nor so expressly for sense, everywhere . . . no cause therefore why the word translated should be denied to be the word, or forbidden to be current, notwithstanding that some imperfections and blemishes may be noted in the setting forth of it."

As happens so often, God's richest treasures are found in earthen vessels. The vessels may be marred by human frailties, but the treasure is divinely perfect.

So if your Bible happens to be a copy of the New Revised Standard Version or the New International Version or the *Revised English Bible* or the *New Jerusalem Bible*, or a "modern-speech translation" by Weymouth, Moffatt, Goodspeed, or Phillips, or an old favorite like the Douay or the King James Version, never mind. Read on. Read all the versions you can obtain. You will find great good in every one of them. But be sure as you read to keep listening for the voice of the Author. For through this Book, in all its multiplicity of versions and translations, God has chosen to speak to human hearts in all the world.

EVIDENCES OF INSPIRATION

Onder divine direction is its unity. Though extraordinarily diversified, its 66 sections all have one predominant purpose. Some are poetry, others prose. Some are historical, others prophetical. Some are missionary reports, others are church letters or personal correspondence. Yet all speak of the same God, all uplift the same standards of righteousness, all tell of the same plan of salvation, and all look forward to the same day of divine judgment and eternal reward. None contradicts another. This could not have just happened.

Nor could the Bible have been preserved from its many enemies if God had not watched over it with special care. Because of its essential goodness, evil men have always hated this Book. Because it champions the cause of the poor and needy, it has always been derided by callous exploiters of labor. Because it advocates the rights of the individual, claiming that the humblest human being is of utmost value in the sight of God, it has always been a thorn in the flesh of tyrants and dictators.

Time and again down the centuries deliberate efforts have been made to get rid of this Book, but always in vain. No persecution, however severe, no subtle attacks, however cunning, have been able to destroy it or diminish its influence for good.

Angered by its obvious power to turn men from the worship of heathen gods to Christ, Roman emperors decreed its extinction, with that of the early church. The precious copies were ferreted out and burned. But always a few were overlooked, carefully hidden by loyal, courageous, and daring souls.

Later there came worse trouble from within the church itself. As growing spiritual laxness brought on the great apostasy, men came to power in the church whose lives were the very antithesis of the teachings of Christ. Consequently they bitterly resented all efforts to translate and circulate the Bible into the common language of the people lest their sham caricature of Christianity be exposed. Historians record the strange spectacle of priests, bishops, and even popes bitterly condemning those engaged in this work.

The hatred of such people pursued Wycliffe throughout his life and beyond. After his death his body was exhumed and burned, the ashes being scattered on a tributary of the Severn River. But those floating ashes, carried to the ocean and so to the far corners of the globe, were a symbol of the future worldwide circulation of the Bible.

The bishop of London ordered that all copies of Tyndale's translation should be gathered up and burned. Later Tyndale himself was strangled. But a century later his work became immortalized in the King James Version.

It is hard to believe, but during the Middle Ages thousands of godly people were put to death because of their love for and devotion to the Bible. Even possession of a copy of the Book was evidence enough to condemn a person to torture and the stake. Foxe's *Book of Martyrs* tells the tragic tale. Yet despite all the senseless killing and maiming, all the ferocious burning of the books, the Bible lived on, protected by God's providence. It was marvelously multiplied by the printing press, which soon produced more copies than either church or state could ever hope to suppress.

Then a new peril arose. When it became obvious that the circulation of the Bible could not be stopped by frontal assault, an effort was made to minimize the value of its content. Critics arose who laughed at its history, derided its science, and scorned its predictions. It was described as folklore, a collection of myths and fables.

For a time the critics enjoyed a field day. Moses, they said, couldn't possibly have written the first five books, because the art of writing wasn't known in those days. People living in 1500 B.C. couldn't have been much above ignorant nomads and cave dwellers. A global flood, they claimed, was ridiculous. As for the Genesis record of Creation, nothing so vast as the earth could possibly have been made in so short a time.

Even staunch believers in the Bible were concerned. Could the critics be right? they wondered. Could it be possible that the Bible wasn't God's Word after all? Was it indeed inaccurate, unreliable, untrustworthy?

Then the tide turned.

Archaeologists began to dig into the tombs of ancient Egypt and the long-buried cities of Palestine and Babylonia. Soon they were bringing forth amazing evidence in confirmation of even the smallest details of the Bible story.

Biologists, after innumerable experiments, amply corroborated the simple Genesis declaration concerning the reproduction of species.

Geologists and paleontologists gleaned facts from the rocks in widely scattered areas of the earth, which demonstrate beyond doubt that Noah's flood was no fiction.

Nuclear scientists, investigating the power of the atom, came to the conclusion that sudden creation and dissolution even of stars and planets is not by any means unreasonable.

Astronomers, with their mighty modern telescopes and radar-scopes, revealed a universe in perfect harmony with the majestic concept of the Hebrew seers of long ago.

Some specific archaeological discoveries are of special interest.

Digging into a mound of earth in Babylonia, a group of archaeologists found it to contain the remains of the very ancient city of Erech, which is coupled with Babel in Genesis 10:10. After going down through 50 feet of debris of reed huts and mud-brick houses, they came across the foundations of a great temple and the base of a ziggurat, or artificial mountain. Such buildings prove the existence of an educated, highly organized community, with considerable knowledge of arts, crafts, and religion, as far back as 2000 B.C.

Similar results were obtained by Sir Charles Woolley at Ur of the Chaldees, where in the now-uncovered streets the modern tourist may see the kind of houses people lived in during the days of Abraham, what utensils they used, how they conducted their correspondence, and what gods they worshiped.

In Egypt a find of cuneiform tablets proved to be correspondence between the Egyptian court and the princes of Canaan at the beginning of the fourteenth century B.C. Known as the Tell el-Amarna Letters, they throw a flood of light on conditions in Canaan at that time. Many scholars believe that they have reference to the beginning of the Hebrew invasion of Palestine under Joshua.

In 1928 a group of French archaeologists began to excavate the mound of Ras Shamra, which turned out to be the site of the ancient city of Ugarit on the Syrian coast. In one of the temples they found a number of tablets inscribed in cuneiform, which proved to be an alphabetic script, a rival of the Phoenician alphabet, the parent of all Western alphabets. Translated, the tablets provided a wealth of information regarding Canaanite religious beliefs and practices in the middle of the second millennium B.C., conforming exactly to the Bible's description of what the children of Israel found when they occupied their Promised Land.

While the French were exploring Ras Shamra, a group of British archaeologists, led by J. L. Starkey, was busy at Tell ed-Duweir, known in the Bible as Lachish. In the guardroom by the city gate they found a number of inscribed pieces of pottery, which proved to be remains of correspondence between the governor of Lachish and the commanding officer of a neighboring stronghold during Nebuchadnezzar's invasion of Judah toward the close of the seventh century B.C. The Hebrew script, dating from the time of Jeremiah, provides a priceless sidelight on conditions at that time.

In the words of S. H. Hooke, emeritus professor of Old Testament, London University: "One important contribution which archaeology has made to our understanding of the conditions under which the transmission of the biblical record took place has been the light which it has thrown on the history and development of writing in the ancient Near East. We now know that the knowledge of writing was more general at a much earlier date than was supposed by scholars in the nineteenth century. The well-known Gezer tablet, sometimes called a farmer's calendar, dated by archaeologists to the time of David, contains a list of the farming operations appropriate to each month of the year, and carries the implication that an ordinary person could read and write as early as the tenth century B.C. The Ras Shamra texts with their extensive collection of myths and sagas, probably dating back to the fifteenth century B.C., make it possible to suppose that early Hebrew records may have been committed to writing far earlier than scholars were wont to assume. . . . Much more might be said about the fresh light thrown by archaeology upon the patriarchal period, but, to sum up briefly, it may be said that Genesis has been shown to reflect faithfully the life and customs of Canaan and the movement of peoples in the first half of the second millennium B.C."(*The Bible Today,* pp. 18-20).

Thus the Bible has again emerged triumphant over its enemies. The charges leveled against it have been proved false. The critics have been silenced and the Bible lives on, more strongly entrenched than ever as the Word of God.

Many years ago, long before the results of modern scientific research were available, H. L. Hastings wrote: "The Bible is a book which has been refuted, demolished, overthrown, and exploded more times than any other book you ever heard of. Every little while somebody starts up and upsets this book; but it is like upsetting a solid cube of granite. It is just as big one way as the other; and when you have upset it, it is right side up, and when you overturn it again, it is right side up still. Every little while somebody blows up the Bible; but when it comes down, it always lights on its feet, and runs faster than ever through the world. They overthrew the Bible a century ago, in Voltaire's time—entirely demolished the whole thing. In less than a hundred years, said Voltaire, Christianity will have been swept from existence, and will have passed into history. . . . But the word of God 'liveth and abideth for ever' " *(Will the Old Book Stand?* p. 11).

Said Jesus 1900 years ago: "Heaven and earth shall pass away, but my words shall not pass away" (Matthew 24:35). At that moment nothing seemed more improbable. Yet time has proved the accuracy of His prediction. The synagogue in which He so often preached crumbled into ruin with the passing centuries; of the Jerusalem in which He walked, not one stone is left upon another; but His words remain to this day in the Holy Scriptures. As one commentator has written: "His words have passed into laws, they have passed into proverbs, they have passed into consolations, but they have never 'passed away.' "

If perchance, in spite of all the evidence offered above, you still have some lingering doubt whether your Bible is indeed God's Book, consider this last impressive fact. Unlike any other book, this one is welcomed by the honest in heart in all the world. It has universal appeal. Its message is for all people.

Many books, when translated, lose their original emphasis. Often the purpose of the author is lost altogether. Not so with the Bible. The Author's message can always be understood in any language. It never loses its life-giving power. Wherever it goes a river of life flows with it. It has a strange reforming influence, changing people's lives, filling them with courage and hope, and helping them to live aright.

Wonderful Book! Not only has God's hand been over it down the ages, but His hand is over it now. Divinely inspired in the long ago, it has been divinely preserved—for you.

WHAT THE BIBLE
CAN DO FOR YOU

IN 1931 two young men landed on the sandy shore of Mussau, a small island in the South Pacific. They had gone there fully aware that the inhabitants were notorious for their savagery and licentiousness.

Born and bred on a neighboring island, they had had none of the advantages of Western culture. Their education was limited to what they had received in a mission school. Their language was pidgin English, and the only book with which they were in any way familiar was the Bible.

All they had to offer their neighbors on Mussau was the message of the Bible as they understood it. Yet within 10 months the entire population had turned to God. Churches were built. Schools were established. Evil habits were discarded. A passion for cleanliness seized the people.

Shortly thereafter a British government official visited the island and wrote his impressions to the missionary society involved: "I am astonished at what I have seen," he said. "I cannot realize that such a change is possible. The people have taken hold of your religion with a fervid zeal that cannot be described, but must be seen to be appreciated. I have never seen, read, or heard of such a movement before. What is it that you have done to the people? They are changed.

They seem to be now living for something which I cannot understand. I took a case of tobacco over with me and it was returned unopened. Betel-nut chewing is not seen anywhere. I marvel and say it is a miracle."

It was a miracle. And it was wrought by the power of the Word of God—power that operated despite the poor quality of the language and the inadequacy of the education of the messengers.

Famous Pitcairn Island, home of the descendants of the mutineers of the *Bounty*, is another shining example of the Bible's life-changing power. Though once the scene of shocking crimes, it has become renowned throughout the world for the uprightness, integrity, and cleanliness of its people. Today it has no crime, no alcoholics, no police. The reason? Fletcher Christian's Bible, still to be seen in the island's chapel.

Today the South Seas are studded with atolls large and small where similar transformations have taken place. Many were brought to the attention of the world as a result of the war in the Pacific. Hundreds of American servicemen, cut off from their units by enemy action, discovered to their surprise that many of the indigenous people were not savage cannibals as they had supposed, but godly, noble, self-sacrificing Christians.

In his book *The Bible Speaks*, Dr. Francis Carr Stifler, public relations secretary of the American Bible Society, tells the story of Stanley Tefft, who was shot down in the South Pacific. With six other marooned airmen he was guided through the Japanese shore patrols to a hideout, where they remained for 87 days before escape became possible.

"The first thing they did," Tefft said, referring to his newfound friends, "proved to be the best. One native, who spoke pretty good English, handed us a Bible—it was one that some missionaries had given him years ago when they came to the island. Every night we had a religious service. . . . Those were the only moments when I forgot my wounds, my tormented nerves, my starving tissues. . . . For these natives do not simply have the Bible in their hands. They have it in their hearts. They are living it. They are as gentle and thoughtful and clean-living as any church folks you ever saw. God had become from the pages of that Book very real to them" (pp. 91, 92).

In the Solomon Islands, says Dr. Stifler, a soldier sought out a quiet spot just off a jungle trail. As he took out his Bible and began to read, a huge native appeared, club in hand. Instead of raising the club, however, the native pointed to the soldier's book. "That Bible?" he asked. When the soldier said Yes the native took it from him and reverently read aloud a chapter from Isaiah. Then with a smile he walked away.

In 1852 a missionary named Snow landed on the island of Kusaie, between Tarawa and Saipan in the Carolines. At that time it was a place of unspeakable horrors, but Snow patiently reduced the native language to writing and began to translate the Bible into it. Ultimately, after many years had passed, the whole Bible was printed in that language by the American Bible Society. Dr. Stifler reports an interview with the king of Kusaie, John Sigrah.

" 'How many murders a year now?' the king was asked.

" 'There has not been a native murder in my lifetime,' said the king, and he was 60 years old when he said it.

" 'Well, then, how many minor offenses? How many cases of detention in your jail this year?'

" 'Jail!' exclaimed the king. 'There is no jail.'

" 'But you must have some place to put the tipsy ones.'

" 'But there is no drinking on Kusaie' was the answer. 'No native has been known to taste alcohol in the past 30 years.'

"Marriage is a sacred thing on Kusaie. Divorce is unknown" (*ibid.*, p. 94).

Every missionary could tell similar stories of deliverance through the power of the Bible. So could every evangelist. Ask Billy Graham! For it is a remarkable fact that whenever the message of this Book is preached or read or discussed, no matter where, or by whom, its dynamic words begin to take effect.

Sometimes no missionary or evangelist is involved at all.

Not long ago, in a certain South American country, an intolerant church official tore up a copy of the Bible and threw the fragments into a tributary of the Amazon. Several miles down the river they were seen by an Indian who picked them out of the water, dried them, and read their message. His heart was so touched that he told his family and friends. Some months later when a missionary reached this place he found upward of four hundred people eager to know more about God. Many of them became wonderful Christians, leaving all the sadness and darkness of heathenism behind them forever.

I recall meeting a man who handed me a small, well-worn paperback copy of the Gospel of John. "This changed my whole life," he told me. He had been a confirmed drunkard, but one day, as he staggered down the street, a little girl handed him this book. He read it and gave his heart to God. Some weeks later he joined a church, of which he became the deacon.

Another young man told me that he too had been a drunkard, a terror to his wife and children. But he had found the Word of God in a wastepaper basket. Curiosity made him read it. And he read on until his life was changed. He is now a church member, holding weekly Bible studies in his home with a dozen of his neighbors.

This same wonderful life-changing power is in every copy of the Bible. It is in every version, every language edition. It is in your Bible. And it is available to you whenever you want it.

In your hands at this very moment is a source of divine energy greater than you have ever encountered before. It can make you a better man, a better woman; it can deliver you from your besetting sins; it can give you victory over every temptation; it can enable you to live a noble, beautiful life; it can help you to set an example of gracious Christian godliness before your children, your neighbors, your friends.

How can you release this power and channel it into your life?

Very simply. Just open the Book. Begin to read it in a spirit of reverence, humbly seeking after truth. Without your realizing it, the power will begin to flow.

HOW TO READ
YOUR BIBLE

PEOPLE have the strangest ideas about reading the Bible. Some treat it as if it were a charm, or amulet. They open it at random and read the first text that happens to catch their eye, feeling sure that God will speak to them in this way.

Others act as if it were a sort of spiritual smorgasbord, taking a text here and a text there and trying to make a meal of them.

Still others, from a stern sense of duty, believe that they must start at the beginning and read every word from Genesis to Revelation.

Such approaches to the Bible leave much to be desired.

True, the random reading of some precious text has occasionally brought sudden and much-needed blessing to some needy soul. But as a way to full and rich understanding of the Bible, such a method could hardly be recommended. It could even lead to entirely unwarranted inferences, such as when a careless text sampler turned abruptly from "Cain rose up against Abel his brother, and slew him" (Genesis 4:8) to "Go, and do thou likewise" (Luke 10:37)!

Jumping from one favorite passage to another is better than not reading the Bible at all, but at best it is superficial. The shepherd psalm (Psalm 23) is indeed comforting; Isaiah's description of the coming Messiah (chapter 53) is poignantly beautiful; Christ's effort to

37

comfort His disciples (John 14) is most touching; and Paul's dissertation on love (1 Corinthians 13) is an incomparable literary gem; but to keep reading these same passages over and over needlessly limits one's comprehension of the divine purpose of the Book. It is somewhat like living in a beautiful little garden and never looking over the fence at the flower-strewn meadows, the rolling hills, and the snowcapped mountains beyond.

As to beginning at Genesis 1:1 and reading clear through to Revelation 22:21, many good Christians do this annually as a pious exercise or to refresh their memory of the content of the Book. For those already well acquainted with the Bible this is commendable, but the beginner would do well to be less ambitious. Too many get through Genesis and Exodus all right but bog down permanently in Leviticus or Deuteronomy. Even if they manage to struggle through these heavier books, they almost certainly give up by the time they reach Ezekiel, Daniel, or the minor prophets.

Here are a few suggestions that will help you to enjoy your Bible and discover what a very beautiful and wonderful Book it really is:

1. Begin with one of the simplest books, such as the Gospel of Mark. Read it through. It won't take long, not more than an hour at the most.

Here is the earliest record of the life and death of Jesus Christ, as told by eyewitnesses to John Mark. The many references to Peter suggest that much of the information was provided by the big fisherman himself, which makes the story even more interesting.

Mark's Gospel is full of action, and you will find it very easy reading. It will introduce you not only to the New Testament but also to the great basic facts of the Christian faith.

2. Next read the Gospel of Matthew. This book was written several years later than Mark and repeats almost every line of it. In addition, however, it gives many of the teachings of Jesus that Mark omitted.

Matthew reports six of the sermons of Jesus, the first and most familiar being the Sermon on the Mount. In this are found the Beatitudes, the golden rule, and the Lord's Prayer.

The second sermon (chapter 10) tells how the gospel should be preached; the third (chapter 13) deals with the growth of the kingdom in a series of parables, or stories; and the fourth (chapter 18) concerns forgiveness and humility.

The fifth (chapter 23) is a rebuke to the Pharisees because of their hypocrisy; and the sixth (chapters 24, 25) is a prophecy of the destruction of Jerusalem and the end of the world.

These six sermons will give you a clear picture of the beautiful message Jesus gave to the people of His day.

3. Next read the Gospel written by Luke, who has been called the first church historian because of his attention to important details, such as the name and year of the Roman emperor who was on the throne when John the Baptist began to preach (Luke 3:1).

Luke's obvious interest in medical matters gave him a humanitarian outlook, which no doubt is the reason that he recorded the parables of the good Samaritan, the prodigal son, and the rich man and Lazarus.

When you have completed Luke—and it won't take you much more than an hour and a half—your appreciation of the true greatness of Jesus will have been still further enhanced.

4. Now read the Gospel of John, which is very different from the others but in some respects is the most beautiful of all. It was written at least a half century after the Gospel of Luke, and many changes had taken place during that time. Two generations had passed since Jesus had died on the cross. The Christian church had become established despite much suffering and hardship, and John was led to record for its encouragement his most treasured memories of Jesus.

When you have read the four Gospels, you will have had the finest possible introduction to the Bible. You will be prepared to go forward to the book of Acts to read Luke's story of the early church, or, if you prefer, turn back to Genesis to find the beginning of the tragedy of sin, which ultimately caused Christ's death. Or you may branch out in any one of several directions, as you please.

5. Look for stories in the Bible. There are hundreds, covering an amazing variety of subjects. For many years I have told Bible

stories to children. In studying these stories, and retelling them in simple language, I have found the Bible to be the most fascinating book. It glows with interest. You can make the same discovery.

6. Pick out the biographies. The Bible is full of them. Unlike many books of biography, it tells the bad as well as the good points of its various characters.

You could concentrate first on Joseph and read all that is said about him from his birth as Rachel's firstborn to the proud day when Pharaoh placed the destiny of Egypt in his hands. See Genesis 37 to 50.

Then take Moses, the great emancipator of the Hebrews, and follow his amazing course from the day his mother placed him in an ark of bulrushes by the river Nile till he stood on Mount Sinai and talked with God "face to face." Exodus 1 to 20, 24, 31 to 35, and Numbers 10 to 27 will bring you the highlights of his story.

Joshua will give you many thrilling moments, from the time he won Israel's first battle with the Amalekites (Exodus 17:9) through to the capture of Jericho, Ai, and finally all Palestine. See Joshua 1 to 24.

David, of course, you will enjoy. From the moment he steps on the Bible stage as an innocent shepherd lad to his last stirring oration as the dying king of Israel, his story will grip your heart. Incidentally, his is the longest biography in the Old Testament, covering about one thirteenth of the whole. You will find most of it in 1 Samuel 16 to 31, all of 2 Samuel, and the first and second chapters of 1 Kings.

If you want to know more about Solomon, the king who was renowned for his wisdom (and for threatening to cut a disputed baby in half), turn to the first 11 chapters of 1 Kings.

Elijah is another outstanding character you will want to study. He and his successor, Elisha, were the greatest Hebrew prophets of the ninth century B.C. As few others have done, they learned how to cause the power of God to work for them. They brought fire from heaven, raised the dead, and performed all manner of other miracles. See 1 Kings 17 to 2 Kings 13.

In the New Testament the most notable biography, apart from the story of Jesus and occasional glimpses of His disciples, is that of Paul.

He steps on the scene in Acts 7:58 as an official of the Sanhedrin at the stoning of Stephen, moves to the center of the stage in chapter 8, and stays there until the last verse of the book. His three missionary journeys are described in much detail as he strives to bring the story of Christ to Jerusalem, Damascus, Antioch, Tarsus, Athens, Corinth, Philippi, Ephesus, and Rome. He was the great city evangelist of the first century A.D. with a story you should not fail to read.

7. Another highly profitable approach to the Bible is to look upon it as a library in which to pursue a variety of studies. For this purpose a good concordance is necessary. Also very helpful is a reference Bible and a Bible study guide such as *Bible Readings for the Home*, published by Review and Herald® Publishing Association.

You might decide to study the subject of prayer. A glance at a concordance will show you hundreds of uses of the word, or its equivalent. You will discover the names of people who prayed, why and when they prayed, and with what results. From such a study will emerge the reasons that God answers prayer—and the reasons that sometimes He doesn't.

Faith offers another intriguing subject. What is it? How does God value it, and why? How important is it in the Christian life? Your Bible will answer all such questions.

Obedience and disobedience is another theme you will find illuminated with many case histories, also love and hatred, faithfulness and unfaithfulness, greed and liberality, justice and injustice, joy and sorrow.

You will want to look into the mercy of God and His judgments, the importance of law and grace, and the reward of the righteous and the wicked.

Another fascinating subject is prophecy. The Bible is full of it. All manner of predictions are on record, with their fulfillment, as we will note in detail later. Nothing will increase your confidence in your Bible so much as the discovery that the forecasts of its prophets have unfailingly come to pass.

If you are in a practical mood, look up all the references to scientific facts, which prove that your Bible was ever far in advance of modern research. Here are a few:

a. "He . . . hangeth the earth upon nothing" (Job 26:7). Not till A.D. 1530 was the suspension of the earth in space discovered by Copernicus.

b. "He looketh to the ends of the earth . . . to make the weight for the winds" (Job 28:24, 25). Not till A.D. 1630 did Galileo first affirm that air had weight.

c. "For the life of all flesh is the blood thereof" (Leviticus 17:14). Not till A.D. 1615 did William Harvey discover the function of the blood.

d. "The heavens shall pass away with great noise, and the elements shall melt with fervent heat" (2 Peter 3:10). Only in recent years have scientists learned that global destruction is possible through nuclear fission, though God may indeed use some other method when He brings earth's history to a fiery end.

Should you feel that you do not have time to pursue one particular study to a conclusion at one sitting, at least continue until you find a thought that stirs your soul.

Don't hesitate to mark your Bible if you feel so disposed. Underlining texts neatly and carefully, in various colors, has proved a great help to many.

Much more might be said on how to read the Bible, for the subject is, in fact, limitless. But more important than any plan or method is the spirit in which you read it. If you approach the Bible critically, looking for faults and flaws, it won't do you much good. On the other hand, if you read it with a prayer in your heart for God's guidance and blessing, you will find it to be not only an endless source of wisdom and enjoyment, but also "a well of water springing up into everlasting life" (John 4:14).

THE GOD
YOUR BIBLE REVEALS

IT IS not without reason that the Bible is called God's Book, or the Word of God. It begins with God and ends with God. All the content is related to Him. Indeed, if all mention of God were eliminated from the Bible, there wouldn't be much left worth reading.

Actually the Bible is a revelation of God, an effort on His part to let us know what He is like and what our relationship to Him should be.

True, it draws no exact picture of God that could be copied on canvas, or in stone or metal, lest men be encouraged in idolatry, which God hates. The costliest image men could make would be but a tawdry caricature of the glorious Lord of the universe.

Contrasting idols with God, Jeremiah wrote: "Beaten silver is brought from Tarshish, and gold from Uphaz. They are the work of the craftsman and of the hands of the goldsmith; their clothing is violet and purple; they are all the work of skilled men. But the Lord is the true God; he is *the living God* and the everlasting King" (Jeremiah 10:9, 10, RSV).

Here then is the Bible's first great revelation of God:

God is a living person. He is not merely an idea, a myth, a figment of the imagination. He is a real being: "He is the living God, and stedfast for ever" (Daniel 6:26).

He has a dwelling place: "Hear thou in heaven thy dwelling place" (1 Kings 8:39).

He can see and hear: "The eyes of the Lord are over the righteous, and his ears are open unto their prayers" (1 Peter 3:12).

He thinks and remembers: "For he knoweth our frame; he remembereth that we are dust" (Psalm 103:14).

He is generous: "No good thing will he withhold from them that walk uprightly" (Psalm 84:11).

He is eager to be helpful: "I am the Lord thy God which teacheth thee to profit, which leadeth thee by the way that thou shouldest go" (Isaiah 48:17).

He is approachable: "Let us therefore come boldly unto the throne of grace, that we may obtain mercy, and find grace to help in time of need" (Hebrews 4:16).

The second revelation is:

God is eternal. He endures. He is not here today and gone tomorrow. He is "the same yesterday, and to day, and for ever" (Hebrews 13:8).

There never was a time when He did not exist: "Before the mountains were brought forth, or ever thou hadst formed the earth and the world, even from everlasting to everlasting, thou art God" (Psalm 90:2).

There never will be a time when He will cease to exist: "For I lift up my hand to heaven, and say, I live for ever" (Deuteronomy 32:40).

His kingdom is everlasting: "Thy kingdom is an everlasting kingdom, and thy dominion endureth throughout all generations" (Psalm 145:13).

He is immortal: "Now unto the King eternal, immortal, invisible, the only wise God, be honor and glory for ever and ever" (1 Timothy 1:17).

The third revelation is:

God is omnipotent. He has all power at His command: "Both riches and honour come of thee, and thou reignest over all; and in thine hand is power and might; and in thine hand it is to make great, and to give strength unto all" (1 Chronicles 29:12).

There is nothing He cannot do: "I know that thou canst do every thing, and that no thought can be withholden from thee" (Job 42:2).

He does as He pleases: "But our God is in the heavens: he hath done whatsoever he hath pleased" (Psalm 115:3).

He considers nothing impossible: "With men this is impossible; but with God all things are possible" (Matthew 19:26). "The Lord God omnipotent reigneth" (Revelation 19:6).

The fourth revelation is:

God is omniscient. He knows everything. There is nothing hidden from Him: "For his eyes are upon the ways of man, and he seeth all his goings" (Job 34:21).

There is nothing He does not understand: "His understanding is infinite" (Psalm 147:5).

There is no word that He does not hear: "For there is not a word in my tongue, but, lo, O Lord, thou knowest it altogether" (Psalm 139:4).

There is nothing He does not see: "Whither shall I go from thy spirit? or whither shall I flee from thy presence? If I ascend up into heaven, thou art there: if I make my bed in hell, behold, thou art there. If I take the wings of the morning, and dwell in the uttermost parts of the sea; even there shall thy hand lead me, and thy right hand shall hold me" (verses 7-10).

Darkness hides nothing from Him: "Yea, the darkness hideth not from thee; but the night shineth as the day; the darkness and the light are both alike to thee" (verse 12).

He is the source and wellspring of all knowledge and wisdom: "O the depth of the riches both of the wisdom and knowledge of God! how unsearchable are his judgments, and his ways past finding out" (Romans 11:33).

The future is as clear to Him as the past: "Behold, the former things are come to pass, and new things do I declare: before they spring forth I tell you of them" (Isaiah 42:9).

He sees the end from the beginning: "Declaring the end from the beginning, and from ancient times the things that are not yet done" (Isaiah 46:10).

There are no secrets He does not know: "He revealeth the deep and secret things: he knoweth what is in the darkness, and the light dwelleth with him" (Daniel 2:22).

The fifth revelation is:

God is infinite. He is without limitations of any kind. Not only in power, wisdom, and knowledge, but also in righteousness: "My righteousness shall be for ever, and my salvation from generation to generation" (Isaiah 51:8).

In every thought, word, and deed He is altogether holy: "The Lord is righteous in all his ways, and holy in all his works" (Psalm 145:17).

His infinite realm is ruled eternally in perfect rectitude: "Righteousness and judgment are the habitation of his throne" (Psalm 97:2).

His kindness is perpetual: "For the mountains shall depart, and the hills be removed; but my kindness shall not depart from thee" (Isaiah 54:10).

His mercy is likewise limitless: "The mercy of the Lord is from everlasting to everlasting upon them that fear him" (verse 13). "As one whom his mother comforteth, so will I comfort you" (Isaiah 66:13).

Such is the God your Bible reveals. He is infinitely powerful but infinitely compassionate; infinitely wise but infinitely good; infinitely just but infinitely merciful.

Being omnipotent, He could be a tyrant.

Being omniscient, He could be intolerant.

Being eternal, He could be indifferent to the needs of short-lived creatures on a small and insignificant planet.

But, wonder of wonders, all His limitless power, wisdom, and knowledge are so blended with infinite goodness, mercy, and truth that He is the one supreme being, utterly perfect in all His attributes, and the only being worthy of universal worship.

WONDERFUL CREATOR

A S YOU continue to study your Bible you will become aware that it takes for granted the existence of a Supreme Being who is not only omnipotent, omniscient, eternal, and infinite but is also the Creator of the universe.

This Supreme Being, whom the Bible calls God, is the first cause of all that exists, the architect and designer of everything animate and inanimate, from the largest sun to the smallest insect. He hung the stars in space and painted the butterfly's wing. He made the mountains and the atom.

"In the beginning God created the heaven and the earth," says the first verse of the Bible; and this great affirmation is made again and again throughout the Book.

"Thou, even thou, art Lord alone," says Nehemiah; "thou hast made heaven, the heaven of heavens, with all their host, the earth, and all things that are therein, the seas, and all that is therein, and thou preservest them all" (Nehemiah 9:6).

The psalmist confidently declares: "Of old hast thou laid the foundation of the earth: and the heavens are the work of thy hands" (Psalm 102:25).

"Lift up your eyes on high," urges the prophet Isaiah, "and behold who hath created these things, that bringeth out their host by

47

number: he calleth them all by names by the greatness of his might, for that he is strong in power; not one faileth. . . . Hast thou not known? hast thou not heard, that the everlasting God, the Lord, the Creator of the ends of the earth, fainteth not, neither is weary?" (Isaiah 40:26-28).

To the pagan priests of Lystra who sought to worship him, Paul says, "Sirs, why do ye these things? We also are men of like passions with you, and preach unto you that ye should turn from these vanities unto the living God, which made heaven, and earth, and the sea, and all things that are therein" (Acts 14:15).

To the Athenians he declares the "God that made the world and all things therein," the one who is "Lord of heaven and earth" who "giveth to all life, and breath, and all things" (Acts 17:24, 25).

And John bids us all, "Fear God, and give glory to him . . . : and worship him that made heaven, and earth, and the sea, and the fountains of waters" (Revelation 14:7).

Have you wondered *how* God made the universe?

Your Bible has a simple answer.

"Through faith we understand that the worlds were formed by the word of God, so that things which are seen were not made of things which do appear" (Hebrews 11:3).

The Revised Standard Version renders this verse: "By faith we understand that the world was created by the word of God, so that what is seen was made out of things which do not appear."

Notice that this text does not say exactly how God created. It does not go into detail. It just says that He made invisible things become visible, which may well be a succinct statement of the scientific truth that energy can be converted into mass.

How long did it take God to perform each mighty miracle? Only as long as it took to speak the word.

"By the word of the Lord were the heavens made; and all the host of them by the breath of his mouth. . . . For he spake, and it was done; he commanded, and it stood fast" (Psalm 33:6-9).

"Praise him, ye heavens of heavens, and ye waters that be above the heavens. Let them praise the name of the Lord: for he commanded, and they were created" (Psalm 148:4, 5).

This does not mean that God made everything in the universe at once; it merely reveals His method of creation. God has but to speak, to state a desire, and the atoms conform to His will.

Consequently, He doesn't need long periods of time to accomplish His purposes. He can act swiftly.

To say that eons and eons of time are required to bring about the evolution of a world or the creatures upon it puts an unwarranted limitation upon God's power. He can use time if He so pleases, or He can dispense with it altogether.

Astronomers, with their marvelous new telescopes, can photograph the light of a star that was in existence a thousand million years ago. But that star could have been made by the eternal, omnipotent Creator in a moment "by the breath of his mouth."

When God decided to create our world, He chose to take six days to do it. That was His privilege. He didn't need six days. Six minutes would have been sufficient, or even six seconds.

Why did He take six days and not six years or 6 million years? For a special purpose, which will become apparent as you read the story in the first two chapters of Genesis.

On the first day He said, "Let there be light: and there was light" (Genesis 1:3). That was the beginning of the sequence of evenings and mornings, of day and night.

On the second day He said, "Let there be a firmament," and there came a space between oceans and clouds (verse 6).

On the third day the dry land appeared, and was suddenly covered with vegetation (verses 9-12).

On the fourth day God said, "Let there be lights in the firmament," and the sun and the moon appeared (verse 14).

On the fifth day God said: "Let the waters bring forth abundantly the moving creature that hath life, and fowl that may fly above the earth in the open firmament of heaven. And God created great whales" (verses 20, 21). Suddenly the birds began to sing and the seas were filled with fish.

On the sixth day God said: "Let the earth bring forth the living creature after his kind, cattle, and creeping thing, and beast of the earth" (verse 24). And animals of all kinds frolicked in the lovely forests and fields.

It was a beautiful world that God made. It was full of treasures—gold, silver, and precious stones; full of food—nuts and fruits and grains, and pure, sparkling water; full of loveliness—trees and ferns and flowers; full of marvelous living creatures—birds, fish, and animals of every kind and color.

Then, still on the sixth day, when all was in readiness for His crowning masterpiece of creation, God said, "Let us make man in our image, after our likeness. . . . So God created man in his own image, in the image of God created he him; male and female created he them" (verses 26, 27).

In so saying, He fulfilled His original purpose for this earth, as revealed by the prophet Isaiah: "Thus saith the Lord that created the heavens; God himself that formed the earth and made it; he hath established it, he created it not in vain, he formed it to be inhabited" (Isaiah 45:18).

The inhabitants had now arrived, marvelously equipped to "multiply, and fill the earth and subdue it" (Genesis 1:28, RSV). Fresh from the hands of God, they were such wonderful creatures that your Bible says Adam and Eve were "crowned . . . with glory and honour" and only "a little lower than the angels" (Psalm 8:5).

With their God-given power to see and hear, to smell and feel, to think and decide, to choose and remember, to understand and love, they were indeed created in the image of God. As near as could be, they were His son and daughter, and therefore inexpressibly dear to Him.

With this thought in mind David says, "Know ye that the Lord he is God: it is he that hath made us, and not we ourselves; we are his people, and the sheep of his pasture" (Psalm 100:3).

And Malachi comments: "Have we not all one Father? hath not one God created us?" (Malachi 2:10).

But why did God take six days to create this world?

Your Bible answers: "For in six days the Lord made heaven and earth, the sea, and all that in them is, and rested the seventh day: wherefore the Lord blessed the sabbath day, and hallowed it" (Exodus 20:11).

The full story is told in the second chapter of Genesis: "Thus the heavens and the earth were finished, and all the host of them. And on the seventh day God ended his work which he had made. . . . And God blessed the seventh day, and sanctified it; because that in it he had rested from all his work which God created and made" (verses 1-3).

Thus God founded the weekly cycle — not for His benefit, but for man's. Because He cared so much for the two wonderful creatures He had made, He planned that every seventh day throughout their lives should be a dedicated day. Each Sabbath, as He called it, was to be for them a day devoted to thinking about Him. Free from life's regular duties, they were to walk and talk with Him and meditate upon His goodness and love.

It was a wonderful plan to keep man forever linked with God. Had Adam and Eve and their children followed it, they would have been saved innumerable sorrows, and His promised blessings would have been theirs eternally.

Fortunately, these blessings were not offered to Adam and Eve alone. God enshrined them in His unique and perpetual memorial of Creation. They have been available every seventh day through all the centuries since. They are available now. You may share them.

If you do so in all sincerity, the Sabbath blessings will be yours. God has promised: "If thou turn away thy foot from the sabbath, from doing thy pleasure on my holy day; and call the sabbath a delight, the holy of the Lord, honourable; and shalt honour him, not doing thine own ways, nor finding thine own pleasure, nor speaking thine own words: then shalt thou delight thyself in the Lord; and I will cause thee to ride upon the high places of the earth, and feed thee with the heritage of Jacob thy father: for the mouth of the Lord hath spoken it" (Isaiah 58:13, 14).

SUPREME LAWGIVER

THE moment God brought the universe into existence laws became essential for its orderly continuance. Without them the multitude of suns and planets He scattered through space would long since have been destroyed in cataclysmic pandemonium.

Some of these laws are known, being named after the scientists who discovered them. There are Newton's law of gravitation, Kepler's laws of planetary motion, Snell's law of the refraction of light, Ohm's law of the relation of electrical forces, Boyle's law of gases, Mendel's laws of heredity, Fechner's law of psychology. Of course, they are not man's laws, but God's. The scientists merely discovered what God instituted millenniums ago.

Your Bible declares the profound truth that "there is one lawgiver" (James 4:12). And it identifies Him as God: "For the Lord is our judge, the Lord is our lawgiver, the Lord is our king" (Isaiah 33:22).

Being a God of order, He is "not the author of confusion, but of peace" (1 Corinthians 14:33). Consequently, having planned the movement of the stars with perfect precision, and having arranged the interplay of molecular and atomic forces with infinite exactitude, it was but natural that when He set out to create our world and populate it with a new race of beings He should do so in harmony with basic laws of His own devising.

When He said, "Let the earth bring forth grass, the herb yielding seed, and the fruit tree yielding fruit after his kind, whose seed is in itself" (Genesis 1:11), He was expressing not merely a wish but a law, as horticulturists long ago discovered in propagating plants.

The same is true of His declaration: "Let the earth bring forth the living creature *after his kind*, cattle, and creeping thing, and beast of the earth *after his kind*." Enshrined herein is a law of heredity that causes modern biologists to marvel.

And when God said to Adam concerning the fruit of the tree of the knowledge of good and evil, "In the day that thou eatest thereof thou shalt surely die" (Genesis 2:17), He was revealing to him another fundamental law: that disobedience brings punishment or, as Paul succinctly stated it, "The wages of sin is death" (Romans 6:23).

All life on this planet was regulated by laws that, although not written on paper, parchment, or stone, were nonetheless real. And it is but reasonable to suppose that God imparted to Adam, His precious masterpiece of Creation, a knowledge of the great basic principles of right living, which later became embodied in the Ten Commandments. Certainly Abraham knew of them, for God said, four centuries before Sinai: "Abraham obeyed my voice, and kept my charge, my commandments, my statutes, and my laws" (Genesis 26:5).

During Israel's harsh captivity in Egypt, knowledge of God's rules of conduct gradually faded. A restatement became urgently necessary. Hence the majestic scene on "the mount of God" when the Supreme Lawgiver came down and talked with Moses and gave him "two tables of testimony, tables of stone, written with the finger of God" (Exodus 31:18).

Upon these two "tables," or tablets, of stone were ten commandments, divinely designed for man's well-being, to direct him in paths of righteousness and preserve him from evil.

You will find these Ten Commandments in Exodus 20:3-17. Memorize them. God planned them for your good. Here they are:

1. *"Thou shalt have no other gods before me."*

We are to put God first in our lives.

2. *"Thou shalt not make unto thee any graven image, or any likeness of any thing that is in heaven above, or that is in the earth beneath, or that is in the water under the earth: thou shalt not bow down thyself to them, nor serve them: for I the Lord thy God am a jealous God, visiting the iniquity of the fathers upon the children unto the third and fourth generation of them that hate me; and shewing mercy unto thousands of them that love me and keep my commandments."*

God will permit no rival to share our adoration. Therefore we must shun idolatry in all its forms. We must not bow down to images, pictures, people, money, or any worldly possession. Our worship must be reserved for God alone.

3. *"Thou shalt not take the name of the Lord thy God in vain; for the Lord will not hold him guiltless that taketh his name in vain."*

We are to be reverent in all matters concerning God. To use His name as an idle swearword is a grievous sin in His sight.

4. *"Remember the sabbath day, to keep it holy. Six days shalt thou labour and do all thy work: but the seventh day is the sabbath of the Lord thy God: in it thou shalt not do any work, thou, nor thy son, nor thy daughter, thy manservant, nor thy maidservant, nor thy cattle, nor thy stranger that is within thy gates: for in six days the Lord made heaven and earth, the sea, and all that in them is, and rested the seventh day: wherefore the Lord blessed the sabbath day and hallowed it."*

This, the longest of the Ten Commandments, bids us remember the day of rest and worship that God set apart in the beginning for man's highest spiritual good. The seventh day of every week is to be regarded as a holy day, God's day, a day of special fellowship and communion with Him.

5. *"Honour thy father and thy mother: that thy days may be long upon the land which the Lord thy God giveth thee."*

We are to be respectful to our parents, with all that this implies of law and order in the home.

6. *"Thou shalt not kill."*

We are to value the lives of others as our own, and have no hateful thought toward a single soul. There must be no murder in our hearts.

7. *"Thou shalt not commit adultery."*

We are to be pure in all our thoughts and actions, avoiding even the appearance of evil.

8. *"Thou shalt not steal."*

We are to be honest in all our relationships with our fellow men, in our business affairs, our money matters, and our service to God and man.

9. *"Thou shalt not bear false witness against thy neighbour."*

We are to be truthful at all times and under all circumstances, albeit "speaking the truth in love" (Ephesians 4:15).

10. *"Thou shalt not covet thy neighbour's house, thou shalt not covet thy neighbour's wife, nor his manservant, nor his maidservant, nor his ox, nor his ass, nor any thing that is thy neighbour's."*

We are to be content with what God has given us, without envy toward those who may be better off. We are to be generous, not greedy; considerate, not selfish.

Such is the law of God as found in your Bible. Its provisions are simple enough and most reasonable. Yet they are so profound that they penetrate to "the thoughts and intents of the heart" (Hebrews 4:12).

Concerning this law Charles Haddon Spurgeon wrote: "There is not a commandment too many; there is not one too few; but it is so *incomparable* that its *perfection* is a proof of its divinity" (*Sermons*, vol. 2, p. 280).

David said: "The law of the Lord is perfect, converting the soul: the testimony of the Lord is sure, making wise the simple" (Psalm 19:7). "O how love I thy law!" he exclaimed. "It is my meditation all the day" (Psalm 119:97). And his continual prayer was: "Open thou mine eyes, that I may behold wondrous things out of thy law" (verse 18).

Paul called this law "holy, and just, and good" (Romans 7:12), and James declared it to be "the perfect law of liberty" (James 1:25).

It is all this and more. And no wonder, for it was fashioned by the Supreme Lawgiver to meet the needs of beings whom He Himself had created and whom He dearly loved.

We cannot value the Ten Commandments too highly. They have been neglected too long by too many.

"The plight of our times," says John Drewett, "is due to the breaking of the commandments, and only when men order their social and individual lives in accordance with God's law, as revealed in the Old Testament and fulfilled in the incarnate life of Jesus Christ, will peace, justice, and reason be established in the earth" (*The Ten Commandments in the Twentieth Century*, p. 13).

During his evangelistic campaigns Billy Graham has made similar statements concerning the indispensability of the Decalogue.

These men and many others are rediscovering God's purpose in giving His law. They are perceiving the great truth stated long ago by Moses: "The Lord commanded us to do all these statutes, to fear the Lord our God *for our good always*, that he might preserve us alive" (Deuteronomy 6:24).

God intended His law to be a blessing. As David said: "Blessed is the man that walketh not in the counsel of the ungodly, nor standeth in the way of sinners, nor sitteth in the seat of the scornful. But his delight is in the law of the Lord; and in his law doth he meditate day and night. And he shall be like a tree planted by the rivers of water, that bringeth forth his fruit in his season; his leaf also shall not wither; and whatsoever he doeth shall prosper" (Psalm 1:1-3).

Significantly, this blessing is repeated in the final benediction in your Bible: "Blessed are they that do his commandments, that they may have right to the tree of life, and may enter in through the gates into the city" (Revelation 22:14).

ETERNAL LOVER

OF ALL the glimpses your Bible gives of God, none is more wonderful than that expressed in the three brief words "God is love" (1 John 4:8).

Here indeed is the crowning revelation concerning Him. Not only does God possess all power and wisdom, not only is He infinite in goodness and truth, but He is the source and fountain of love.

He is the wonderful Creator, the Supreme Lawgiver, and the Eternal Lover.

"This," says Godet in his commentary on the Gospel of John, "is the initiation of the earth into the deepest secret of heaven. God is from all eternity Father—that is to say, Love."

"Love is indeed the very Being of God," says Stephenson in his *Chief Truths of the Christian Faith*. "Love is His Nature and Essence, so that whatever God intends and designs, Love intends and designs. Love is the supreme directing principle in all His actions. It is the supreme relation between Himself and all created life—yea, the supreme relation between the Persons of the ever-blessed Trinity. Were the Divine Nature capable of being expressed in a single word, that one word would assuredly be Love."

Because of this stupendous fact, this "deepest secret of heaven," because indeed God is love, He made the sublime decision to take upon Himself human flesh, and in the person of His Son, live upon this earth as a man.

Says your Bible: "God so loved the world that he gave his only Son, that whoever believes in him should not perish but have eternal life" (John 3:16, RSV).

Why did God do this? Love is the only answer. He saw that this was the only way to reclaim the human race from the bondage of sin into which it had fallen as a result of the sad tragedy described in the third chapter of Genesis. Because the inhabitants of earth were the creatures of His hand, He loved them, deploring the sorrow and suffering that had come upon them. He longed to bring them again into full fellowship with Himself, such as He had enjoyed with Adam and Eve in the Garden of Eden.

Man could not restore himself to that relationship. He had gone too far. He had sunk too low. He was morally enfeebled by sin and doomed by God's own edict to die (Genesis 2:17).

There was nothing God could do but receive in Himself the penalty He had decreed for sin. True, He could have set aside His law and said that it was of no consequence; but had He done so, He would have jeopardized the foundation on which the government of His whole vast universe depends. The penalty for disobedience is death, and this penalty had to be paid either by the offender or by the Lawgiver in His own person.

Because God is love, He chose the latter course, though He knew it must lead to Calvary.

So in His own appointed time He came to this earth to dwell among His human creatures in the ever-mysterious, ever-glorious Incarnation. "God was in Christ, reconciling the world unto himself" (2 Corinthians 5:19).

It was a brief sojourn, yet replete with love. All the way from Nazareth to Olivet He sought to convince mankind of His undying affection. From His tender heart love poured forth in a ceaseless stream of gentle words and kindly deeds.

Like the good Samaritan of His own parable He bound up the wounds of His enemies. Graciously He befriended the poor, the sick, the outcast. He loved the children, the young people, the old folks.

Calling a little child to Him, He said to His disciples, "It is not the will of your Father which is in heaven, that one of these little ones should perish" (Matthew 18:14).

"Suffer little children to come unto me," he added, "and forbid them not; for of such is the kingdom of God." Only someone with a love-filled heart could have used such words.

When He met the rich young ruler, your Bible says, "Jesus beholding him loved him" (Mark 10:21).

"Behold *how* he loved him!" exclaimed the bystanders as they saw Jesus weeping in sympathy with Mary and Martha over the death of their brother.

Love was the central theme of His teaching. His disciples, He said, were to love not only their friends but also their enemies. They were to do good to those who hated them and pray for those who did them harm (Matthew 5:44).

They were to love God with all their heart, soul, mind, and strength, and their neighbors as themselves (Matthew 22:37-39).

"He that loveth me," He said, "shall be loved of my Father, and I will love him" (John 14:21).

"The Father himself loveth you," He assured His followers, "because ye have loved me" (John 16:27).

He taught men to call God "Father," which was a new idea to most of them. They had wandered so far away from God that they pictured Him as stern, cruel, and inaccessible. God wasn't like that at all, Jesus said. Instead He was tender, kind, thoughtful, and understanding. "When you pray," He told them, "say, Our Father which art in heaven" (Luke 11:2).

Many people, He suggested, are like prodigal sons who leave home proudly and self-confidently to enjoy the pleasures of sin. In consequence, they get into much trouble and sorrow. But if they repent and return to God, they will find a loving heavenly Father waiting with outstretched arms to welcome them.

Completing His revelation of the love of God, Jesus went at last to the cross. There, as the Son of God and at the same time as the one sinless representative of the race, with His divine and human natures inseparably blended, He offered up a complete, perfect, and all-sufficient sacrifice for the sins of men.

Thus was the penalty paid. And "as by one man's disobedience many were made sinners, so by the obedience of one shall many be made righteous" (Romans 5:19).

This sacrifice was in no sense intended to appease an angry deity. Rather it was God offering Himself. As we read above, "God so loved . . . that he gave"; and the sharing in this sublime transaction of all three Persons of the blessed Trinity is revealed in the beautiful words: "Christ . . . through the eternal Spirit offered himself without spot to God" (Hebrews 9:14).

Moreover, Christ's sacrifice was altogether voluntary. "The Son of man came not to be ministered unto, but to minister, and to *give his life* a ransom for many" (Matthew 20:28).

"No man taketh it from me," He said concerning His life "but *I lay it down of myself*" (John 10:18).

"Our Saviour Jesus Christ," said Paul, "*gave himself for us*, that he might redeem us from all iniquity" (Titus 2:13, 14).

"*He offered up himself*" (Hebrews 7:27).

He "*gave himself a ransom for all*" (1 Timothy 2:6).

"*He gave himself for our sins*, that he might deliver us from this present evil world, according to the will of God and our Father" (Galatians 1:4).

Here indeed was perfect love, made manifest by an act of utter self-surrender and submission, the willing yielding up of life that others might live.

What the Incarnation cost God the Father we shall never know. How much it meant for God the Son to die for the human race must also remain a mystery. Even the angels do not understand it; and it will be the theme of endless discussion and wonderment through all eternity (1 Peter 1:11, 12).

Nevertheless, the results are clear.

God "hath made him to be sin for us, who knew no sin; that we might be made the righteousness of God in him" (2 Corinthians 5:21).

"Christ redeemed us from the curse of the law, having become a curse for us" (Galatians 3:13, RSV).

"He was wounded for our transgressions, he was bruised for our iniquities; the chastisement of our peace was upon him; and with his stripes we are healed. . . . The Lord hath laid on him the iniquity of us all" (Isaiah 53:5, 6). "He was numbered with the transgressors; and he bare the sin of many" (verse 12).

What awfulness of suffering this bearing of sin brought upon the Son of God we shall never know, but it reached the ultimate limit because of the utter perfection of His character. As Bishop B. F. Westcott says: "Man as he is cannot feel the full significance of death . . . but Christ in His sinlessness perfectly realized its awfulness. In this fact lies the immeasurable difference between the death of Christ, simply as death, and that of the holiest martyr."

Upon Him who came from God, with mind attuned to that of His holy Father, and with all the delicate sensitiveness of a perfect character, fell the terrible impact of the penalty of sin. No wonder we read in the Scriptures that we have been bought "with a price" (1 Corinthians 6:20). What a price!

Only perfect love, in the heart of the Eternal Lover, could have devised a plan of salvation such as this and endured so much to carry it through to its consummation.

Trying to bring home to the people of Philippi the stupendous nature of the divine sacrifice, the apostle Paul wrote this sublimely beautiful description: "Though he was in the form of God, [Jesus] did not count equality with God a thing to be grasped, but emptied himself, taking the form of a servant, being born in the likeness of men. And being found in human form he humbled himself and became obedient unto death, even death on a cross. Therefore God has highly exalted him and bestowed on him the name which is above every name, that at the name of Jesus every knee should bow, in heaven and on earth and under the earth, and every tongue confess that Jesus Christ is Lord, to the glory of God the Father" (Philippians 2:6-11, RSV).

Thus did God seek to bridge the gulf that sin had made. As Peter wrote: "Christ also hath once suffered for sins, the just for the unjust, that he might bring us to God" (1 Peter 3:18).

Because of the wonder and glory of the divine sacrifice and the intensity of love that it revealed, look again at Jesus hanging on the cross. Behold Him in whom all truth is centered dying for those in error! Behold Him who is the author of light dying for those in darkness! Behold Him who is wisdom personified dying for the foolish and the ignorant! Behold Him from whom all life springs giving Himself for the dead in sin! Behold Him who is Himself holiness, purity, and righteousness dying for the unholy, the impure, and the depraved! Behold Him in whom all power is centered submitting to every indignity, dying for the wayward and the weak! Behold Him who is all Love yielding His poor, marred body as a sacrifice on this despised and accursed altar—Love suffering, Love nailed to the cross, Love dying, that the unlovely, the vicious, the hateful, might be saved!

"O God, help us to realize it!" cries A. C. Dixon as he ponders the glories of the cross. "Put all into one . . . all Truth, all Light, all Life, all Wisdom, all Power, all Holiness, all Love incarnate in one Man, Who gives Himself for the untruthful, for the darkened, for the dead, for the weak, for the unholy, for the unlovely—and you have some conception of what the Cross of Jesus Christ is in its deepest meaning" (*The Glories of the Cross*, pp. 12, 13).

No wonder Charles Wesley exclaimed, as he contemplated this stupendous spectacle:

"O love divine, what hast Thou done!
    The incarnate God hath died for me!
  The Father's well-beloved Son
    Bore all my sins upon the tree!
  The Son of God for me hath died—
    My Lord, my Love, is crucified."

GLORIOUS SAVIOUR

G LORIOUS indeed is the salvation offered in your Bible. Here are glad tidings of deliverance not only from the penalty of sin but also from its power. And the good news is for everybody, everywhere, in every age.

Under no condition should you feel that you are left out, that this rich provision is not for you.

Your Bible says: "God our Saviour . . . will have *all men* to be saved, and to come unto the knowledge of the truth. For there is one God, and one mediator between God and men, the man Christ Jesus; who gave himself a ransom for all" (1 Timothy 2:3-6).

Again and again this great truth is repeated.

Says the apostle Paul to Titus: "The grace of God that bringeth salvation hath appeared to *all men*" (Titus 2:11).

"We see Jesus," says the writer to the Hebrews, "who was made a little lower than the angels for the suffering of death . . . that he by the grace of God should taste death *for every man*" (Hebrews 2:9).

He "delivered him up *for us all*," is Paul's message to the Romans (Romans 8:32), supplemented by the great declaration that "there is no difference between the Jew and the Greek: for the same Lord over all is rich unto *all that call upon him*. For *whosoever* shall call upon the name of the Lord shall be saved" (Romans 10:12, 13).

When Jesus died on Calvary, He reconciled *the world* unto God (2 Corinthians 5:19). He paid the price of sin. He bridged the gulf that sin had made. After that there was no excuse for anybody to be separated from God anymore.

He made it possible for a sinful race to come back into full fellowship with its Maker. As Son of God and Son of man He became "the way, the truth, and the life" (John 14:6) — the way back to the Father, back to God, for all men, for all time.

The glorious transaction is summed up and crystallized in the most exquisite of all Scripture passages: "God so loved the world, that he gave his only begotten Son, that *whosoever* believeth in him should not perish, but have everlasting life" (John 3:16).

There it is again — that wonderful *whosoever!*

How it must have touched the hearts of the first disciples! For "whosoever" meant fishermen as well as rabbis, tax gatherers as well as priests, little people up in Galilee as well as the lords of the Sanhedrin in Jerusalem. It took in the lame, the blind, the crippled, the leper. It left out nobody who wished to be included.

When on the day of Pentecost Peter saw around him a crowd of strangers from "every nation under heaven" the same lovely word came rushing into his mind. Eagerly he cried aloud, "*Whosoever* shall call on the name of the Lord shall be saved" (Acts 2:21).

Again, when he visited the home of Cornelius, the Roman centurion, he recalled the blessed word. As he talked about Jesus he said, "To him give all the prophets witness, that through his name *whosoever* believeth in him shall receive remission of sins" (Acts 10:43).

Almost the last message from Jesus in your Bible is a reminder of the same gracious, unlimited invitation. "I Jesus have sent mine angel to testify unto you these things in the churches. . . . And the Spirit and the bride say, Come. And let him that heareth say, Come. And let him that is athirst come. And *whosoever* will, let him take the water of life freely" (Revelation 22:16, 17).

Some words may be bigger and some deeper, but none is broader than "whosoever." It makes God's plan for man's salvation a very personal matter. It declares that every individual on the face of the earth is included. Nobody is left out. Not a single man or woman. Not the smallest boy. Not the tiniest girl. Most definitely it takes in you.

Wherever you read "whosoever" in your Bible, you can substitute your own name, for in its all-comprehensive offer of salvation it takes in the whole human race. The poor and the well-to-do. The sick and the well. The educated and the uneducated. Laborers, businessmen, miners, goldsmiths, carpenters, clerks, sailors, shipbuilders, actors, authors, preachers—everybody!

Whatever you are, wherever you live, whoever you may be, God's offer of salvation is for you.

It doesn't matter how big a sinner you may have been. God welcomes you just the same.

If you feel that your life has been too ungodly for Him to receive you, open your Bible to Romans 5:6 and read the blessed assurance: "In due time Christ died for the ungodly."

If you think that your life has been too deeply steeped in sin, remember that "God commendeth his love toward us, in that, while we were yet sinners, Christ died for us" (Romans 5:8).

If you feel that you have been so unjust, unkind, and cruel that God couldn't possibly take you into His kingdom, do not worry, for "Christ also hath once suffered for sins, the just for the unjust, that he might bring us to God" (1 Peter 3:18).

If you think that you have sunk so low that even the love of Jesus could not possibly reach you, you are mistaken, for "he is able also to save them *to the uttermost* that come unto God by him, seeing he ever liveth to make intercession for them" (Hebrews 7:25). And "whosoever will" may come.

John Bunyan once wrote: "If God had written with His own hand, 'If John Bunyan will come to me I will save him,' I should have hesitated, for I would have said, 'To be sure, it is not this poor drunken tinker; it is another John Bunyan that lived hundreds of years ago, or some John Bunyan that will live hundreds of years hence; or it is a John Bunyan across the seas. To be sure it cannot be this poor miserable sinner.' But when God says 'Whosoever,' I know that it takes in this John Bunyan."

And it does. Where sin abounds, Paul assures us, grace does much more abound. In other words, there is no sinner Christ cannot save. No life is too degraded for Him to transform. His grace is sufficient for every need and in every case.

"I have read," wrote Charles H. Spurgeon, "of one who dreamed a dream when in great distress of mind about religion. He thought he stood in the outer court of heaven, and he saw a glorious host marching up, singing sweet hymns, and bearing banners of victory. They passed by him through the gate, and he heard in the distance sweet strains of music.

" 'Who are they?' he asked an angel.

" 'The goodly fellowship of the prophets' was the answer.

"He heaved a deep sigh as he said, 'Alas, I am not one of them, and never shall be, and I cannot enter there.'

"By and by there came another band equally lovely in appearance and equally triumphant, robed in white. They passed within the portals, and again the shouts of welcome were heard.

" 'Who are they?' he asked.

" 'They are the goodly fellowship of the apostles' was the reply.

" 'Alas,' he said, 'I do not belong to that fellowship either.'

"Still he lingered in the hope that he might yet go in; but the next multitude was the noble army of martyrs, and he could not go in with them nor wave their palm branches.

"At last he saw a larger host than all the rest put together marching and singing melodiously. In front walked the woman who was a sinner and the thief who died on the cross. As he looked he saw there Manasseh, and many like him, and as they passed nearer to enter the gate he could see clearly who they were and he thought, There will be no shouting about them.

"But to his astonishment it seemed as if all heaven was rent with sevenfold shouts as they passed in. And the angel said to him, 'These are they that were mighty sinners, saved by mighty grace.'

" 'Blessed be God,' he cried. '*I can go in with them.*' "

So can you! So can I! So can anybody who is willing to accept God's gracious offer of salvation through Jesus.

And there's nothing to pay for it. It is absolutely free. This greatest gift of Heaven comes to you "without money and without price."

Thank God we are "justified *freely* by his grace through the redemption that is in Christ Jesus" (Romans 3:24). We are "accepted in the beloved. In whom we have redemption through his blood, the forgiveness of sins, according to the riches of his grace" (Ephesians 1:6, 7).

Says Paul again, "God who is rich in mercy, for his great love wherewith he loved us, even when we were dead in sins, hath quickened us together with Christ . . . : that in the ages to come he might shew the exceeding riches of his grace in his kindness toward us through Christ Jesus. For by grace are ye saved through faith; and that not of yourselves: *it is the gift of God"* (Ephesians 2:4-8).

Those who think they must do something to win God's favor and bring His power into their lives are sadly mistaken. No amount of money, no lengthy pilgrimage, no painful penance, no sacrificial service, not even meticulous observance of His commandments, can buy His wonderful salvation. It must be accepted as a gift.

The story is told of a wealthy young man who, for a wager, walked down the main street of his city offering bills of high denomination to passersby. Nobody took one, for all assumed they must be counterfeit—because they were free! Surely, they thought, no one would give away good money like this. But it *was* good money, and the people to whom it was offered lost the opportunity of a lifetime.

Likewise God's offer is good—the best ever made—and we need to be careful that we do not value it lightly because it is free.

Perhaps you are wondering just what you should do about it. Maybe you are asking, like the Philippian jailer, "What must I do to be saved?" (Acts 16:30).

There is but one answer. It is the same as Paul and Silas gave to that poor, distraught man as the prison still trembled from the earthquake: "Believe on the Lord Jesus Christ, and thou shalt be saved" (verse 31).

It is as simple as that. Believe! Take God at His word. Accept what He offers.

Says Peter: "We *believe* that through the grace of the Lord Jesus Christ we shall be saved" (Acts 15:11).

To the Ethiopian official who requested baptism, Philip said, "If thou *believest* with all thine heart, thou mayest. And he answered and said, I *believe* that Jesus Christ is the Son of God" (Acts 8:37).

Here a most important fact should be noticed. It is not sufficient to say "I believe that Jesus Christ was a real person" or "I believe that Jesus Christ was a good man" or even "I believe that Jesus Christ lived, died, and rose again." Something more is necessary. It is "I believe that Jesus Christ is the Son of God."

To see in Christ the divine Son of God is the greatest discovery any man or woman can make. It is the one and only way to receive salvation and to bring into one's life all the power and blessing God has promised.

Accept Christ as the Son of God, see in His life and death God's sublime effort to redeem mankind, and God, overjoyed that you have found Him, will welcome you as His child and will, by His Holy Spirit, come and dwell in your heart. See John 14:23.

In the third chapter of the book of Revelation you will find this marvelous concept summed up in that exquisite verse where Jesus is portrayed as a suppliant outside the door of somebody's heart.

"Behold, I stand at the door and knock: if any man hear my voice, and open the door, I will come in to him, and will sup with him, and he with me" (Revelation 3:20).

What an indescribably beautiful picture! The Son of God, creator of the heavens and the earth, supreme lawgiver and eternal lover, pleading gently, eagerly, with one of His humblest creatures! He knocks, He calls, waiting and hoping.

"Open the door," He asks. "Please let Me in."

What will your answer be?

EVERLASTING FRIEND

ACCEPTING Jesus as your Saviour can be the beginning of a friendship that will last through all eternity.

"You are my friends," He said to His disciples (John 15:14, RSV). Not servants, but friends, He emphasized; which was very wonderful when you stop to think that He was the Lord of heaven in human form, and they but fishermen, revenue men, and the like. Despite the infinite difference in background, He enjoyed their companionship and took them into His confidence. And "having loved his own which were in the world, he loved them unto the end" (John 13:1).

This close, abiding friendship He offers to all who believe in Him. He offers it to you. He would be your friend too.

"I will never leave thee, nor forsake thee," He promises (Hebrews 13:5).

And there is no reason that you should not accept this assurance of His constant presence and watchcare.

This promise was first made to Jacob at a very sad and lonely moment in his experience. He was fleeing from home after sinning grievously against his brother, Esau. Well might he have thought that God had finished with him forever and cut him off permanently from His list of friends. But that very night he saw a ladder linking earth with heaven, with angels on it, "ascending and descending." It was God's way of telling him that contact had not been severed. The way back was still there, right beside him. His repentance and God's love would solve the problem sin had created.

Then it was that God said to him, "Behold, I am with you and will keep you wherever you go . . . ; for I will not leave you until I have done that of which I have spoken to you" (Genesis 28:15, RSV).

Thousands of years later Jesus repeated this pledge, likening Himself to a shepherd with his sheep.

"My sheep hear my voice," He said, "and I know them, and they follow me; and I give them eternal life, and they shall never perish, and no one shall snatch them out of my hand" (John 10:27, 28, RSV).

When a shepherd is with his flock no wild animal or bird of prey can steal a sheep. In like manner Jesus stands guard over His own. No enemy can harm the least of His friends while He is around. And He will be around for a long, long time.

This assurance of everlasting friendship is no less real and precious because Jesus no longer walks the earth as He did 19 centuries ago. Though He is now in heaven "on the right hand of God" (Hebrews 10:12), there is nothing He does not know about you. And because He knows and loves and "continues for ever," "he is able for all time to save those who draw near to God through him, since he always lives to make intercession for them" (Hebrews 7:24, 25, RSV).

Here Jesus is pictured as a priest, a "great high priest," ministering in the heavenly sanctuary; and the writer of this Epistle says that He "had to be made like his brethren in every respect, so that he might become a merciful and faithful high priest in the service of God, to make expiation for the sins of the people. For because he himself has suffered and been tempted, he is able to help those who are tempted" (Hebrews 2:17, 18, RSV).

So in going to heaven Jesus did not take Himself clear away from humanity and all its problems. On the contrary, He is better able to help us than ever. Because He suffered so much we may be sure He understands when we suffer. Because He was tempted so sorely we may know that He can help us whenever we are tempted.

"Since then we have a great high priest who has passed through the heavens, Jesus, the Son of God, let us hold fast our confession. For we have not a high priest who is unable to sympathize with our weaknesses, but one who in every respect has been tempted as we are, yet without sinning. Let us then with confidence draw near to the throne of grace, that we may receive mercy and find grace to help in time of need" (Hebrews 4:14-16, RSV).

So Jesus is both able and eager to be a real friend to His people now. He has not changed with the changing years. His love is as strong, His understanding as perfect, His sympathy as deep, as ever it was in the days of old. He is just as eager to be helpful today as at any time in the past.

In the book of Proverbs we read that "a friend loveth at all times, and a brother is born for adversity" (Proverbs 17:17), and how very true this is of Jesus! He loves at all times and He was surely born "for adversity." This glorious truth is reiterated time and again in your Bible.

"He shall deliver thee in six troubles: yea, in seven there shall no evil touch thee" (Job 5:19).

"The Lord also will be a refuge for the oppressed, a refuge in times of trouble" (Psalm 9:9).

"The salvation of the righteous is of the Lord: he is their strength in the time of trouble" (Psalm 37:39).

"He that dwelleth in the secret place of the most High shall abide under the shadow of the Almighty. . . . Surely he shall deliver thee from the snare of the fowler, and from the noisome pestilence. He shall cover thee with his feathers, and under his wings shalt thou trust: his truth shall be thy shield and buckler.

"Thou shalt not be afraid for the terror by night; nor for the arrow that flieth by day; nor for the pestilence that walketh in darkness; nor for the destruction that wasteth at noonday. A thousand shall fall at thy side, and ten thousand at thy right hand; but it shall not come nigh thee. . . .

71

"Because thou hast made the Lord, which is my refuge, even the most High, thy habitation; there shall no evil befall thee, neither shall any plague come nigh thy dwelling. For he shall give his angels charge over thee, to keep thee in all thy ways" (Psalm 91:1-11).

Amazing assurances! And they are as trustworthy as the One who made them and who left them on record for the encouragement of His people in every age.

If perchance at this moment you are troubled, perplexed, afraid, it may be because you have forgotten that you have such a friend as this to help you.

Your Bible says that He is "a very present help in trouble" (Psalm 46:1), so why not take Him at His word and go "boldly" and "with confidence" to the throne of grace and tell Him all that is on your heart?

Sometimes, like the patriarch Job, God's children are called upon to pass through periods of trial and hardship. Darkness settles upon them. Their future seems hedged with difficulties. Their faith and loyalty are tested to the limit. But never does He desert them. He stands in the shadows "keeping watch above His own." Ever loyal and true, He awaits the right moment to come to their rescue.

Should you be passing through such an experience just now, do not lose faith in your Friend. Instead, say with Job, "Though he slay me, yet will I trust in him" (Job 13:15).

The night will not last forever. Dawn will surely break.

Just when your river Jordan is overflowing its banks, making a crossing seem impossible, He will open a way through.

An acquaintance once told me this personal experience. Prolonged sickness and unemployment had eaten up all the family savings. At last a day came when there was not even a morsel of food in the house. The little girl had to go to school without breakfast, and there was no dinner to offer her when she came home.

The parents wept as the child said to her mother, "Surely Jesus does not want us to starve like this."

"I don't think He will let us starve," replied the mother, "but I wish He would do something soon."

As she spoke her courage returned. Going over to the old piano in the living room, she began to play the familiar hymn "The Lord Will Provide."

"Now let us pray once more," she said. "I cannot believe Jesus will forget us."

So they all knelt in prayer and asked God to help them in their need.

As they rose to their feet the mother said with conviction in her voice, "I believe that when the mailman comes there will be a letter for us with some money in it."

The little girl laughed with high hope and ran out to meet the mailman.

He did have a letter for them. Eagerly the mother opened it. Out fell a money order for a dollar!

Only a dollar! But both child and parents accepted it as a token of God's abiding friendship.

Strangely enough, the very next day a gentleman called at the home and offered the husband work, which he gladly accepted. It was the turning point in their experience. They were never in want again.

Someone may say, "It just happened that way." No. Nothing "just happens" in the lives of those who love God. They are His friends. He loves them. He cares for them. He will never leave them nor forsake them.

Similar stories could be told by the thousand. Miracles of healing. Miracles of protection. Miracles of provision. Miracles of guidance.

And all because the wonderful Creator, the Supreme Lawgiver, the Eternal Lover, the glorious Saviour, is also an everlasting friend—my friend and your friend. Today, tomorrow, always, "even unto the end of the world."

YOU MAY HAVE PEACE

THE more you study your Bible, the more clearly you will see how much it has to say about your life. It is full of good counsel as to how you can make the most of it. Obviously its Author is deeply concerned for your welfare and is anxious that you shall be happy, contented, cheerful, and a source of spiritual strength to your family and community.

Take, for instance, the subject of peace of mind, which has become so very important to multitudes in these trying times. While millions of nervously upset people visit psychiatrists and spend fortunes on tranquilizers, your Bible offers a most reasonable and inexpensive remedy.

All too many nowadays chainsmoke "to soothe their nerves," then drink stimulants to spur themselves on to do their work. But the peace they seek eludes them. They are never really at rest, never truly happy. Such living is a poor substitute for the good way of life revealed in that wonderful Book of yours.

True, your Bible states that "there is no peace . . . to the wicked" (Isaiah 57:21), yet it is equally definite in declaring that those who put their trust in God shall be kept in "perfect peace" (Isaiah 26:3).

There is a reason for this, and it is given in the same beautiful passage:

"Thou wilt keep him in perfect peace, whose mind is stayed on thee: because he trusteth in thee. Trust ye in the Lord for ever: for in the Lord Jehovah is the rock of ages" (verses 3, 4, margin).

Peace is to be found in God because He is more durable than the mountains. With Him there is a stability and permanence that invite the fullest confidence. He is ever the same, unaffected by forces that work changes in others. The passing of time brings no alteration to His person or His character. He endures "from everlasting to everlasting" (Psalm 90:1, 2). Forever and ever all power in heaven and earth belongs to Him (Matthew 28:18).

How restful it is to trust in a God such as this—to have a Friend who never changes, whose love will never die! The very thought suffuses the soul with delicious tranquillity. As the old hymn says:

"Unlike our friends by nature,
Who change with changing years,
This Friend is always worthy
The precious name He bears."

There will never come a time when God's love for His children will lessen. There will never be an occasion when He will cease to hear their petitions and supply their needs. Always He will be to them a tower of strength, a sure refuge. His wisdom and power will ever be available to assist them in every emergency.

That is why peace of mind is to be found through trusting Him. With such a wonderful Friend ever thinking of us, ever caring for us, there can never be any need to worry.

Your Bible says that God is a "God of peace" (Hebrews 13:20). Nothing ever disturbs Him. No earthborn storms invade the holy calm of His presence. He is always at peace. With perfect vision He sees the end from the beginning. In the working out of His plans and purposes there is neither haste nor delay.

Can you imagine God being anxious? Impossible! There is no problem to which He does not know the solution. Nor is there any difficulty so great but He knows the way out. "There is nothing too hard" for the Lord (Jeremiah 32:17).

The Son of God is called the "Prince of Peace," and it is said of

75

Him that "of the increase of his government and peace there shall be no end" (Isaiah 9:7). That is because He understands the secret of peace. Having dwelt with His Father from "the days of eternity" (Micah 5:2, margin), He knows, as no other being can ever know, what perfect peace is and how it is maintained.

When He came to this earth and lived as a man among men, one feature of His life that deeply impressed both His friends and enemies was His perfect poise. Harsh criticism left Him unmoved. Unkind words never made Him angry. Rejection left Him sad but not revengeful. Even on the cross He prayed for those who drove the nails through His hands and feet.

Again and again He invited the weary, worried people who followed Him to share His placidity of spirit. "Come unto me," He said to them with loving sympathy and understanding. "Come and learn My secret." "Come unto me, all ye that labour and are heavy laden, and I will give you rest. Take my yoke upon you, and learn of me; for I am meek and lowly in heart: and ye shall find rest unto your souls. For my yoke is easy, and my burden is light" (Matthew 11:28-30).

The farmers who heard Him say these words understood them perfectly. They knew that a "yoke" joins the animals who pull the plow. So to them this was an invitation to share their troubles and cares with Him. It was an offer to carry the heaviest part of their load.

Many accepted this "yoke" and felt their burdens vanish. Tired mothers, anxious fathers, found peace in Jesus. They learned to rest in the Lord and wait patiently for Him. See Psalm 37:7. They began to understand what the psalmist meant when he said, "Cast thy burden upon the Lord, and he shall sustain thee" (Psalm 55:22).

Especially concerned that His disciples discover the secret of peace, Jesus said to them again and again, in various ways, "Let not your heart be troubled, neither let it be afraid" (John 14:27). He was not afraid of the future Himself, even though He knew it would lead Him to Calvary, and He wanted them to share the peace that filled His soul. "Peace I leave with you," He said to them, "my peace I give unto you" (verse 27).

A little later they were disturbed again, this time by His statement that He was soon going back to His Father in heaven. So He added: "These things I have spoken unto you that in me ye might have peace. In the world ye shall have tribulation; but be of good cheer; I have overcome the world" (John 16:33).

They had no need to worry. His overcoming of the world, of the flesh, and of the devil made certain the ultimate triumph of righteousness. His victory was theirs. They could share its glorious results with Him through all eternity.

So no tribulation or disappointment should ruffle our peace of mind or weaken our reliance upon the promises of God.

It may be that you feel that you have a proper reason for worrying. Perhaps you are thinking about some sin you committed years ago. You confessed it to God and asked His forgiveness, but you are convinced that He still holds it against you.

If so, you are suffering needlessly. If confessed and forsaken, your past sins should be dismissed from your mind. Your Bible says, "If we confess our sins, he is faithful and just to forgive us our sins, and to cleanse us from all unrighteousness" (1 John 1:9). As a result, "we have peace with God through our Lord Jesus Christ" (Romans 5:1).

To every repentant sinner God says: "I have blotted out, as a thick cloud, thy transgressions, and, as a cloud, thy sins: return unto me; for I have redeemed thee. Sing, . . . shout, . . . break forth into singing" (Isaiah 44:22, 23).

He wants us to be glad and rejoice in the salvation He has provided for us. And if He has blotted out our sins, why should we continue to worry about them?

"As far as the east is from the west," we are assured, "so far hath he removed our transgressions from us" (Psalm 103:12). And that is a long, long way. It is, in fact, an infinite distance, beyond human measurement.

"If the wicked restore the pledge, give again that he had robbed, walk in the statutes of life, without committing iniquity," He says to us through the prophet Ezekiel. "He shall surely live, he shall not die.

77

None of his sins that he hath committed shall be mentioned unto him" (Ezekiel 33:15, 16).

"Who is a God like unto thee," exclaims the prophet Micah, "that pardoneth iniquity, and passeth by the transgression of the remnant of his heritage? he retaineth not his anger for ever, because he delighteth in mercy. He will turn again, he will have compassion upon us; he will subdue our iniquities; and *thou wilt cast all their sins into the depths of the sea"* (Micah 7:18, 19).

Only in recent years has the full wonder of this promise dawned upon human minds. For scientists have but lately discovered how deep the ocean really is. Parts of the Pacific are now known to go down nearly seven miles. Anything buried so deep would be buried forever.

That is what God does with your sins when you repent of them and ask His pardon. He casts them into the depths of the sea, eternally beyond reach, never to come to the surface again.

And if that is God's intention, why worry about them any longer?

Why not leave them where He has put them and find rest for your soul in Him?

It could be, of course, that your present disquietude is a result not of past sins but of present temptations. You are worried lest you may fall into some trap the enemy of all good is laying for you. But here again God has made provision for the dispelling of your fears. "The Lord knoweth how to deliver the godly out of temptations," says the apostle Peter (2 Peter 2:9). He is right. God does know how to do it. As Jude says, He "is able to keep you from falling, and to present you faultless before the presence of his glory with exceeding joy" (verse 24).

But, you say, maybe I shall sin again. Suppose you do. This will not take God by surprise. He has made provision for such a slip on your part. Should your conscience ever tell you that you have done something displeasing to Him, remember that you have "an advocate with the Father, Jesus Christ the righteous" (1 John 2:1). He who died on Calvary for our redemption is now "even at the right hand of God, who also maketh intercession for us" (Romans 8:34).

"Likewise the Spirit also helpeth our infirmities: for we know not what we should pray for as we ought: but the Spirit itself maketh intercession for us with groanings which cannot be uttered" (verse 26).

So we have strong help in heaven. Father, Son, and Holy Spirit, who together form the Holy Trinity of love, are eager to help us in our struggle with sin. They yearn for our victory. All the angels, too, are dedicated to be "ministering spirits, sent forth to minister for them who shall be heirs of salvation" (Hebrews 1:14).

There is nothing God is not willing to do to help those who have surrendered their lives to Him. With such ample assurances, why worry so?

This divine concern reaches into the temporal details of our lives. No child of God should ever become unduly anxious about the provision of his daily necessities. Jesus made this abundantly plain in His memorable Sermon on the Mount.

Pointing to the wildflowers blooming about Him, He said, "If God so clothe the grass of the field . . . shall he not much more clothe you, O ye of little faith? Therefore take no thought, saying, What shall we eat? or, What shall we drink? or, Wherewithal shall we be clothed? . . . for your heavenly Father knoweth that ye have need of all these things. But seek ye first the kingdom of God, and his righteousness; and all these things shall be added unto you" (Matthew 6:30-33).

What peace of mind we all would have if we followed this precious counsel! Of course, it does not mean that we should be slothful in our business arrangements, for indolence and improvidence are forbidden by other equally forceful passages of Scripture; but it does mean that we should cease from worrying so much about temporal matters and trust more confidently in the loving-kindness of God toward us.

To overburdened Martha, Jesus said, "Martha, Martha, thou art careful and troubled about many things: but one thing is needful: and Mary hath chosen that good part, which shall not be taken away from her" (Luke 10:41, 42).

In so saying He did not mean to minimize the importance of

home duties. He knew that such work has to be done. But He saw that Martha was more concerned with the housework than with God's work. She was rushed and bothered because she thought she had no time to be with Jesus. Had she taken but a few moments to talk with Him, her soul would have been set at rest.

Taking a little time now and then to think about God and to talk with Him is one of the surest ways of keeping your mind at peace.

If you know you are overwrought, nervous, quick-tempered, worried, it may well be because you are not praying enough. Communion with God is the most soul-calming force known. It will lift you out of the wild tumult of a busy life into the serenity that surrounds His throne. It will correct your perspective and give events, people, and things their proper value. It will help you to realize that "the things which are seen are temporal; but the things which are not seen are eternal" (2 Corinthians 4:18).

Of course, it is easy to tell ourselves that there isn't time to pray, what with the keen pace of modern life and radio, television, newspapers, and magazines filling every vacant moment. Yet the more rushed life is, the more crowded our daily program, the more we need God. And if we would have His peace, we must find time to pray. Indeed, we must learn to bring *all things* to Him in prayer. As the apostle Paul wrote to the Philippians, "Have no anxiety about anything, but *in everything* by prayer and supplication with thanksgiving let your requests be made known to God" (Philippians 4:6, RSV).

With what result? "And the peace of God, which passes all understanding, will keep your hearts and your minds in Christ Jesus" (verse 7).

So peace of mind is possible. God has made provision for it. It is one of the rich gifts of His love. You may have it if you want it. And you may have it now.

YOU MAY HAVE POWER

NO CHILD of God need be a spiritual weakling. Your Bible reveals that an unlimited source of power is available to all who wish to make use of it.

The gospel of Christ, Paul states, is "the power of God unto salvation to every one that believeth" (Romans 1:16). By bringing a man in touch with God, it opens to him all the resources of Omnipotence.

How does this power come to us? Through the Holy Spirit. Says Jesus: "If you then, who are evil, know how to give good gifts to your children, how much more will the heavenly Father give the Holy Spirit to them who ask him?" (Luke 11:13, RSV).

When explaining to Nicodemus the necessity for a spiritual rebirth, Jesus told as simply as He could how this flow of divine power proceeds.

"The wind blows where it wills," He said, "and you hear the sound of it, but you do not know whence it comes or whither it goes; so it is with every one who is born of the Spirit" (John 3:8, RSV).

Perhaps at that very moment, in the darkness of the night, the wind was blowing hard over the mountains round about Jerusalem, rushing down the narrow streets of the city, waving the branches of trees, tugging at the garments of passersby. It could be heard rattling the shutters and banging the doors of nearby houses. They could not see the wind, but they could feel it and hear the effects of it as it swept by.

"So," said Jesus, "it is with every one who is born of the Spirit."

The moment a man opens the door of his heart to God the divine Wind blows in, blowing the dust and dirt of sin from every nook and corner and filling his life with every spiritual blessing.

Jesus called this powerful, invisible force the "Comforter" or the "Counselor," and told His disciples to pray for it.

"The Counselor," He explained to them, "the Holy Spirit, whom the Father will send in my name, he will teach you all things, and bring to your remembrance all that I have said to you" (John 14:26, RSV).

"It is to your advantage that I go away," He added, "for if I do not go away, the Counselor will not come to you; but if I go, I will send him to you" (John 16:7, RSV). "When the Spirit of truth comes, he will guide you into all the truth" (verse 13).

After His resurrection from the dead He recalled these assurances to their minds. "Behold," He said to them, "I send the promise of my Father upon you; but stay in the city, until you are clothed with *power from on high*" (Luke 24:49, RSV).

This was His last recorded command before ascending to heaven. You will find it repeated in the first chapter of the book of Acts.

"While staying with them," the record states, "he charged them not to depart from Jerusalem, but to wait for the promise of the Father, which, he said, 'you heard from me, for John baptized with water, but before many days you shall be baptized with the Holy Spirit. . . . [And] you shall *receive power* when the Holy Spirit has come upon you; and you shall be my witnesses in Jerusalem, and in all Judea and Samaria and to the end of the earth' " (Acts 1:4-8, RSV).

Obediently, expectantly, the disciples waited, continuing "with one accord in prayer and supplication" for 10 days, wondering how the promise of the Father would be fulfilled and what it would mean to them to receive the power from God.

Then came Pentecost. And "suddenly a sound came from heaven like the rush of a mighty wind, and it filled all the house where they were sitting. And there appeared to them tongues as of fire, distributed and resting on each one of them. And they were all filled with the Holy Spirit and began to speak in other tongues, as the Spirit gave them utterance" (Acts 2:2-4, RSV).

Thus was Christ's promise fulfilled. Into the waiting, open, surrendered hearts of His faithful followers burst the dynamic force of the Spirit of God.

The first effect was to empower them for service. They found themselves able to speak freely to the thousands of visitors who had come to Jerusalem from all parts of the Roman Empire to celebrate the Feast of Pentecost. And what a story they had to tell of the life, death, and resurrection of their beloved Lord and Master! Incidents and remarks that normally they might have forgotten were brought back to their minds with great vividness by the Holy Spirit.

Peter was transformed from an obscure, discouraged fisherman into an impassioned preacher—so much so that on that very day, as a result of his ministry, three thousand persons accepted Jesus Christ as the Son of God and were baptized.

Gradually the first exciting weeks of victorious witnessing passed, but as long as the disciples remained humble and prayerful the power of God remained with them. Miracles of healing were wrought. A beggar at the Beautiful Gate of the Temple, lame from birth, was restored to perfect health and went "walking, and leaping, and praising God" to the amazement of everybody around. See Acts 3:2-11.

At Samaria, as a result of Philip's preaching, there was a mighty stir among the people, for "unclean spirits, crying with loud voice, came out of many that were possessed with them: and many taken with palsies, and that were lame, were healed. And there was great joy in that city" (Acts 8:7, 8).

At Lydda there lived a man called Aeneas, who had been bedridden eight years, paralyzed. Peter said to him: " 'Aeneas, Jesus

Christ heals you; rise and make your bed.' And immediately he rose" (Acts 9:33, 34, RSV).

At Joppa, where the saintly Tabitha lay dead, Peter prayed that she might be restored to life. "Then turning to the body, he said, 'Tabitha, rise.' And she opened her eyes, and when she saw Peter she sat up" (verse 40).

At Troas, a young man named Eutychus, having fallen out of a window during one of Paul's long sermons, was likewise raised from the dead.

But the power of the Holy Spirit was not confined to healing the body and restoring life to the dead. It energized every activity of the newborn church.

When, owing to the rapid growth of membership, it was found imperative to appoint men to care for all matters of business, the deacons chosen were men "full of the Spirit and of wisdom" (Acts 6:3, RSV). Stephen, their leader, became almost apostolic in his accomplishments. "Full of grace and power," he "did great wonders and signs among the people" (verse 8).

Later, when persecution arose, "they that were scattered abroad went every where preaching the word" (Acts 8:4). In those first glorious years of devotion and enthusiasm the whole membership was quickened and inspired to great and glorious deeds by the power of the Holy Spirit.

And the Spirit moved on with the advancing church. As new companies of believers were raised up in various parts of Asia Minor, Greece, Italy, and beyond, He filled them also with power, imparting gifts of various kinds. These gifts, your Bible says, "were that some should be apostles, some prophets, some evangelists, some pastors and teachers, for the equipment of the saints, for work of ministry, for building up the body of Christ" (Ephesians 4:11, 12, RSV).

Is this power available today? It is. The gifts of the Spirit, says the apostle Paul, are to remain with the church "until we all attain to the unity of the faith and of the knowledge of the Son of God, to mature manhood, to the measure of the stature of the fullness of Christ" (verse 13).

Says the apostle Peter: "The promise is unto you, and to your children, and to all that are afar off, even as many as the Lord our God shall call" (Acts 2:39).

This promise is as inclusive as the great "whosoever" we have already considered. It takes in everybody of every generation till the end of time. It means that the power of the Holy Spirit is available for you today. If you have heard and accepted the call of God, you are in line to receive your share of the promised blessings. All the gifts of the Spirit may not be granted you, but you will receive those best suited to your capacity for service.

Here is power that will develop every latent talent of yours to the utmost and make your witness for God abundantly effective.

As F. B. Meyer once wrote: "There is no limit to the possibilities of a life that is fully surrendered to God, which has become the aperture or channel through which God can pour Himself forth" (*Moses: The Servant of God*, p. 10).

Such possibilities are within your reach. They are yours for the asking. The Holy Spirit awaits your invitation. Why not open the door of your heart at this moment and let the glorious Wind of God blow in?

This beautiful prayer by Andrew Reed may be yours:

> "Spirit divine, attend our prayer,
>   And make our hearts Thy home;
> Descend with all Thy gracious power:
>   Come, Holy Spirit, come!
>
> "Come as the fire, and purge our hearts
>   Like sacrificial flame;
> Let our whole soul an offering be
>   To our Redeemer's name.
>
> "Come as the wind, with rushing sound,
>   With Pentecostal grace;
> And make Thy great salvation known,
>   Wide as the human race."

YOU MAY BE A
NEW PERSON

THE power of the Holy Spirit is so great, so limitless, that it can bring about a complete transformation of an individual's life. It can change you into an entirely new person.

As the apostle Paul said: "If any one is in Christ, *he is a new creation*; the old is passed away; behold the new has come" (2 Corinthians 5:17, RSV).

Everything mean, unkind, and critical disappears, being replaced by graciousness, gentleness, and unselfishness. The change is so complete that a person is hardly recognizable by his friends. It is as though he has been "born again" (John 3:3).

So absolute is this transformation that it corresponds to a death and resurrection—death of the old nature, with all its sinful tendencies, and life for the new nature, with all its glorious possibilities in Christ.

Drawing an illustration from the Christian ordinance of baptism by immersion, Paul said, "Do you not know that all of us who have been baptized into Christ Jesus were baptized into his death? We were buried therefore with him by baptism into death, so that as Christ was raised from the dead by the glory of the Father, we too might walk in newness of life" (Romans 6:3, 4, RSV).

Baptism by immersion involves a lowering of the body under

water. Should a person be allowed to remain there, he would die. So by taking part in this ceremony a Christian proclaims his willingness to die to his past life.

When brought up out of the water by the officiating minister he reenacts, symbolically, the resurrection—the miracle of living again. Thus he declares his intention to "walk in newness of life" in Christ.

Such a change involves nothing short of a total revolution in all his thoughts and actions. It affects his home life, business life, and recreational life. It alters his eating habits, drinking habits, and spending habits.

He has, perchance, been a user of profane language. Profanity has become so interwoven with his ordinary speech that he no longer thinks anything of it. Suddenly, however, as the Holy Spirit floods his heart and he is "born again," he becomes conscious of the evil words and senses their cheapness and vulgarity. He wonders why he ever soiled his lips with them, and he cuts them out of his vocabulary forever.

Maybe he has become accustomed to drinking alcoholic beverages, or smoking tobacco, or indulging in other habits that detract from his physical fitness and make him less than his best. But immediately God comes into his heart with His marvelous re-creating power, and all desire for such things fades away. He resolves never to indulge in them again.

His attitude at home is different. Willingness to serve replaces expectation to be waited on. Thoughtfulness supersedes selfishness. Ill temper dissolves into pleasantness. Quarrelsomeness is submerged by consideration for others. While before he had no time for prayer or Bible study now he establishes a family altar.

He has a new attitude toward worldly pleasures. Dances, races, and movies lose their fascination as deeper and more lasting joys are found in the things of God. He finds holy hymns and the music of the masters infinitely more satisfying than the silly songs of the nightclubs. Ministry to the poor and needy becomes more enjoyable than the most alluring pastimes.

The commandments of God are seen in a new light. No longer

YOUR BIBLE AND YOU

do they seem legalistic and burdensome. He now counts it a privilege to live in harmony with God's revealed will. With Jesus he desires to "magnify the law and make it honourable" (Isaiah 42:21).

The Sabbath, instead of being a nuisance, is welcomed with joy as an opportunity for communion with the Lord. The holy hours "from sunset to sunset" (Leviticus 23:32; Mark 1:32) are no longer used for business or pleasure seeking, but rather for worship, rest, and prayer. As they recur from week to week they seem to him like islands of peace amid the rushing torrent of life, where spiritual resources may be replenished.

Money takes on a new significance. Instead of using it merely for satisfaction of personal needs, vanities, and ambitions, he regards it as a sacred trust. The "new man," reborn by the power of God, considers himself a steward rather than an owner, administering his affairs "as unto the Lord." He proves the truth of the ancient proverb: "There is that scattereth, and yet increaseth" (Proverbs 11:24), and learns by experience that "God loveth a cheerful giver" (2 Corinthians 9:7).

Is such a total transformation possible?

It must be, or God would not have promised it. You may be sure that He can make you into a new person if you want Him to do so.

Actually it isn't as difficult as it may seem. Jesus revealed the secret in one of His prayers.

"Neither pray I for these alone," He said concerning the disciples who were with Him at the time, "but for them also which shall believe on me through their word; that they all may be one; as thou, Father, art in me, and I in thee, that they also may be one in us. . . . I in them, and thou in me, that they may be made perfect in one" (John 17:20-23).

Perfection can be attained only by unity with God, or, in other words, by complete surrender to the will of God. When your life is thus given to Him, He will dwell within you by His Holy Spirit and live His life in you.

Paul understood it thus, for he prayed this prayer for the Ephesians:

88

"I bow my knees before the Father," he said, "that according to the riches of his glory he may grant you to be strengthened with might *through his Spirit in the inner man*, and that Christ may dwell in your hearts through faith; that you, being rooted and grounded in love, may have power to comprehend with all the saints what is the breadth and length and height and depth, and to know the love of Christ which surpasses knowledge, that you may be *filled with all the fullness of God"* (Ephesians 3:14-19, RSV).

"Filled with all the fullness of God" implies that there is no room left for self or sin. The new life, the better, nobler life, is an inevitable result.

This way the old, hopeless struggle with sin ends and the day of victorious living begins.

If this seems hard to understand, think of this: In every forest there are usually a few trees that retain some of their leaves throughout winter. Storms may rage, gales may blow, torrents of rain may fall, but still the leaves remain. You may take a stick and beat the branches with all your might, but you will not be able to dislodge them. But let a few weeks pass. Let spring come. Some fine morning you will discover that the tree is bare. In a single night every leaf has fallen to the ground!

Why? The sap has risen. That's all. Life is flowing through the tree once more. Rushing up like a torrent from the roots, it is surging out into the farthermost twigs with a power that makes all things new, causing a million lovely leaves to appear and cover the naked branches with verdant beauty.

Thus it is with the God-filled life. Without the aid of the Holy Spirit you could wrestle with sin for a lifetime without success. But let Him flow in! Let the life of God rise like sap in a tree and radiate through every part of your being! Instantly old besetting sins will drop away. Conscience will awake. The will, now under divine control, will express itself in a thousand gracious words and deeds.

Such is the new life your Bible portrays and that God says you may live. You may not understand all its mysteries. He doesn't expect you to. All He asks is that you believe His promise and accept His offer. If you do, the transformation can begin now. This moment He can make you a new person, a "new creation," created, like Adam, "in the image of God" (Genesis 1:27).

YOU MAY HAVE
ANYTHING

SOME of God's promises are absolutely breathtaking. They almost seem to be too good to be true. They suggest that there is nothing He will not do for those who love Him.

If you want to feel like a millionaire, open your Bible and read Psalm 84:11: "*No good thing* will he withhold from them that walk uprightly."

The same pledge is given in Psalm 34:10: "They that seek the Lord shall not want *any good thing.*"

And look at this in Psalm 37:4: "Delight thyself also in the Lord; and *he shall give thee the desires of thine heart.*"

Now turn to the book of Deuteronomy and read what God was prepared to do for Israel in the days of Moses: "If thou shalt hearken diligently unto the voice of the Lord thy God, to observe and to do all his commandments . . . all these blessings shall come on thee and overtake thee. . . . Blessed shalt thou be in the city, and blessed shalt thou be in the field. . . . Blessed shall be thy basket and thy store. Blessed shalt thou be when thou comest in, and blessed shalt thou be when thou goest out" (Deuteronomy 28:1-6). "The Lord shall open unto thee his good treasure" (verse 12).

It was as though God said to them, "I will give you all these blessings, and if there is anything else you need, it is yours for the asking. Just come and take it. My treasure is open to you."

That these amazing promises were not intended only for His people in ancient times is made abundantly clear in the Scriptures. Again and again the glorious truth is repeated that God wants to be equally generous to everybody in every age. "*Whatsoever ye shall ask in my name*," said Jesus, "that will I do, that the Father may be glorified in the Son" (John 14:13).

Notice that word "whatsoever." It recalls the wonderful "whosoever" of John 3:16. It is equally limitless. It suggests infinite wealth and an infinite willingness to share it with others.

To make sure that no one would mistake His intention or underestimate the extent of His promise, Jesus added: "If ye shall ask *any thing* in my name, I will do it." A little later He repeated the assurance in these words: "If ye abide in me, and my words abide in you, ye shall ask *what ye will*, and it shall be done unto you" (John 15:7).

Here are some of the most remarkable promises of help and blessing ever made. Read them again in the Revised Standard Version:

"Whatever you ask in my name, I will do it."

"If you ask anything in my name, I will do it."

"Ask whatever you will, and it shall be done for you."

If words mean anything, then God has made provision for every holy wish of ours to be granted. If our lives are wretched, impoverished, and spiritually emaciated, the fault must be ours, not His. He has planned greatly for us. He stands ready to be very gracious to us and fill our lives with blessings. If we "have not," it is because we "ask not." See James 4:2.

One reason that Jesus came to this earth and died on Calvary's cross was to make rich those who accept and love Him. "You know the grace of our Lord Jesus Christ," wrote the apostle Paul, "that though he was rich, yet for your sake he became poor, so that by his poverty you might become rich" (2 Corinthians 8:9, RSV).

Not rich necessarily in material things, for these count little in the sight of God, but rich in the things of the Spirit, which, after all, alone have lasting value. Through Him we can become rich in wisdom, in knowledge, in faith, in mercy, in love. "Has not God chosen those who are poor in the world to be rich in faith and heirs of the kingdom which he has promised to those who love him?" (James 2:5, RSV).

"If any of you lacks wisdom," wrote James, "let him ask God who gives to all men *generously* and without reproaching, and it will be given him" (James 1:5, RSV).

This emphasizes again God's attitude to all our needs and requests. He is generous. Very generous. And His generosity is measurable only by His love, which is infinite.

With this thought in mind the apostle Paul asked, "He that spared not his own Son, but delivered him up for us all, how shall he not with him also *freely give us all things?*" (Romans 8:32).

It seemed only reasonable to him that if God loved us enough to give His Son to die for us, He would never withhold anything else that might contribute to our present and eternal happiness.

His reasoning was right, of course; and it helps us to appreciate more fully the infinite weight of eternal truth behind Christ's promise: "If you ask *anything* in my name, I will do it."

Of course, the word "anything" does not mean anything bad, or anything harmful to us or to others. But it does imply anything that will be good for us, anything that is in harmony with the will of God, anything that will advance His cause and His kingdom.

And because He says "anything," we should not hesitate to bring large requests to Him. By so doing we shall honor Him, for it will demonstrate that we believe He is able to grant them.

Judging by some people's prayers, one would think they believe that God is concerned only with the smaller interests of life. They seem afraid to mention the great burdens they are carrying, or the real desires of their hearts. But God wants us to bring all such larger matters to Him. It is His joy to do great things for His children, for "he is able to do exceeding abundantly above all that we ask or think" (Ephesians 3:20).

Notice that Jesus did not say, "If you shall ask any *little* thing in

My name, I will do it," but "If you ask *any thing*." And that surely takes in the great things, the seemingly impossible things, the things that seem far beyond our reach.

"Call unto me," the Lord said to the prophet Jeremiah, "and I will answer thee, and *shew thee great and mighty things*, which thou knowest not" (Jeremiah 33:3).

That is what He wants us all to do—to call upon Him in faith, expecting mighty results from our prayers.

Many people have accepted this invitation, and, as a result, have seen God work for them in marvelous ways.

Your Bible tells the story of the prophet Elijah, who asked that fire be sent from heaven—not for his glory, but for God's.

"Lord God of Abraham, Isaac, and of Israel," he prayed, "let it be known this day that thou art God in Israel, and that I am thy servant, and that I have done all these things at thy word" (1 Kings 18:36).

It was a very short and simple prayer, but it revealed the complete consecration of the prophet, and his single-minded desire to bring honor to God's holy name. As a result, there and then, "the fire of the Lord fell."

This is the kind of prayer God answers. As John says: "If we ask anything according to his will he hears us" (1 John 5:14, RSV).

King Hezekiah prayed a similar prayer when he received a letter from the king of Assyria demanding the immediate surrender of Jerusalem. He took the letter "and went up unto the house of the Lord, and spread it before the Lord. And Hezekiah prayed unto the Lord, saying, O Lord of hosts, God of Israel, that dwellest between the cherubims, thou art the God, even thou alone, of all the kingdoms of the earth: thou hast made heaven and earth. Incline thine ear, O Lord, and hear; open thine eyes, O Lord, and see: and hear all the words of Sennacherib, which hath sent to reproach the living God. . . . Now therefore, O Lord our God, save us from his hand, that all the kingdoms of the earth may know that thou art the Lord, even thou only" (Isaiah 37:14-20).

As a result of this prayer, which was also for the glory of God, the Assyrian army was mysteriously destroyed and Sennacherib returned to Nineveh without so much as shooting an arrow at Jerusalem.

Examples of great results from earnest prayers uttered by faith-filled men and women are not confined to Bible characters.

Everybody has heard of George Müller and his world-famous orphanage at Bristol, England. When he began his work for orphans in 1836, he resolved to depend solely upon God for help. Over the years his institution has received multiplied millions of dollars solely in answer to prayer and without anyone's being asked for a donation. Think of praying for millions! But God sent it, and nearly 18,000 orphans have been blessed thereby.

Müller's faith became almost proverbial, and inspired countless others to put their trust in God. All his needs, great and small, he spread out before the Lord, with absolute assurance that they would be supplied.

On one occasion when he was crossing the Atlantic his ship ran into a fog. Approaching the captain, he said, "I have come to tell you that I must be in Quebec on Saturday afternoon."

"Impossible," said the captain.

"Very well," replied Müller, "if your ship cannot take me, God will find some other means. I have never broken an engagement in 57 years."

"I would willingly help you if I could," said the captain, "but there's nothing anyone can do."

"Do you know how dense the fog is?" asked the captain.

"No," was Müller's answer. "My eye is not on the density of the fog, but on the living God, who controls every circumstance of my life."

Together they went to the chartroom, and Müller prayed: "O Lord, if it is consistent with Thy will, please remove the fog in five minutes. You know the engagement You made for me in Quebec on Saturday. I believe it is Your will."

When he had finished, the captain was about to pray, but Müller touched him on the shoulder and told him not to do so. "First," he said, "you do not believe He will; and second, I believe He has, so there is no need for you to pray about it."

The captain looked amazed and Müller continued: "Captain, I have known my Lord for 57 years, and there has never been a single day that I have failed to gain an audience with Him. Get up and open the door. You will find the fog gone."

The captain opened the door. The fog had disappeared!

Many similar stories have come out of the trials and anguish of our fighting forces. Chaplain W. H. Bergherm tells of meeting a devout admiral who once sent up 25 planes on a reconnaissance flight and lost sight of them in impenetrable mist. Anxiously he waited for their return, but they couldn't find the carrier. Knowing their gas was running low, he began to lose hope of saving the gallant young pilots. Then he thought of God. Going to his cabin, he prayed for a break in the fog. Returning to the deck, he saw that a streak of blue sky had appeared. Through this the planes came hurtling down one after another, till all were safely aboard. Then, just as suddenly and mysteriously, the sky closed in again.

In his book *We Thought We Heard the Angels Sing*, Lt. James C. Whittaker tells of the days he spent on a rubber raft after his plane had crashed in the ocean. Hungry, thirsty, and blistered with the heat, he and his companions turned to God for help.

On the thirteenth day of their terrible experience, hope revived as a rain squall blotted out the scorching sun and moved toward them. Then when the cloud was less than a quarter of a mile away, the wind blew it in another direction! The disappointment was crushing. "But somehow," says Lieutenant Whittaker, "my faith did not die. For the first time I found myself leading the rest in prayer. Like many of the others, I didn't know how to address God properly. I talked to Him, therefore, as I would have to a parent or a friend.

" 'God,' I prayed, 'You know what that water means to us. The wind has blown it away. It is in Your power, God, to send back that rain. It's nothing to You, but it means life to us.' "

Nothing happened, but he continued to pray. In agony of soul he cried out:

" 'God, the wind is Yours. You own it. Order it to blow back the rain to us who will die without it.' "

They waited, watching and hoping. Then the miracle happened. Says Lieutenant Whittaker:

"There are some things that can't be explained by natural law. The wind did not change, but the receding curtain of rain stopped where it was. Then, ever so slowly, it started back toward us — against the wind!

"Maybe a meteorologist can explain that to your satisfaction. One tried it with me; something about crosscurrents buffeting the squall back. I tell you that there was no buffeting. It moved back with majestic deliberation. It was as if a great and omnipotent hand was guiding it to us across the water."

They caught a great store of rainwater, washed the salt from their poor, blistered bodies, and gathered courage for the rest of their ordeal. They knew then that God would not desert them.

Forced down at sea while on a flight to Australia, Maj. Allen Lindberg, of Westfield, New Jersey, found himself and his crew of nine on rubber rafts after their Flying Fortress had plunged to the bottom of the ocean.

"The boys were pretty worried," Major Lindberg said afterward, "all except Sgt. Albert Hernandez, our tail gunner. Right away that lad from Texas started praying, and pretty soon he startled us by announcing that he knew God had heard him and would help us out."

Retelling the story in *Cosmopolitan* magazine, Percy Waxman wrote:

"Drifting beneath a broiling sun with their lips too cracked and their tongues too swollen to join Hernandez in singing hymns, their prayers continued just the same. On the third day just before nightfall they saw the outline of a small island, and soon after that the almost unbelievable spectacle of three canoes filled with naked men coming toward them. Their rescuers turned out to be Australian aborigines — black-skinned, kinky-haired fishermen from the mainland several hundred miles away. These men told Lindberg that the day before they had been homeward bound with their catch when a strange urge came over them. Something impelled them to change their course and steer for this uninhabited and worthless bit of coral. And from that atoll they spied Lindberg and his companions."

Yet it is not only amid the crises of war that God draws near to deliver those who seek His help. He watches over His loved ones "in every time of need."

Some years ago a woman told me this personal experience: Her father, a farmer in Canada and a faithful servant of God, had fallen upon hard times. It was winter, and there was food enough for but one last meal for the family of five. In desperation he called them all to prayer, not seeing any escape from starvation. After praying, he sent one of the boys through the snow to the post office, several miles away. The lad brought back a letter, and in it was a draft for $100—money the father had lent to a man 13 years before!

Would you like to see God work for you? You may. He loves you very dearly. He wants to help you. He wants to do great things for you. Just give Him a chance. Tell Him your needs, your hopes, your dreams. Ask for specific blessings and watch them come to pass.

"Call," He says, "and I will answer."

"If you ask *anything* in my name, I will do it."

YOU MAY OPEN THE
WINDOWS OF HEAVEN

Y OU may open the windows of heaven. This is another of the
wonderful promises in your Bible.

Not that heaven has windows made of plate glass or plastic.
Obviously the phrase is a word picture intended to express in a very
graphic way God's willingness to do great and glorious things for
those who love Him.

You will find the promise in Malachi 3:10: "Bring ye all the tithes
into the storehouse, that there may be meat in mine house, and prove
me now herewith, saith the Lord of hosts, if I will not *open you the
windows of heaven, and pour you out a blessing, that there shall not
be room enough to receive it.*"

In olden times it was a custom on feast days, at weddings, and
other celebrations, for rich people to open the upper windows of
their homes and throw gold and silver coins to passersby below. This
may well have prompted the prophet to say that God would open His
windows too, with this difference: the blessing He would bestow
would be so bountiful that the recipients would not know where to
put it. Their pockets would not be large enough.

"Empty out" a blessing is the marginal reading, which is even
more expressive of God's limitless generosity. He is prepared to give
everything He has. He will exhaust the whole vast treasury of heaven,

if need be, on behalf of His faithful children.

The next verse outlines some additional rewards:

"I will rebuke the devourer for your sakes, and he shall not destroy the fruits of your ground; neither shall your vine cast her fruit before the time in the field, saith the Lord of hosts."

Malachi was talking for the most part to small farmers, who understood His language perfectly. Their whole living depended on the preservation of their crops. No doubt they had often longed for some way to fight successfully the many harmful pests that preyed upon them. Often, too, they must have hoped to find a way to ensure the adequate pollination of their vines so that they would not fail to bear fruit. Now they had no more reason for worry. The God of nature would take over. Marvelously, invisibly, but certainly, He would control the activities of the tiny creatures He had created so that the fullest possible harvest might be reaped. The harmful insects would be restrained while the helpful ones would be assisted in their beneficial operations.

As a result of this divine intervention the whole country would be enriched and beautified. Prosperity would abound. Israel would become the envy of the world. "All nations will call you blessed, for you shall be a land of delight, says the Lord of hosts" (Malachi 3:12, RSV).

These blessings, like all God's promises, were available to all, but not everybody would receive them. People who hated God or were careless and indifferent about His requirements would not participate in the benefits.

One big trouble with the people of Malachi's day was that they had failed to pay the tithe that God had said was to be used to support the religious activities of the country. They had spent God's money on themselves, and as a result the ministers in the Temple were starving. Hence the prophet's urgent plea, "Bring . . . all the tithes into the storehouse, that there may be meat in mine house."

For those who heeded that call and did what was right in the sight of God the windows of heaven would be opened. For the others they would remain shut.

For the obedient there would be blessings innumerable. For the disobedient there would be nothing. They would be "cursed with a curse" (Malachi 3:9). Does this mean that a person can buy God's favors by giving 10 percent of his "increase" to charity? No indeed. God's blessings are not for sale.

Then why does He ask for a tithe at all?

It cannot be because He needs the money, for "the silver is mine, and the gold is mine" (Haggai 2:8), He says, and "the cattle upon a thousand hills" (Psalm 50:10). He is rich beyond all human conception, and our paltry gifts could add nothing significant to His infinite resources.

But it could be that God wants us to pay one tenth of our "increase" to Him as a reminder that all we possess belongs to Him and we are but stewards of His property.

Tithe paying goes back a long, long way in history—before there were any Israelites. Your Bible tells how Abraham paid tithe to "the priest of the most high God" (Genesis 14:18), and how Jacob promised to do so (Genesis 28:22). Later the principle was woven into the laws of Moses as the best way to support the priests and Levites (Leviticus 27:30; Deuteronomy 14:22). Thereafter, down through the centuries, the tithe was considered "holy unto the Lord."

Jesus made but one reference to this custom, and it is of special interest. In His day tithe paying was scrupulously practiced by the religious leaders of Israel, but it had become a matter of law, not of love. They did it to acquire merit and build up a good reputation for themselves while neglecting other matters much more important to God.

"Woe to you, scribes and Pharisees, hypocrites!" Jesus said to them. "For you tithe mint and dill and cummin, and have neglected the weightier matters of the law, justice and mercy and faith; these you ought to have done, without neglecting the others. You blind guides, straining out a gnat and swallowing a camel!" (Matthew 23:23, 24, RSV).

Here is clear proof that it is love that matters most to God. By their meticulous attempts to tithe even the lowly herbs they had been

101

"straining out a gnat," while by their shocking lack of justice, mercy, and faith—the fruits of love—they had been "swallowing a camel."

This was no attack on the tithing system as such—which everybody agrees is the finest way ever devised to raise money for church purposes—but rather a rebuke at its abuse. To give money to God while being unjust, unmerciful, and faithless is the worst kind of hypocrisy. It demonstrates a total lack of understanding of God and of His purpose in establishing the tithing plan.

Only tithe accompanied by love is pleasing to God. Paid as a legal requirement, it will never bring the promised blessings.

Should Christians pay tithe today? That is a question that has been debated for a long time. But Christ's statement that it should not be left "undone" is not without significance, especially when linked with Paul's declaration that "the Lord ordained that they which preach the gospel should live of the gospel" (1 Corinthians 9:14). In addition, there is a great deal of evidence that suggests that it is a very wise, as well as a very desirable, thing to do.

I know thousands who are following this plan, and they all seem to be getting along quite well. Somehow they seem to accomplish more with nine tenths than those who spend all ten tenths on themselves.

There is a blessing in it. And a very rich blessing it is—just as God promised through Malachi. The windows of heaven are opened and His bounties are bestowed beyond all expectation.

This blessing is not necessarily monetary. God does not promise to make us wealthy just because we tithe. On the other hand, some wealthy people have added their witness to the tithe principle. H. J. Heinz of "57 Varieties," H. P. Crowell of Quaker oats, J. L. Kraft of Kraft cheese, M. W. Baldwin of the Baldwin Locomotive Works, F. W. Woolworth of the well-known five-and-ten chain, William Wrigley of chewing gum, M. S. Hershey of Hershey's chocolate, and William Colgate of toothpaste fame all put God first in their finances.

Sometimes—when needed—God fulfills His promise to "rebuke the devourer" and care for a faithful Christian's harvest.

Some years ago I visited a farmer near Hollister, California, where this actually occurred. His crops were coming up satisfactorily when one day he noticed that the dreaded army beetle had settled in a corner of one of his fields. Realizing that it would be but a matter of hours before his entire farm would be bare, he was filled with despair.

Whereupon his little girl spoke up. "Daddy," she said, "you pay your tithe, don't you? Then why not ask God to keep His promise and drive the beetles away?"

Together they knelt in prayer, earnestly claiming the promise of Malachi 3:11.

Looking up, they saw some blackbirds alighting on the field where the beetles were. More came, and still more. Soon, the farmer told me, they resembled a cloud in the sky. They remained on the ground only a few minutes, but when they flew away there wasn't a beetle left. The blackbirds had devoured them all.

A missionary in East Africa, a personal friend of mine, once told me this story: During the great plague of locusts that swept over Kenya colony during August 1931, when every green thing was consumed and the government had to step in to save the people from starvation, a Christian African decided to ask for God's protection. He was a faithful tithepayer and knew the promise in Malachi by heart. Now he wanted to see whether it would come true for him.

As the locusts advanced, they settled on all the surrounding country, leaving not a blade of grass or a stalk of corn, or even a leaf on a tree. Yet when they had passed by, the little garden of that humble Christian African stood out green and beautiful, like an oasis amid the universal desolation. People came from miles around to see the amazing sight.

Why not put Him to the test? He invites you to do so. Should you decide to bring your tithe—lovingly and gratefully—into His storehouse, you too may open the windows of heaven. Into your life may flow blessings so great and so many that there will not be room enough to receive them.

YOU MAY LIVE VICTORIOUSLY

NOT only does God want to make you happy and prosperous, and to bless you with "every spiritual blessing"; it is His plan and desire that you shall live victoriously every day. With head high and shoulders back, you may tread the earth like a conqueror. Not in pride, of course, but in sheer joy of serving Him and with full confidence in His direction of your life.

Some indication of His purpose can be seen by reading His messages to ancient Israel. Take your Bible and turn to the book of Deuteronomy. Here you will find some of the most striking promises of this sort.

"If you will be careful to do all this commandment which I command you to do, loving the Lord your God, walking in all his ways, and cleaving to him," He said through Moses, "then the Lord will drive out all these nations before you, and you will dispossess nations greater and mightier than yourselves. . . . *No man shall be able to stand against you*" (Deuteronomy 11:22-25, RSV).

"The Lord will cause your enemies who rise against you to be defeated before you; *they shall come out against you one way, and flee before you seven ways*" (Deuteronomy 28:7).

"The Lord will establish you as a people holy to himself, as he has sworn to you, if you keep the commandments of the Lord your

God, and walk in his ways. And all the peoples of the earth shall see that you are called by the name of the Lord; and *they shall be afraid of you"* (verses 9, 10).

Notice that the power of the people would reside not in military might but in holiness. They would be respected because of their lofty principles and noble lives. No one would dare to harm them because of their obvious identification with the God of heaven.

The same spiritual significance can be seen in this promise also: *"The Lord will make you the head, and not the tail;* and you shall tend upward only, and not downward; if you obey the commandments of the Lord your God, . . . being careful to do them"* (verse 13).

Later, as Israel was about to enter the Promised Land, God said to their new leader, Joshua, "Only be strong and very courageous, being careful to do according to all the law which Moses my servant commanded you; turn not from it to the right hand or to the left, that *you may have good success wherever you go"* (Joshua 1:7, RSV).

Again: "Have I not commanded you? Be strong and of good courage; be not frightened, neither be dismayed; for *the Lord your God is with you wherever you go"* (verse 9).

Accepting these glorious promises at their face value, Joshua went on from victory to victory until God's purpose in Canaan had been achieved. At the close of his life he was able to say, "There failed not ought of any good thing which the Lord had spoken unto the house of Israel; all came to pass" (Joshua 21:45).

May we claim these promises today? By all means. Why not? God has not changed His plans for those who love Him and keep His commandments.

After Joshua's day the people of Israel lost their way and forsook the worship of God for idols, at very great cost to themselves. The promised blessings were withdrawn. But not forever. They were merely held in reserve until there should appear on earth a people who could be trusted with them.

At last such a people appeared. To the eager, innocent, zealous followers of Jesus, who made up the church of the first century, God said through the apostle Peter, "You are a chosen race, a holy nation, *God's own people*, that you may declare the wonderful deeds of him who called you out of darkness into his marvelous light" (1 Peter 2:9, RSV).

Because *they* were now "God's own people," doing what was pleasing in His sight, the blessings were bestowed on them. Like a river in full flood the power of the Holy Spirit came upon them and they "went forth conquering, and to conquer" (Revelation 6:2).

Each individual member believed, as did Joshua, that God was with him wherever he went. Remembering the Master's promise, "I give unto you power . . . over all the power of the enemy" (Luke 10:19), he talked victory and expected victory. So, irresistibly, the church moved on to win an empire for Christ.

This glorious, conquering spirit was specially manifest in the life of that greatest of all missionaries, the apostle Paul. Nothing seemed to discourage him.

After his conversion life was not easy for him. He endured much. "Five times I have received at the hands of the Jews the forty lashes less one," he told the church in Corinth. "Three times I have been beaten with rods; once I was stoned. Three times I have been shipwrecked; a night and a day I have been adrift at sea; on frequent journeys, in danger from rivers, danger from robbers, danger from my own people, danger from Gentiles, danger in the city, danger in the wilderness, danger at sea, danger from false brethren; in toil and hardship, through many a sleepless night, in hunger and thirst, often without food, in cold and exposure" (2 Corinthians 11:24-27, RSV).

All this was enough to make any man depressed. But not Paul.

"For the sake of Christ," he added, "I am content with weaknesses, insults, hardships, persecutions, and calamities; for when I am weak, then I am strong" (2 Corinthians 12:10, RSV).

"We are afflicted in every way, but not crushed," he said; "perplexed, but not driven to despair; persecuted, but not forsaken; struck down, but not destroyed. . . . Knowing that he who raised . . . Jesus will raise us also with Jesus and bring us with you into his presence" (2 Corinthians 4:8, 9, 14, RSV).

"So we do not lose heart," he went on. "Though our outer nature is wasting away, our inner nature is being renewed every day. For this slight momentary affliction is preparing for us an eternal weight of glory beyond all comparison, because we look not to the things that are seen but to the things that are unseen; for the things that are seen are transient, but the things that are unseen are eternal" (verses 16-18).

What marvelous faith! What incredible courage! Here indeed was the spirit of a conqueror. Sustained by absolute confidence in God, sure of His love, leadership, and ultimate deliverance, Paul faced each day's trials and defeats as though God had already turned them into victories.

"Wherever I go, thank God," he wrote, "he makes my life a constant pageant of triumph in Christ" (2 Corinthians 2:14, Moffatt).

No doubt he had often seen Roman generals departing on foreign expeditions at the head of mail-clad legions. And he had seen them return, bringing the spoils of war to lay at the emperor's feet.

"My life is like that," he said. "A constant pageant of triumph. Only I serve not Caesar but the King of kings."

"Who shall separate us from the love of Christ?" he asked the Christians in Rome. "Shall tribulation, or distress, or persecution, or famine, or nakedness, or peril, or sword? . . . No, *in all these things we are more than conquerors through him who loved us.* For I am sure that neither death, nor life, nor angels, nor principalities, nor things present, nor things to come, nor powers, nor height, nor depth, nor anything else in all creation, will be able to separate us from the love of God in Christ Jesus our Lord" (Romans 8:35-39, RSV).

To the end of life's journey this conquering spirit remained with him. In his last letter, written just before his execution, he said, "I have fought a good fight, I have finished my course, I have kept the faith: henceforth there is laid up for me a crown of righteousness, which the Lord, the righteous judge, shall give me at that day: and not to me only, but unto all them also that love his appearing" (2 Timothy 4:7, 8).

How did he manage to keep up his courage so long, through so many terrible trials? There is a hint of the secret in that word of his to the Corinthians: "Our inner nature is being renewed every day" (or as the King James Version puts it: "The inward man is renewed day by day"). His was a day-by-day experience. He never let himself get far away from God. He kept close to the fountain of spiritual strength. Instead of taking trials and insults to heart and grieving over them, he told God about them. When threatened and persecuted, he thought of God's long-range plans and laughed at his fears.

But it was to the Ephesians that he spoke most plainly on this subject. He wanted them to be as "strong in the Lord, and in the strength of his might" as he was himself. He wanted them also to live the victorious life. So he gave them this admonition:

"Put on the whole armor of God, that you may be able to stand against the wiles of the devil. For we are not contending against flesh and blood, but against the principalities, against the powers, against the world rulers of this present darkness, against the spiritual hosts of wickedness in the heavenly places. Therefore take the whole armor of God, that you may be able to withstand in the evil day, and having done all, to stand.

"Stand therefore, having girded your loins with truth, and having put on the breastplate of righteousness, and having shod your feet with the equipment of the gospel of peace; above all, taking the shield of faith, with which you can quench all the flaming darts of the evil one. And take the helmet of salvation, and the sword of the Spirit, which is the word of God" (Ephesians 6:10-17, RSV).

Notice this armor carefully, for you too must wear it if you would live victoriously.

First there is the garment of *truth*; next the breastplate of *righteousness*; then the shoes of *peace*, the shield of *faith*, the helmet of *salvation*, and finally the sword of the Spirit, "which is the *word of God.*"

Obviously this armor is not material but spiritual. It has to do with the mind and the heart rather than the body. But once donned, it will preserve the whole being from "all the flaming darts of the evil one."

Truth will give us certainty and keep our thoughts balanced and reasonable.

Righteousness will give us confidence and free us from fear of criticism.

Peace will give us gentleness and enable us to ignore all slights and slurs upon our character and way of life.

Faith will give us courage and buoyancy and place all disappointments and hardships in their true perspective.

The Word of God will supply every weapon we need in our warfare with the powers of darkness. Like the flaming sword over the gate of Eden, it will turn "every way" in the battle with evil.

Notice particularly that last piece of equipment suggested by the apostle—"the word of God." That, of course, is the Bible. Your Bible!

This means that the very Book you have in your home can help you to triumph over every difficulty, every sorrow, every setback, and to live victoriously here and hereafter.

YOU MAY WALK
WITH GOD

HERE is God's crowning blessing. In addition to every other good thing, He offers us His company. It is hard to understand why the omnipotent Creator would want to associate with such lowly creatures, but the fact remains that He does.

"If you walk in my statutes and observe my commandments and do them," He said to Israel of old, "I will walk among you, and will be your God, and you shall be my people" (Leviticus 26:3, 12, RSV).

Here was a wonderful offer. "If you walk . . . I will walk." In other words, If you want to go along with Me, I will go along with you. It was a gracious invitation to walk together.

Like all God's offers and promises, it was not made to Israel alone. It was open to all. Anyone who loved God enough to want to walk with Him could do so.

It is said of Enoch that he "walked with God after he begat Methuselah three hundred years" (Genesis 5:22).

Something about the birth of his son changed his life. He gave his heart to God as he had never done before. He resolved to try to please Him in every thought, word, and deed (Hebrews 11:5). As a result they became such intimate companions that eventually "God took him" by translation so that he did not need to die. By walking with God, he walked clear into heaven.

Noah also was "a just man and perfect in his generations, and Noah walked with God" (Genesis 6:9). "Thee have I seen righteous before me in this generation" was God's personal tribute to him (Genesis 7:1). And although he was not translated as was Enoch, yet he and his family were afforded the unique experience of being delivered from the Flood that overwhelmed the rest of mankind.

When Abraham was 99 years old, God appeared to him and said, "Walk before me, and be thou perfect" (Genesis 17:1). Abraham obeyed, and they enjoyed such intimate fellowship that God called him His friend (Isaiah 41:8). "*I know him*," God said, "that he will command his children and his household after him, and they shall keep the way of the Lord, to do justice and judgment" (Genesis 18:19).

As for Moses, there is no doubt that he walked with God through the long, weary wilderness years. Your Bible says that the Lord spoke to him "face to face, as a man speaketh unto his friend" (Exodus 33:11).

Likewise Joshua was conscious of God's continual presence during the conquest of Canaan. When all the battles were over and he was sending the warriors back to their homes, he exhorted them to live as he had. "Take diligent heed to do the commandment and the law," he urged them; "to love the Lord your God, and to *walk in all his ways*, and to *keep his commandments*, and to *cleave unto him*, and to *serve him with all your heart and with all your soul*" (Joshua 22:5).

King David, despite all his faults and failings, inwardly coveted the experience of unbroken communion with God. Contrite and humble, he prayed: "For thou hast delivered my soul from death, mine eyes from tears, and my feet from falling. I will walk before the Lord in the land of the living" (Psalm 116:8, 9).

In the New Testament we read how the disciples walked with God in person for three and a half years, a walk they never forgot. They talked of it and wrote of it to the end of their days.

Said John: "If we say we have fellowship with him while we walk in darkness, we lie and do not live according to the truth; but if we

111

YOUR BIBLE AND YOU

walk in the light, as he is in the light, we have fellowship with one another, and the blood of Jesus his Son cleanses us from all sin" (1 John 1:6, 7, RSV).

Again: "He who says he abides in him ought to walk in the same way in which he walked" (1 John 2:6, RSV).

With the same thought in mind Peter wrote: "Christ also suffered for you, leaving you an example, that you should follow in his steps" (1 Peter 2:21, RSV).

In other words, if we want to walk with God, we must go where He goes. We cannot choose our own way or go off in some direction He does not approve.

"Can two walk together, except they be agreed?" asked the prophet Amos, and the obvious answer was no. There must be agreement on direction, objective, and even topics of conversation, or the journey will come to an abrupt end. People don't go very far together unless they are in harmony.

It could be that at this moment you are saying to yourself, "Does God mean what He says? Does He really seek the companionship of someone like me?"

Here is your answer: "He has showed you, O man, what is good; and what does the Lord require of you but to do justice, and to love kindness, and to *walk humbly with your God?*" (Micah 6:8, RSV).

So He *does* want you to walk with Him. Unbelievable though it may seem, the God of heaven is so interested in you that He wants you for His friend. He actually invites you to be His life companion. He wants you to walk with Him every day for the rest of your life.

Before accepting the offer, you had better think what it means.

There will have to be identity of purpose. If God wants to take you to heaven and you don't want to go there, the arrangement will not last very long.

There will have to be identity of wills. An impossible situation would arise if God wanted to follow one set of rules and you another. You could hardly tell God that He must change. So before you begin to walk with Him it would be wise to look again at His commandments and resolve with His help to bring your life into harmony with them. If conscience tells you that you are breaking the first, the fourth, the seventh, the tenth, or any one of them, you had better make it right with God now.

There will have to be identity of ideals. You must love the things that God loves and hate the things He hates. Justice, mercy, truth, must be as precious to you as to Him. Greed, self-seeking, and worldly pleasures must be as distasteful to you as to Him.

You must learn to find joy in forgiving your enemies, in sacrificial giving, and in being tolerant over nonessentials, because such matters mean so much to Him. You must learn to hate all cruelty and unkindness, all tyranny and injustice—in fact, everything that hurts or harms a fellow creature—because God hates them too.

You will have to "seek . . . first the kingdom of God" because that, naturally, will be His first interest also.

Church, not the golf course or the supermarket, will have to be your choice on the Sabbath day, because that is where *His* steps will lead. For the same reason evangelistic services will have to take precedence over ball games, and the baptismal pool over swimming pools.

Do you still want to walk with Him? Are you willing to pay the price? Will you make His purpose yours? Will you surrender your will to His? Will you give up your ideals for His? If so, there will open up before you possibilities of spiritual growth of which you have never dreamed. Your future will begin to glow with the light of heaven into which it will ultimately blend. Your path of life will lead on into the infinite distances of eternity.

And close beside you—all the way—will be Someone who loves you dearly, who will be your guide, companion, deliverer, and friend through all the days to come.

MARRIAGE
CAN BE HAPPY

MARRIAGE is the oldest institution known to man. It dates back to Creation and the Garden of Eden.

God Himself performed the first marriage ceremony. He also gave away the first bride.

You will find the beautiful story in the first two chapters of your Bible.

On the sixth day of Creation week, having fashioned the world into a very lovely home for the bride- and bridegroom-to-be, God said, "Let us make man in our image, after our likeness; and let them have dominion over the fish of the sea, and over the birds of the air, and over the cattle, and over all the earth, and over every creeping thing that creeps upon the earth" (Genesis 1:26, RSV).

And so He did. The Sacred Record says: "So God created man in his own image, in the image of God he created him; male and female he created them" (verse 27).

How this miracle was wrought is described in the following chapter, where we are told that after making Adam, God said to Himself, "It is not good that the man should be alone; I will make a helper fit for him" (Genesis 2:18, RSV).

"So the Lord caused a deep sleep to fall upon the man, and while he slept took one of his ribs and closed up its place with flesh;

114

and the rib which the Lord had taken from the man he made into a woman and brought her to the man.

"Then the man said, 'This at last is bone of my bones and flesh of my flesh; she shall be called Woman, because she was taken out of Man.' Therefore a man leaves his father and his mother and cleaves to his wife, and they become one flesh" (verses 21-24).

The exquisite loveliness of this scene is all too frequently overlooked. People smile at the "rib" story as if it were only a hoary legend or a foolish fable. How much they miss!

Granted, it does seem, at first thought, a strange thing for God to do. Having made the earth by saying "Let the dry land appear"; having made the forests by saying "Let the earth put forth vegetation"; having filled the oceans with fish by saying "Let the waters bring forth swarms of living creatures," why did He not say "Let there be a woman"? Why, after making Adam the most marvelous creature in the wonderful new world, did He take a rib from his perfect body to make a life companion for him?

There must have been a good reason for God acting thus, and there was. God wanted man to know right from the beginning that his wife was truly a part of him, so that he would ever treat her as he would himself.

Your Bible says—in the King James Version—that God made Eve to be "an help meet" for Adam—from which our lovely word "helpmate" has come. She was to stand by his side always, helping him, working with him, planning with him, and sharing life's joys with him. She was to be the model, the forerunner, of all such helpmeets.

But to catch the full significance of that first marriage, look at it again more carefully. Watch God at work. See how He brought it about.

Adam is asleep. God has removed one of his ribs. Out of this, with infinite skill and wisdom, He makes a woman.

Even as He had "formed" man of the dust of the ground, giving him a body, a brain, a nervous system, a breathing apparatus, and a blood circulatory system, together with the ability to see, hear, taste, feel, think, remember, and judge—which are still the marvel of the medical profession—He now with equal ingenuity fashions the one who is to be the mother of the whole human race.

How perfectly He molds her features! How gracefully He arranges her long, flowing hair! With what loving thought He places within her mind and heart all the tenderness, gentleness, sweetness, patience, and longsuffering love that He wants every future mother to possess!

It does not take Him long. Suddenly there stands before Him the fairest creature of all creation, her eyes sparkling with the joy of life, a tender smile giving her face a beauty beyond compare.

Slowly and gracefully she takes her first few steps as God brings her "unto the man."

She looks down at the sleeping form before her. Who can this be? she wonders.

Adam opens his eyes and looks up. Before him stands a being so beautiful, so choice, so noble, so altogether lovely that he can scarcely believe she is real.

It is love at first sight. Instantly both realize that they belong to each other. Clasping hands, they walk away together under the smiling benediction of their Creator.

Reading the dear old story again reminds us of God's primary purpose in marriage. It was to make two people happy. When He linked the first man and the first woman He did so with their best good in mind. He knew that only by sharing life together could they taste its richest joys.

Nor should we overlook the fact that it was really Christ who performed that first wedding ceremony. See Colossians 1:16. Thus it was the first Christian marriage, a fact that lends special significance to His comments upon matrimony.

The Pharisees had come to Him with the tricky question "Is it lawful to divorce one's wife for any cause?" Jesus answered, "Have you not read that he who made them from the beginning made them male and female, and said, 'For this reason a man shall leave his father and mother and be joined to his wife, and the two shall become one'? So they are no longer two but one. What therefore God has joined together, let no man put asunder" (Matthew 19:3-6, RSV).

Thus, as on other occasions, He answered His opponents by stating a fundamental truth—in this case that marriage was divinely intended to unite two persons for eternity.

Here He touched upon the first of five vital steps of a happy marriage.

1. *Preserve Unity at All Costs.* "The two shall become one," said Jesus. "So that they are no longer two but one." Obviously it was the gracious design of the divine Architect of the marriage institution that the man and woman should be united not only legally but totally.

A wedding should see two hearts laid upon an altar that is aglow with the fire of divine love, here to be fused and forged into one sacred instrument for God and coming forth more strong, more efficient, more durable, than ever one could be alone.

It should be a trysting place at the crossroads of life where two travelers meet, and linking arms and minds and hearts, stride on together with tenfold more confidence and zeal toward one noble purpose, one holy goal.

It should be the beginning of a lifelong experience of thinking together, talking together, planning together, hoping together, praying together. The beautiful oneness should pervade every phase of life from wedding day till journey's end.

It is not without good reason that the formal words employed at a wedding ceremony include the solemn pledge "I take thee . . . for better for worse, for richer for poorer, in sickness and in health, to love and to cherish, till death us do part." It is based on six millenniums of experience. And it is vital to married happiness. How tragic that so many brides and grooms recite the words all too carelessly, without a thought for the solemnity of the promise!

The precious unity of marriage should be guarded with the utmost diligence. Never should it be spoken of facetiously. It is too valuable to fritter away in idle jesting. How many have wished, too late, that the first hint of separation had never been spoken!

Encircle the vital unity with protecting walls of love. Loving words. Loving deeds. Mutual thoughtfulness. Mutual tolerance. Mutual forgiveness. Above all, with a determination to stick together always, come what may.

This way lies happiness.

2. *Keep Confidence.* From the moment two young people leave on their honeymoon they should resolve that there are some things they will tell nobody else on earth. Because henceforth they belong together they should keep their innermost secrets to themselves.

Nothing will contribute more to preserving unity than keeping private matters within the walls of the new home. That is where they belong. That is where they should be kept. They are nobody else's business. Not even of close relatives or old friends.

Each home, if it is to last, must have a sacred citadel of exclusiveness where no prying eyes or gossiping tongues are permitted.

Mutual trust, thus fostered, will grow with the passing years. No outside influence will ever beget suspicions or insert the first wedge of doubt.

This way lies happiness.

3. *Settle Misunderstandings at Once.* Two persons of different background and upbringing, sometimes of different nationality and language, are bound to have misunderstandings. It would be unrealistic to expect otherwise. These are part of the adjustment that marriage entails. But they should never be allowed to develop into long drawn-out quarrels. Your Bible suggests that they should be settled on the same day they arise — before nightfall. "Do not let the sun go down on your anger," counsels the apostle Paul (Ephesians 4:26, RSV), and his advice is particularly good for married couples.

Agreement may come only as a result of one party's backing down from a position taken in the heat of argument, or saying "I'm sorry" for an unkind word or ungenerous deed. But it is a rewarding attitude to take, infinitely preferable to letting the misunderstanding fester until it bursts into open enmity. The costliness of petty grievances cherished and unresolved is beyond calculation. Every highway to a divorce court is strewn with the resulting wreckage.

At the onset of any quarrel read these temper-cooling words: "I . . . beg you to lead a life worthy of the calling to which you have been called, with all *lowliness* and *meekness*, with *patience, forbearing one another in love, eager to maintain the unity of the Spirit in the bond of peace*" (verses 1-3).

This way lies happiness.

4. *Let Love Prevail.* This is the solution for most difficulties. "Above all hold *unfailing* your love for one another," wrote the apostle Peter, "since love covers a multitude of sins" (1 Peter 4:8, RSV).

Never let love die out. Keep it alive whatever may have been said or done. Keep it "unfailing" and, sooner or later, it will cover all sins. The hurts will be healed, the mistakes will be forgotten, the impatience and unkindness will be forgiven.

Given a chance, love will prevail—always.

This was the burden of Paul's letter to the Ephesians: "Husbands, love your wives, as Christ loved the church and gave himself up for her, that he might sanctify her, having cleansed her by the washing of water with the word, that the church might be presented before him in splendor, without spot or wrinkle or any such thing, that she might be holy and without blemish.

"Even so husbands should love their wives as their own bodies. He who loves his wife loves himself. For no man ever hates his own flesh, but nourishes and cherishes it, as Christ does the church, because we are members of his body" (Ephesians 5:25-31, RSV).

He couldn't have spoken more plainly and helpfully. Husbands should love their wives with the same selfless, sacrificial love that Christ has shown for His church. Wives are to respond in like manner.

With such love motivating and sustaining a marriage, what else could it be but a success?

This way lies happiness.

5. *Let God Direct.* A dedicated marriage will never break up. When husband and wife gladly put God first in everything and look to Him for direction in all their affairs, they will be blessed with a

peace, harmony, and contentment that will be the envy of their friends. Unity of worship, unity of devotion, unity of sacrifice, will do more than anything else to keep a marriage durable.

Therefore if you want your marriage to last, share your Christian experience. Pray together. Read the Bible together. Go to church together. Say with Joshua, "As for me and my house, we will serve the Lord" (Joshua 24:15).

This way, too, lies happiness.

HOME CAN BE
BEAUTIFUL

TO BE beautiful, a home does not have to have a wonderful location, a panoramic view, an elaborate entrance, or fine landscaping. It can be a modest apartment in town or a humble cottage in the country and still be lovelier than a royal palace.

It does not have to boast expensive draperies, deep-piled carpets, or the latest electrical appliances. Its furniture can be all hand-me-downs or items picked up at secondhand stores. Chrome, tiling, and stonework may all be absent. Yet it can possess a holy radiance beyond description.

How can this be? Your Bible tells you.

First notice Deuteronomy 5:29. Here God expresses His deep yearning for the happiness and contentment of His people.

"O that there were such an heart in them," He says, "that they would fear me, and keep all my commandments always, that it might be well with them, and with their children for ever!"

He was concerned about their homes. He wanted every one of them to be truly beautiful and happy. He wanted them to be orderly, peaceful, and godly, with parents and children walking together along the highway of righteousness, fearing Him and keeping His commandments.

Knowing that the Israelites were about to move into a new

country where they would soon set up tens of thousands of new homes, He was eager for them to begin properly, making no mistakes. So, through His servant Moses, He went on to instruct them how to go about it.

First and foremost, undergirding all else, was this counsel:

Keep the Commandments in Love

He did not ask them to build their houses according to a certain type of architecture or paint lovely pictures on the walls or buy the choicest silverware for their tables. No. Seeking only enduring beauty, He asked them to memorize His commandments and observe them.

"Now this is the commandment, the statutes and the ordinances which the Lord your God commanded me to teach you," said Moses, "that you may do them in the land to which you are going over to possess it; that you may fear the Lord your God, you and your son and your son's son, by keeping all his statutes and his commandments, which I command you, all the days of your life; and that your days may be prolonged. Hear therefore, O Israel, and be careful to do them; that it may go well with you" (Deuteronomy 6:1-3, RSV).

"Hear, O Israel," he went on. "The Lord our God is one Lord; and *you shall love the Lord your God with all your heart, and with all your soul, and with all your might.*

"And these words which I command you this day shall be upon your heart; and you shall teach them diligently to your children, and shall talk of them when you sit in your house, and when you walk by the way, and when you lie down, and when you rise. And you shall bind them as a sign upon your hand, and they shall be as frontlets between your eyes. And you shall write them on the doorposts of your house and on your gates" (verses 4-9).

Here, in these few brief sentences, God revealed the secret of the truly beautiful home.

That secret is love. Full, unstinted love, for God and man. Love for God demonstrated by wholehearted obedience to the first four of His Ten Commandments, and love for man revealed by the self-restraints suggested in the last six.

Law and love, discipline and affection, perfectly blended, will preserve the home from all peril and bring upon it the continual blessing of Heaven.

Long years afterward Jesus repeated this good counsel. When a lawyer asked Him which was "the great commandment in the law" He replied in almost the words of Deuteronomy 6:5: "Thou shalt love the Lord thy God with all thy heart, and with all thy soul, and with all thy mind. This," He added, "is the first and great commandment. And the second is like unto it, Thou shalt love thy neighbour as thyself. On these two commandments hang all the law and the prophets" (Matthew 22:37-40).

He was so right. *Everything* hangs on them. Love is so basic, so fundamental. It is the wellspring of all human joys, the secret of happy marriages and beautiful homes.

To be effective, however, it must be manifested in harmony with God's revealed will. Otherwise it would not be true love.

In other words, the truly beautiful home is a love-filled home where God is honored and His commandments are observed.

But God's second piece of advice is almost as important as the first.

It can be summed up in these five words:

Teach the Commandments in Love

Immediately following Moses' exhortation "You shall love the Lord your God with all your heart," this additional command, so often overlooked, was given: "These words . . . shall be upon your heart; and you shall teach them diligently to your children" (Deuteronomy 6:7, RSV).

Which words? Obviously the Ten Words, or Ten Commandments, recorded in the previous chapter. See Deuteronomy 5:1-21. The Ten Commandments are actually called "these words" in verse 22. They are God's words of instruction, guidance, and counsel to His people in all ages, from the beginning to the end of time.

"These words" are to be "taught diligently" in every home, so that the rising generation may not be ignorant of God's law. From the moment they can discern between right and wrong, children are to be led to understand that the God of heaven requires their adherence to these righteous principles of life. And in the teaching, explaining, simplifying, and illustrating of them, both parents and children will be greatly blessed.

Being principles of love, they are to be taught in love. Not with a mailed fist, but with a tender heart. Not with a stick in the hand, but with a sob in the soul.

To cause children to think of God as a tyrant who says nothing but "Don't" and "Thou shalt not" is to libel His good name. He is not a taskmaster, but a lover. Indeed, He *is* love. Therefore He cannot do anything unloving or unlovely. His commandments must be, as He says Himself, "for our good always." For the good of parents. For the good of children. For everybody's good.

Rightly understood, they are positive, not negative; kind, not harsh; beneficial, not vindictive. Therefore they should be presented to boys and girls as a blessing, not a curse. Otherwise, how will they grow up to think of God as a God of love?

There is a third word of counsel that has great significance in the making of a beautiful home:

Discuss the Commandments in Love

Said Moses: "You shall . . . talk of them when you sit in your house, . . . and when you lie down, and when you rise" (Deuteronomy 6:7, RSV).

This does not mean that the Ten Commandments are to be the only topic of conversation in the home. That would be unreasonable.

To talk solely about God's law, no matter how good and wonderful it is, would lead to fanaticism, boredom, dissatisfaction, and finally, rejection. And God would not want that.

What He had in mind was freedom of discussion. Religion is not to be a closed subject in the home, as it so often is today. Talking about God and His manifold provisions for man's welfare and salvation is to be as natural as talking about the weather or the latest political or social events. Equally free and easy is to be discussion of all Bible topics. It is to be a normal part of life, like breathing out and breathing in.

This means, of course, talking about Christ, for is He not the author of the Ten Commandments? Did He not die on Calvary because His law had been broken and there was no other way to pay the penalty for sin and make everlasting life again available to man? What a theme for endless discussion!

This way, thinking and talking about heavenly things will become second nature to parents and children alike. The thoughts of the whole family will be elevated, as will the conversation at mealtimes. New meaning will be seen in those precious words, which used to hang on the living room wall in many a home:

"Christ Is the Head of This House,

  The Unseen Guest at Every Meal,

  The Silent Listener to Every Conversation."

Thus God will be remembered last thing each night—"when you lie down"—and first thing in the morning—"when you rise."

What home would not be a thousandfold more beautiful with such a program?

The fourth piece of advice has an outreach that is limitless:

Proclaim the Commandments in Love

"You shall bind them as a sign upon your hand, and they shall be as frontlets between your eyes" (Deuteronomy 6:8, RSV).

Some people have taken this instruction literally and affixed parts of the law, written on parchment or cloth, to their wrists and foreheads. But God had a deeper meaning. He wanted His law where it would be really effective for good—in the mind and heart. Here it would guide the conscience, control the judgment, and keep a man in the narrow way that leads to life eternal. All the work of his hands would then testify to his devotion to God.

This advice is none other than a call to every child of God, by divine grace, to live out the principles of the law in his life and so be an example to the world of the joy of doing right and seeking to please the Lord. It has the same meaning that Paul had in mind when he urged the Ephesians to speak the truth in love (Ephesians 4:15).

He wanted them to manifest so much love in their lives that unbelievers would be overwhelmed thereby. They would accept truth because of what they saw rather than because of what they heard. The gentleness, sweetness, thoughtfulness, of a godly life would be the Christian's most powerful argument.

All this God had in mind when He said, through Moses, "You shall write them on the doorposts of your house and on your gates" (Deuteronomy 6:9, RSV).

Painted signs would not do much good. What God really wanted was completely dedicated homes, known everywhere for their virtue, piety, and goodness. He wanted love to shine from the windows and flow out through the doors and gates so that passersby would say, "Such wonderful people live there; the nicest folks in the neighborhood. What makes them so different? What makes their home so beautiful?"

Such things are still being said about some homes today. Perhaps they are being said about yours. I hope so.

If not, they can be. Your Bible makes the way plain. And God makes it easy. His grace is sufficient.

Your home can be beautiful. Beautified by "the commandments of God, and the faith of Jesus" (Revelation 14:12).

SEVEN SECRETS OF CHILD TRAINING

T HE rapid growth of juvenile delinquency affords tragic evidence that bringing up children has well-nigh become a lost art. All too many are not "brought up" at all, but largely left to do as they please. As a result, across the country almost 30 percent of persons arrested for violent crimes are under 18 years old.

Yet it is not necessary that boys and girls should be so troublesome. They don't have to be rude, insolent, disobedient, sadistic little vandals. Right upbringing will make them the nicest youngsters in the world. With proper care and training they can be like little angels. "Train up a child in the way he should go," says your Bible, "and when he is old, he will not depart from it" (Proverbs 22:6).

"Train" is the essential word. It embraces thoughtful planning, unwearying determination, and infinite patience. It is no job for weaklings. The most vital task ever committed to men and women, it demands the utmost and best of them.

The trouble is that many parents have never learned how to train their children. They are at their wits' end to know what to do with them. In their hearts they long to bring them up right, but how to go about it is beyond them. They stand by helpless as their boys and girls get out of hand and join the lost generation of cynical, rebellious youth.

Some of these disappointed parents have poured out their troubles to me. They have expressed consternation that their beautiful plans have gone awry. They are certain that they have had a streak of bad luck. They want to know how it happened that all our six children chose Christian service for their lifework. "You are so fortunate," they say. "You must have had a lot of luck."

Luck indeed! Just as though bringing up a family for God is a matter of luck! Luck hasn't anything to do with it. It's just plain hard work, plus the blessing of God, of course. It means being everlastingly on the job day and night, from childhood to youth, from youth to manhood and womanhood.

Then we tell them our seven secrets of child training. They may not work in every case. Parents are so different. Children are so different. So are circumstances and environments. But these suggestions seem to help some people. Maybe, if you are a parent, they will help you. You will find them strongly supported in your Bible.

Here is the first:

1. *Watch Over Your Children With Ceaseless Vigilance*

If you want to bring up your children right, you cannot leave them half the time with the neighbors. The best baby-sitter in the world is no substitute for the mother.

"But," you say, "in our family mother has to go out to work." More's the pity. If at all possible—and sometimes it *is* impossible— she should stay home with the children.

"But," you argue, "how else would we make our monthly payments on the car, the freezer, the stereo, the TV, the VCR, the computer?"

That is a problem. Maybe you will have to choose between these gadgets and your children. You could end up with a lot of machinery and a broken heart.

"What did *you* do?" you ask. We decided that the interests of the children should come first. The last time my wife went out to work was some months before our first baby arrived. That was a long time

128

ago. All their growing years she spent guiding, training, and helping the children in ways without number.

"You must have had a lot of money then." On the contrary, when the children were small we had very little. We had no refrigerator, no washing machine, no freezer, no disposal, and, of course, no radio or television. We didn't get our first secondhand car till our oldest girl was almost in her teens.

Mother was always there when the children came home from school. Whenever they entered the house there was always that radiant welcome that only a mother can give. Always she was interested in all that concerned them, being ready to meet their needs, answer their questions, help them to make right decisions, and warn them against temptations. No woman worn out from a hard day's work, with all the family chores still to do, can do a job like this properly.

2. *Maintain Your God-appointed Leadership*

God intends that parents, not the children, shall direct the household. See Genesis 18:19. As you value the peace and happiness of your home, don't surrender this leadership. There was a time when some educators advocated leaving children free to do just about what they like, lest they develop a complex, but experience has proved that such ideas are unsound. After all, what are parents for if not to plan the program of their homes and give direction to their children's lives? Upon them is laid the responsibility to guide, to counsel, to lead, and if they fail to live up to this responsibility, they invite only calamity and sorrow.

A colt, a lamb, a calf, or a puppy stays with its mother but a few days or weeks, but boys and girls, under normal circumstances, remain with their parents for years. Why? By accident or design? Surely it is because God planned it so. He meant this precious time to be used by parents to lead their little ones in the way they should go, to bring them up to be obedient, unselfish, and reverent; noble in all their thinking, gracious in all their ways. Parents have a long-term job on their hands, for they are preparing their children not only for this present life, but also for the life to come.

This means discipline—that word which nobody likes to use anymore. But discipline is necessary. It's part of the job of parenthood. It involves setting the right pattern and holding to it. It means saying what is to be done and seeing that it *is* done. It calls for the application of gentle but determined pressure when—and where—necessary.

The apostle Paul had something to say on this subject. First to children.

"Children," he said, "obey your parents in the Lord, for this is right. 'Honor your father and mother' (this is the first commandment with a promise), 'that it may be well with you and that you may live long on the earth' " (Ephesians 6:1-3, RSV).

This may sound like old-fashioned advice, but it has lost no value or virtue with the passing years. Equally timely is his counsel to parents.

"Fathers," he said, "do not provoke your children to anger, but bring them up in the *discipline* and *instruction* of the Lord" (verse 4).

Discipline takes time, thought, care, judgment, but it makes all the difference between an orderly home and a bedlam. Dispense with it for fear of some complex and you will pay for your slackness the rest of your life. So will the children. They will never know the kind of home God planned for them. And they will escape from the confusion as soon as they can.

3. *Help Your Children to Find God for Themselves as Early as Possible*

This is vital. Let their earliest thoughts be about Jesus and His love. As soon as they can read, teach them to study their weekly Bible lesson by themselves. Make sure they know by heart the Ten Commandments, the twenty-third psalm, the Beatitudes, and other great passages of Scripture. Urge them to say their prayers by their own bedsides every night before they go to sleep and every morning when they get up. Thus they will develop priceless habits, which will stay with them through life.

What about family worship? By all means have it as often as you can. Gather the children around you and read to them the grand old Bible stories. Have them all pray aloud and repeat the Lord's Prayer together at the close. It's a glorious thing to do, and will be a precious memory in the children's minds in years to come. But even more important is the personal Bible study, the private praying, whereby each individual child builds up his or her own connection with God.

Children will pray for all sorts of strange and wonderful things. Never mind. Let them. All their prayers may not be answered, but many of them will be. I have come to believe that God takes special delight in answering children's prayers and that He does so in order to strengthen their faith in Him. And children who come to regard Jesus as their firm, true friend in their earliest days will turn to Him in periods of stress and strain in years to come. In youth they will "storm the battlements of heaven" in His name and give their lives to His service.

4. *Keep Your Children Busy*

The old saying that "Satan finds some mischief still for idle hands to do" has a lot of truth in it. Children are normally so full of life that if they are not engaged in something good they will surely be up to mischief.

This doesn't mean that parents should be slave drivers, thinking up one task after another for their children to do. That doesn't make for a happy family. Children must have time to play. But they should be led to understand that it is their responsibility to help keep the home going. Just as soon as they are old enough to do little jobs around the place they should be taught to do them. It isn't right that mother should always be in the kitchen getting the supper ready and washing the dishes while John and Mary watch TV or play Nintendo in the family room.

Children can be a marvelous help around the place if they are taught to do their part when they are very young. Once you get across the idea that it is their duty and privilege to keep the home running and looking nice *because it is their home,* they will stop at nothing in their desire to help. They will do the dusting and the floor washing and the lawn cutting without your having to ask them, and without holding out their hands to be paid for every little service.

5. *Lay Responsibilities Upon Your Children and See That They Carry Them Out*

This will teach them self-reliance and make them trustworthy in days to come. Of course, this will take time too. It's easy enough to give a child a job; but considerably more difficult to see that it's done. And it takes real perseverance to insist that it be done over and over until it is done right. Yet only so can one build character.

One of the curses of the present age is passing the buck, otherwise known as "Let Bill do it." Work is regarded as something to be bypassed if possible, or hurried through no matter how slipshod the way in which the task is carried out. The remedy for this disease of irresponsibility must be applied in childhood. Little Tommy must be made to understand that when mother or father gives him a job he must do it to the best of his ability. Little Marjorie must learn that she cannot escape her responsibilities even with the most subtle excuses.

Children trained like this will grow into dependable youth. It will be natural for them to be faithful to every trust. And when at last they leave home to take up their lifework, the world will welcome them.

6. *Open the Treasure-house of New Ideas*

When the children are old enough to read by themselves, introduce them to good books and magazines. This will take more time. For you will have to read the books and magazines yourself to find out which are good and which are not. Remember that one bad book or comic can poison a child's mind for life. So keep strong control on all reading matter coming into your home. And when opportunity offers, explain *why* some things are good and others are bad.

The same applies to television programs. Keep control of the knob. As the divinely appointed leaders of the home, parents have the right and the duty to decide on the kind of program the children shall look at. And they should take time to explain why they turn one program off and another one on. If the explanation is given wisely, kindly, and firmly, the children will see the correctness of the decision and will make the same right choice when there is no grown-up around to tell them what to do.

7. *Make Home the Central Attraction*

Plan things to make the children happy. Take time to play with them. Make them feel that they are wanted. Let them know you love them. Tell them to invite their friends—at the proper times, of course. Above all, read to them. Children love to be read to; and there's no music like the sound of mother's voice. For many years until she passed away, whenever our children came home—though they were all grown up by then—they still begged mother to read them a story as she had done so often when they were young.

The result of all this will be that the children will look upon home as the most beautiful place in the world. They won't be forever running off to the neighbor's or to the movies or the skating rink or the ball game. For them there will be no joy quite like just being at home.

In years to come such a home will prove an anchor amid the storms of life, and the most treasured memory they will carry with them to the home eternal.

THE ROAD TO
RADIANT YOUTH

THE highway to happy childhood and the road to radiant youth are one and the same. Only the grades are different.

In both cases the essential element is knowledge of God and His Word; but while for children this must be imparted by parents and teachers, for youth it must be personally absorbed and applied.

To the question "How can a young man keep his way pure?" the psalmist answered, "By guarding it according to thy word" (Psalm 119:9, RSV).

The way of life must be *guarded* according to the Word of God. This calls for prayerful study of the Bible and resolute action in harmony with its teachings—two vital phases of a personal experience.

David continued: "With my whole heart I seek thee; let me not wander from thy commandments! I have laid up thy word in my heart, that I might not sin against thee" (verses 10, 11).

Laying up the Word involves memorizing it, thinking about it, and putting it into practice. It means giving God first place in all one's plans and decisions.

Fortunate is the youth who starts out with this understanding of what matters most in life. With God's Word in his heart he will be guarded from all evil. His determination to walk in harmony with

God's law will invite the blessings of Heaven. In simple goodness and humble nobility, his life will become ever more radiant with the glory of God.

This was powerfully illustrated in the life of Daniel, the young prince of Judah who was taken captive by Nebuchadnezzar about 606 B.C.

After he arrived in Babylon with a host of fellow prisoners, he was soon confronted with a serious personal problem. He had to decide whether he should partake of the food and drink that was set before him. The record does not state what the food was, but it may well have been pork, forbidden in the Levitical law. Certainly the wine was fermented. Probably both were first offered to the idols of Babylon.

Daniel was aware that as a slave he had no rights, but as a child of God he had a conscience. Having been brought up to love and obey God, he felt he could not do anything displeasing to Him no matter what the cost. So your Bible says, "Daniel purposed in his heart that he would not defile himself with the portion of the king's meat, nor with the wine which he drank" (Daniel 1:8).

He asked for a more wholesome diet, and his request was granted. But his determination not to violate his conscience marked him as a youth with a future. And what a future it was!

Shortly thereafter he and three friends who had taken the same courageous stand were brought before Nebuchadnezzar. After a lengthy interrogation, "in all matters of wisdom and understanding, that the king enquired of them, he found them ten times better than all the magicians and astrologers that were in all his realm" (verse 20).

Because Daniel walked with God from day to day, he became God's messenger to reveal and interpret the king's forgotten dream. As a result he was made prime minister of Babylon. "Then the king made Daniel a great man, and gave him many great gifts, and made him ruler over the whole province of Babylon, and chief of the governors over all the wise men of Babylon" (Daniel 2:48).

Thus, because of his unswerving resolve to do right, he was led onward and upward to fulfill the great destiny God had marked out for him.

Three successive sovereigns—Nebuchadnezzar, Belshazzar, and Darius the Mede—honored him with the greatest gifts within their power to bestow.

Throughout his long and brilliant career the radiance of his youth never left him. He glowed for God till his dying day. Even in his old age he was prepared to risk his life rather than deny his faith.

Faced with the choice of giving up his lifelong practice of praying three times a day or being thrown into a den of lions, he chose the den of lions. No other course occurred to him. And it was the king, not he, who was afraid of the consequences.

Miraculously he was preserved, and next morning when Darius came to find out what had happened in the night, Daniel was able to say to the king, "My God sent his angel and shut the lions' mouths, and they have not hurt me" (Daniel 6:22, RSV).

It is a wonderful story of a boy who set out on the road to radiant youth and followed it to the end of the journey. Regrettably the lives of all Bible characters did not turn out like this. Many, alas, started out well, then lost their way.

Take Solomon, for instance, Israel's most famous king. From his dying father, David, he received this wise counsel: "Solomon my son, know the God of your father, and serve him with a whole heart and with a willing mind; for the Lord searches all hearts, and understands every plan and thought. If you seek him, he will be found by you; but if you forsake him, he will cast you off for ever" (1 Chronicles 28:9, RSV).

Shortly thereafter Solomon had a dream in which he heard God saying, "Ask what I shall give you." The young king answered: "Thou hast shown great and steadfast love to thy servant David my father, because he walked before thee in faithfulness, in righteousness, and in uprightness of heart toward thee. . . . And now, O Lord my God, thou hast made thy servant king in place of David my father, although I am but a little child; I do not know how to go out or come in. . . . Give thy servant therefore an understanding mind to govern thy people, that I may discern between good and evil" (1 Kings 3:5-9, RSV).

God was much pleased with this humble prayer and replied, "Because you have asked this, and have not asked for yourself long life or riches or the life of your enemies, but have asked for yourself understanding to discern what is right, behold I now do according to your word. Behold, I give you a wise and discerning mind, so that none like you has been before you and none like you shall arise after you. I give you also what you have not asked, both riches and honor, so that no other king shall compare with you, all your days. And if you will walk in my ways, keeping my statutes and my commandments, as your father David walked, then will I lengthen your days" (verses 11-14).

God kept His promise. He showered blessings innumerable upon this devout youth, so that his fame spread all over the world. He "exceeded all the kings of the earth for riches and for wisdom" (1 Kings 10:23). Rulers of other nations made pilgrimages to Jerusalem just to see and hear this king of whose fame they had heard. His life glowed with a Heaven-imparted radiance in which all his people basked.

Never before had Israel known such prosperity, or such perfect peace. "Judah and Israel were many, as the sand which is by the sea in multitude, eating and drinking, and making merry" (1 Kings 4:20).

"And Solomon reigned over all kingdoms from the river [Euphrates] unto the land of the Philistines, and unto the border of Egypt; they brought presents, and served Solomon all the days of his life. . . . He had peace on all sides round about him" (verses 21-24).

Sad to say, however, these good times did not last. But the fault was not God's.

Your Bible says that "King Solomon loved many foreign women" and "his wives turned away his heart after other gods" (1 Kings 11:1, 4, RSV). As a result, "the Lord was angry with Solomon" because "he did not keep what the Lord commanded" (verses 9, 10).

What a tragedy that was! As a young man he had started out well and God had blessed him greatly. By doing what was right in God's sight he had gained wisdom, riches, power, prestige—all that a man could wish for. By forsaking Him he lost everything.

His life, which might have glowed with ever-increasing radiance, faded out in a twilight of ignominy and self-reproach. Yet before he died, the old king, out of his sad experience, left this priceless counsel for the youth of succeeding generations: "Remember now thy Creator in the days of thy youth, while the evil days come not" (Ecclesiastes 12:1). "Let us hear the conclusion of the whole matter: Fear God and keep his commandments; for this is the whole duty of man. For God shall bring every work into judgment, with every secret thing, whether it be good, or whether it be evil" (verses 13, 14).

This shows that he knew all along which was the right and true way. What a pity he did not follow it!

Josiah's story is similar and demonstrates the same truth.

Like Solomon he came to the throne in his youth. In fact, your Bible says he was crowned when he was but 8 years old. "While he was yet young" he began to seek God (2 Chronicles 34:3). When he was 12 he started to remove all evidences of idolatry from Jerusalem and Judah. Later, when Hilkiah the priest brought him the precious copy of the law of Moses that had been found in the Temple treasury, he responded immediately to its message. As he listened to the reading of God's Word he was saddened by all Israel's shortcomings.

"And the king stood in his place, and made a covenant before the Lord, to walk after the Lord and to keep his commandments, and his testimonies, and his statutes, with all his heart, and with all his soul" (verse 31). Then he asked all the people to stand in token of their own solemn intention and pledge to do God's will.

It was a wonderful thing this young man did, and God rejoiced in his love and loyalty. He was another radiant youth who might have gone on from strength to strength and glory to glory had he not made one mistake. In a moment of folly, and against much good advice, he needlessly went to war against Pharaoh Necho of Egypt and was killed.

In the New Testament you will find the story of still another young man who started out on the road to radiant youth only to lose his way and disappear from history—a failure. It is told three times, in Matthew 19:16-22, Mark 10:17-22, and Luke 18:18-23. You should read all three reports to get the full picture.

"Good Teacher," asked the rich young ruler, "what shall I do to inherit eternal life?"

"You know the commandments," said Jesus. "Do not commit adultery, Do not kill, Do not steal, Do not bear false witness, Honor your father and mother."

"All these have I observed from my youth," replied the young man. "What do I still lack?"

So touched was Jesus by his earnestness that "looking upon him," He "loved him."

There must have been something very attractive about this youth. Obviously he was sincere, earnest, and eager to do right. Years of seeking truth and striving to do God's will had left a noble mold upon his face. Here was radiant youth at its best. Yet there was something missing.

"One thing you still lack," said Jesus. "Sell all that you have and distribute to the poor, and you will have treasure in heaven; and come, follow me."

It was a wonderful opportunity Jesus offered him. He could have been one of the apostles. He could have fellowshipped with the Son of God. He could have been present at Gethsemane, Calvary, Olivet. He could have been in the upper room at Pentecost. He might even have contributed a book to the New Testament! But "he went away sorrowful: for he had great possessions" (Matthew 19:22).

Today nobody even knows his name. As for the possessions he prized so highly, they vanished with him centuries ago. This young man's experience proves that merely memorizing the Ten Commandments is not enough. As he grew in stature he should have grown in understanding of them. Somehow, somewhere, his spiritual growth had stopped. He had become a legalist, who was concerned about the letter of the law but failed to discern its deeper, spiritual meaning.

While he knew all the commandments by heart and was prepared to admit that the last six could be summed up in the words "Thou shalt love thy neighbour as thyself," it never occurred to him that this might mean using his wealth to alleviate the sufferings of the poor.

Those who would walk the road to radiant youth must "grow in grace, and in the knowledge of our Lord and Saviour Jesus Christ" (2 Peter 3:18). Besides knowing God's commandments, they must learn to perceive more and more their spiritual implications—so marvelously revealed by the Lawgiver Himself during His brief sojourn among men.

In the book of Joel there is a prophecy concerning youth in the latter days of the world's history. It says that among "portents in the heaven and on the earth, blood and fire and columns of smoke," God will "pour out" His Spirit upon all flesh. As a result sons and daughters will prophesy and *"young men shall see visions"* (Joel 2:28-30, RSV).

If this time has come, as indeed it has, it should be a moment of high expectancy for all youth. For now God is to pour out His Spirit in final full flood tide especially upon the last generation of young men and women.

He wants to give them visions. Not of worldly grandeur, but of service splendid and sublime. Not of secular objectives, but of His plans for the grand consummation of His eternal purpose. Not of vast stores of human learning—valuable though they may be—but of the rich treasures of His Word.

Young people thus richly endowed will find the road to radiant youth to be the very "path of the just" which, as "the shining light . . . shineth more and more unto the perfect day" (Proverbs 4:18).

THE MORE
ABUNDANT LIFE

HOW few really healthy people there seem to be these days! A polite "How are you?" usually elicits a description of some ache, pain, operation, or drugstore remedy for "vitamin deficiency" or "that tired feeling."

Everywhere, by every conceivable means, people are seeking relief from the stresses, strains, and nervous tensions resulting from the fast tempo of modern living. All about us are multitudes of these "walking sick"; while every hospital, sanitarium, clinic, and mental home is crowded to capacity with more serious cases.

Vital statistics issued by the large insurance companies make the picture still worse. From these we learn that vast numbers now living will die of cancer, heart trouble, and other diseases within the next few years.

Surely God did not intend life to be like this! He did not. Your Bible is most definite on this point.

When Adam was created, God gave him a constitution designed to last forever, sustained only by the choice products of nature and the fruit of the tree of life. If he had not sinned, his teeth would never have decayed, his hair would never have fallen out, his eyes would never have grown dim, and his heart would have gone on beating forever and ever. The abounding vitality he experienced on the first day of his life would have been his through all eternity.

Though God told him that, as a result of sin, "dying thou shalt die" (Genesis 2:17, margin), it took a long, long time to wear him down. Your Bible says that Adam lived nearly a thousand years—930, to be exact. His son, Seth, lived 912 years, and his grandson, Enos, 905 years. Cain lived 910 years, Mahalaleel 895 years, Jared 962 years, and Methuselah—the oldest man who ever lived—969 years.

Are these fictitious figures? Not at all. When one considers how close these pioneers of the human race lived to Creation, they no longer seem unreasonable. Not only were their constitutions nearly perfect, unaffected by hereditary disease, but their food also was of highest excellence. The vegetables and fruits, which were their chief articles of diet, grew in soil that had not been denuded of health-building minerals. In those days, too, the stream of life flowed more gently. There were none of the fierce tensions that make people old so soon today. In all probability heart disease and similar ailments were unknown in those far-off times.

As century succeeded century, however, man's life span gradually became shorter. While Noah lived 950 years, his son Shem attained but 600, his grandson Arphaxad, 438, and his great-grandson Salah, 433.

Two generations later Peleg lived only 239 years, and four generations after him Terah died at 205. See Genesis 11:10-32.

Terah's son, Abraham, lived to be 175, and it is significant that the record states that he "died in a good old age, an old man, and full of years" (Genesis 25:8). Evidently by this time, 500 years after the Flood, the average age level had dropped considerably below this figure.

By Moses' time it was only 70. "The days of our years," Psalm 90 declares, "are threescore years and ten; and if by reason of strength they be fourscore years, yet is their strength labour and sorrow; for it is soon cut off, and we fly away" (Psalm 90:10).

Today, especially in some of the underprivileged countries, the period of life expectancy is lower still.

Thus over the years the marvelous piece of machinery God set in

142

motion at Creation has been running down.

This was not, as stated above, His original purpose. He planned for life, not death; for health, not sickness; for radiant energy, not weariness and pain.

When He chose the children of Israel to be His people He lovingly tried to show them how, despite the curse of sin, they could avoid many of its immediate consequences. Through Moses He revealed the elementary secrets of good health and how they could keep well even when living under substandard conditions.

If they would but follow this good advice, Moses assured them, they would save themselves many sorrows.

"If you will diligently hearken to the voice of the Lord your God, and do that which is right in his eyes, and give heed to his commandments and keep all his statutes, *I will put none of the diseases upon you which I put upon the Egyptians; for I am the Lord, your healer*" (Exodus 15:26, RSV).

On another occasion God told them that if they would serve Him with all their heart, they would enjoy abounding health. "I will bless your bread and your water," He said; "and *I will take sickness away from the midst of you*" (Exodus 23:25, RSV).

Some of this divine instruction on healthful living is well worth restudying today.

1. *They were to be careful about their food.* They were "to make a distinction between the unclean and the clean and between the living creature that may be eaten and the living creature that may not be eaten" (Leviticus 11:47, RSV). Some things were good for them and some were not. To be well and healthy, they must watch their diet—a fundamental truth that the world at large has but recently begun to perceive.

2. *They were to be careful about matters of hygiene.* Cleanliness was of the utmost importance. Persons with infectious diseases were to be quarantined, as well as those who had been in contact with them (Numbers 5:2). Special precautions were to be taken with lepers (Leviticus 13:1-59). Meat kept more than three days—they had no refrigerators—was to be burned (Leviticus 7:17). Contami-

nated articles were to be destroyed (verse 19). It was all in harmony with modern medical standards.

3. *They were to avoid immorality.* The seventh commandment of God's law, "Thou shalt not commit adultery," was intended to save them from the dread physical consequences of misuse of the body's most sacred function.

4. *They were to balance work and rest.* Continual work would make them prematurely old. Continual rest would make them lazy and degenerate. To enjoy a happy, healthy life they must blend work and rest in perfect harmony. God's prescription was six days of work and one of rest. "Remember the sabbath day, to keep it holy," He said. "Six days shalt thou labour and do all thy work; but the seventh day is the sabbath of the Lord thy God; in it thou shalt not do any work" (Exodus 20:8-10).

Nothing would contribute more to their total well-being than observance of this good counsel. Not only would it ensure for them adequate relaxation for their bodies, it would also benefit their minds by regularly interrupting their material pursuits with contemplation of the things of God. Spiritual uplift, coming to them every seventh day, would be a powerful healing factor in their lives and bring upon them blessings innumerable.

"If thou turn away thy foot from the sabbath," God told them, "from doing thy pleasure on my holy day; and call the sabbath a delight, the holy of the Lord, honourable; . . . I will cause thee to ride upon the high places of the earth, and feed thee with the heritage of Jacob thy father: for the mouth of the Lord hath spoken it" (Isaiah 58:13, 14).

As long as the children of Israel gave heed to this good counsel, they enjoyed the promised blessings. So healthy were they for a while that your Bible says, "There was not one feeble person among their tribes" (Psalm 105:37). Unfortunately, their faithfulness was short-lived, and it was not long before disease began once more to take its toll.

When the Son of God came among them in person, He found Himself surrounded by the sick and dying. Everywhere He went He was trailed by people clamoring for restoration of health. The blind longed for sight, the deaf for hearing, the lame for power to walk.

As He beheld this mass of suffering humanity His heart of love was "moved with compassion" (Matthew 9:36). And no wonder! He was man's Creator, and now had come to see the frightful wreckage sin had wrought. Without a thought for His own comfort or peace He "went about doing good, and healing all that were oppressed of the devil" (Acts 10:38). While He taught in the synagogues and preached the gospel of the kingdom, He busied Himself "healing all manner of sickness and all manner of disease among the people" (Matthew 4:23).

To these poor folks who were suffering so much He brought the inspiring thought that a new and better life was within their reach. "I am come," He said, "that they might have life, and that they might have it more abundantly" (John 10:10).

Did they need health? Did they want strength? Did they desire peace of mind? Did they seek overflowing vitality? It was all theirs for the asking. "Come unto me, all ye that labour and are heavy laden," He said, "and I will give you rest" (Matthew 11:28). Rest! Yes, and *life*. Life more abundant than they had ever known.

But there were conditions. They must be prepared to "sin no more" (John 8:11). They must turn back to God. They must keep His commandments. Then all their yearnings would come to pass. "If you keep my commandments," He told them, "you will abide in my love" (John 15:10, RSV). And that meant everything.

The underlying principles of healthy, happy living are the same today as then. God has not changed. His compassion for us is as great as it was for the suffering and needy of Galilee in the long ago.

Therefore, if we would have the more abundant life God wants us to enjoy, there is a first step we can take. We can give our hearts to Him, and turning from all known transgression of His commandments, seek by His grace to live in full harmony with His revealed will.

WISE EATING

NO MORE wonderful piece of mechanism was ever devised than that which feeds and nourishes the human body. The tongue for tasting, the teeth for chewing, the stomach for digesting, the intestines for absorbing, the blood for circulating, and the lungs for maintaining the oxygen content.

In addition are the minute and still mysterious glands that supply essential chemicals to aid the process of transforming an endless variety of foods into an equally endless variety of human parts—and keep it up for a lifetime. Surely only the Creator Himself could have constructed anything so marvelous!

Each of us possesses one of these divinely designed systems, and it behooves us to take the best possible care of it. While provision has been made for its repair when damaged, it is much more sensible and far less costly to keep it in good condition.

This can be done by giving thought to what we eat, how we eat, and in some cases when we eat. Eating just anything on the menu regardless of its food value or its possible effect on the body is foolish indeed.

Not that we should worry ourselves unduly about diet and become hypochondriacs. That would do us no good. Nor will it help to become fanatical on the subject.

Here is where your Bible comes in again with wise and reasonable suggestions.

First, it makes clear that man's original diet consisted of fruits, nuts, and grains. You will find the instruction in Genesis 1:29, RSV:

"And God said, 'Behold, I have given you every plant yielding seed which is upon the face of all the earth, and every tree with seed in its fruit; you shall have them for food.' "

This was God's plan before the entrance of sin. Supplemented by fruit from the tree of life, this diet would have kept man in perfect health eternally. He would never have known disease or death. But sin came, and everything was changed. Apparently all nature suffered. See Genesis 3:17, 18.

Having rebelled against God in one matter, man found it easy to disregard His other counsels. Tiring of fruits, nuts, and grains, he began to kill and eat animals. There seems little doubt that this contributed, in some degree at least, to the state of affairs that brought the judgments of God upon the antediluvians. See Luke 17:26, 27; Genesis 7:5-7.

When the Flood had receded and little, if any, vegetation remained, a mixed diet was permitted. Said God: "Every moving thing that lives shall be food for you; and as I gave you the green plants, I give you everything. Only you shall not eat flesh with its life, that is, its blood" (Genesis 9:3, 4, RSV).

Yet while God said "everything," it is clear from the context that He made some reservations. When instructing Noah concerning the animals that were to enter the ark, He emphasized that some were unclean (Genesis 7:2). For various reasons these were not intended for human consumption.

A list of these forbidden mammals, fish, birds, insects, and reptiles is given in the eleventh chapter of Leviticus. Be sure to read it in the Revised Standard Version.

Take the mammals first. All that part the hoof and are cloven-footed and chew the cud are clean and edible. All other animals are unclean and unfit for food. Four are mentioned because of special problems (they meet some but not all of the specifications), namely, the camel, the rock badger, and the hare, cud chewers, and the swine, cloven-footed. "Of their flesh," God says, "you shall not eat."

Fish are mentioned next, although without names. Verse 9 reads: "Everything in the waters that has fins and scales, whether in the seas or in the rivers, you may eat. But anything in the seas or the rivers *that has not fins and scales* . . . is an abomination to you."

As to birds, many familiar names are on the prohibited list, including the eagle, the ossifrage, the osprey, the kite, the falcon, the raven, the ostrich, the nighthawk, the sea gull, the hawk, the owl, the cormorant, the ibis, the water hen, the pelican, the vulture, the stork, the heron, the hoopoe, and the bat.

Forbidden insects are not named, but verse 20 reads: "All winged insects that go upon all fours are an abomination to you." Only exceptions: locusts, crickets, and grasshoppers.

Other "abominations" include the weasel, the mouse, the great lizard, the gecko, the land crocodile, the lizard, the sand lizard, and the chameleon (verses 29, 30).

It is not a very inviting list. With few exceptions these creatures are usually classified as scavengers. There is very little, if any, demand at the best restaurants for roast camel, crocodile steaks, breast of eagle, or sea gull à la king. Nor have we heard of a request for broiled vulture or breaded mouse.

The fact is that if it were not for one animal mentioned here—one that brings much money to a great many people—this list would be universally acclaimed as a most wise provision of a benevolent Creator.

Because of this animal—the swine—people who like pork and those whose business it is to prepare and market it find all sorts of reasons for discounting the entire list. They claim that it was part of the Levitical law and therefore not binding on Christians, overlooking the fact that the distinction between "clean" and "unclean" existed long before there was a Levite, as noted above.

What is the right position for a Christian to take on a matter like this? The answer is simple: Follow God's advice. If He says that the flesh of these mammals, fish, birds, insects, and reptiles is not fit to eat, He must have a very good reason for saying so. He is not a capricious dictator, but a loving Father. All that He does for us, all the counsel He offers us, is "for our good always" (Deuteronomy 6:24; see Deuteronomy 10:13).

Some may not perceive the reason for God's clear prohibition of swine's flesh. They may be carried away by the pork packers' advertisements saying that theirs is the most nourishing food in the world. But in the long run God will be proved right. He does not make mistakes. For the person with an open mind, medical science has already provided adequate explanation that demonstrates His wisdom.

As you continue to study your Bible in search of truth on this matter of diet and health, you will discover that the whole subject was very much to the fore in New Testament times. It was actually on the agenda of the first Christian council in Jerusalem. Luke tells the story in the fifteenth chapter of the book of Acts. As a result of the discussion James, the acting president, said, "My judgment is that we should not trouble those of the Gentiles who turn to God, but should write to them to abstain from the pollutions of idols and from unchastity and from what is strangled and from blood" (verses 19, 20, RSV).

No other details are recorded, but it is interesting to note that the items mentioned predate the Levitical law by hundreds of years. See Genesis 6:5; 9:4; 35:2.

As the apostle Paul traveled among the newly organized churches in Asia Minor, Greece, and Italy, he found the subject of food and religion being widely discussed. Not that members were especially concerned about its health aspects; their big concern was whether they should eat meat that had been offered to idols. But other phases of eating and drinking became involved. Already the matter was dividing the membership and leading to harsh criticism by those who held opposite views. This was particularly the case in Rome, and to this church the apostle sent the finest counsel any group of Christians was ever given on the subject. Powerfully yet tenderly he stressed that love must be the guide in every decision, the motive of every action.

This incomparable passage is so good that you should read it both in the King James and Revised Standard versions. Even more forceful is the rendering by Dr. J. B. Phillips, who makes it read as if the apostle were writing to a church in New York or London today. The great passage begins with Romans 13:11 and runs on to Romans 14:21. Here are some of the most striking paragraphs:

"Why all this stress on behaviour? Because, as I think you have realised the present time is of the highest importance — it is time to wake up to reality. Every day brings God's salvation nearer. . . .

"The night is nearly over, the day has almost dawned. Let us therefore fling away the things that men do in the dark, let us arm ourselves for the fight of the day! Let us live cleanly, as in the daylight, not in the delights of getting drunk or playing with sex, nor yet in quarrelling or jealousies. Let us be Christ's men from head to foot, and give no chances to the flesh to have its fling. . . .

"Why, then, do you criticise your brother's action, why do you try to make him look small? We shall all be judged one day, not by each other's standards or even by our own, but by the judgment of God. . . .

"Let us therefore stop turning critical eyes on one another. Let us rather be critical of our own conduct and see that we do nothing to make a brother stumble or fall. . . .

"If your habit of unrestricted diet seriously upsets your brother, you are no longer living in love towards him. And surely you wouldn't let food mean ruin to a man for whom Christ died. . . . After all, the kingdom of Heaven is not a matter of whether you get what you like to eat and drink, but of righteousness and peace and joy in the Holy Spirit. If you put these things first in serving Christ you will please God and are not likely to offend men. So let us concentrate on the things which make for harmony, and on the growth of one our fellowship together. Surely we shouldn't wish to undo God's work for the sake of a plate of meat!"

This plea for mutual tolerance is Christianity at its best. Because it states an eternal truth, it is as valuable today as when it was written

150

19 centuries ago—and even more greatly needed. For as medical science opens up the mysteries of allergies we can see how very wrong and foolish it is to judge anybody concerning his food. Some people are allergic to milk and all milk products. Others are allergic to wheat and to all wheat products. Others are allergic to nuts, celery, strawberries, and a whole list of fruits, vegetables, and grains, just as others are allergic to cats, horses, house dust, feathers, ragweed, and the pollen of trees. These allergies are not imaginary but painfully real, as any allergic person will testify.

How appropriate then is Paul's searching question, "Who are you to criticize?"

Equally potent is his declaration that "the kingdom of Heaven is not a matter of whether you get what you like to eat and drink, but of righteousness and peace and joy in the Holy Spirit."

The Revised Standard Version renders this passage: "The kingdom of God is not food and drink but righteousness and peace and joy in the Holy Spirit."

No one can eat his way into heaven. Eating unwisely may result in a person's being lost, by ruining his judgment and causing him to sin, but eating even the heavenly manna itself will entitle no one to Paradise. Only acceptance of Jesus Christ as Lord and Saviour can do that.

Does this mean that a person is free to eat anything regardless of the consequences? No indeed. The apostle Paul made this plain in his first letter to the Corinthians. Here again he was not writing about diet and nutrition but concerning food offered to idols; but the great guiding principle is identical: "So, *whether you eat or drink, or whatever you do, do all to the glory of God*" (1 Corinthians 10:31, RSV).

Here the apostle brings us back once more to that fundamental truth so often set forth in your Bible: love matters most. Love for God and our fellowman. By revealing love—to a believer or unbeliever—we glorify God, because only God can make us kind, gracious, thoughtful, and tolerant toward others.

So in all our partaking of food or drink we should ask Is what

I am doing pleasing to God? Will my diet nourish my body so that it will be efficient in His service? Will it make my mind keener, my muscles stronger, my judgment more sound, my influence for good more potent?

You may not always be able to choose your own food. If you are overweight, your doctor may prescribe a high-protein diet. If you have high blood pressure, he may order a salt-free diet. If you have diabetes, he may restrict your carbohydrate intake. Sometimes when you are in other people's homes courtesy may lead you to eat things you don't really like. But when you are free to choose for yourself, choose what you know is best for you. Live as nearly as you can in harmony with God's invaluable suggestions for your well-being, and "thine health shall spring forth speedily" (Isaiah 58:8).

UNWISE DRINKING

WHEN God provided Adam and Eve with a perfect diet of grains and fruits, their drink consisted, presumably, of fruit juices and clear, sparkling water from springs and streams.

Just which of their descendants discovered that fruit juices left too long in heat would ferment and produce a narcotic fluid, no one knows. But within the first 10 chapters of your Bible you will find the first sad and sordid story of drunkenness.

From that day to this, uncounted millions have made the same mistake as Noah. Drinking alcoholic beverages has brought them shame and disgrace, sickness and ruin.

Because God is love and it grieves Him to see men and women made in His image behaving foolishly, He has left on record many strong warnings against this form of self-indulgence.

Best known of all is one of King Solomon's proverbs: "Wine is a mocker, strong drink a brawler; and whoever is led astray by it is not wise" (Proverbs 20:1, RSV).

Alcohol in any form is a mocker because it does not and cannot fulfill the hopes of those who partake of it. They think it will bring them relief from worry. But when their money is spent and the wine is drunk, their troubles remain, accentuated. Another bottle, another glass, will do it, the drinker fondly believes, but each one leads him further from his goal. Each drink makes him less able to appreciate the truly beautiful things of life for which, in his heart of hearts, he longs. The wine mocks him, laughing at his weakness and folly.

"Who has woe? Who has sorrow? Who has strife? Who has complaining? Who has wounds without cause? Who has redness of eyes?" asks the wise man (Proverbs 23:29, RSV). Here is his answer: "Those who tarry long over wine, those who go to try mixed wine" (verse 30).

He adds this warning: "Do not look at wine when it is red, when it sparkles in the cup and goes down smoothly. At the last it bites like a serpent, and stings like an adder."

Graphically picturing the effects of alcohol, he says, "Your eyes will see strange things, and your mind utter perverse things. You will be like one who lies down in the midst of the sea, like one who lies on the top of a mast. 'They struck me,' you will say, 'but I was not hurt; they beat me, but I did not feel it. When shall I awake? I will seek another drink' " (verses 31-35).

This was written 3,000 years ago, but its meaning is timeless; alcohol affects every generation in the same way.

Hundreds of years after Solomon, the prophet Isaiah gave this admonition to the people of Judah: "Woe to those who rise early in the morning, that they may run after strong drink, who tarry late into the evening till wine inflames them! They have lyre and harp, timbrel and flute and wine at their feasts; but they do not regard the deeds of the Lord, or see the work of his hands. Therefore my people go into exile for want of knowledge" (Isaiah 5:11-13, RSV).

A similar warning appears in the same chapter: "Woe to those who are heroes at drinking wine, and valiant men in mixing strong drink, who acquit the guilty for a bribe, and deprive the innocent of his right! Therefore, as the tongue of fire devours the stubble, and as dry grass sinks down in the flame, so their root will be as rottenness, and their blossom go up like dust; for they have rejected the law of the Lord of hosts, and have despised the word of the Holy One of Israel" (verses 22-24).

Your Bible is most definite that there is a terrible price to pay for permitting alcohol to mar God's handiwork by stupefying the brain and confusing the judgment.

To the "drunkards of Ephraim" Isaiah wrote this powerful denunciation:

"Behold, the Lord has one who is mighty and strong: like a storm of hail, a destroying tempest, like a storm of mighty, overflowing waters, he will cast down to the earth with violence. The proud crown of the drunkards of Ephraim will be trodden under foot. . . . These also reel with wine and stagger with strong drink; the priest and the prophet reel with strong drink, they are *confused* with wine, they *stagger* with strong drink; they *err in vision,* they *stumble in giving judgment"* (Isaiah 28:2-7, RSV).

These effects of drinking were also noted by the prophet Hosea, who was a contemporary of Isaiah. "Wine and new wine," he said, "take away the understanding" (Hosea 4:11, RSV).

God spoke some strong words to Aaron regarding the use of wine by those who ministered the priestly office: "Drink no wine nor strong drink, you nor your sons with you, when you go into the tent of meeting, lest you die; it shall be a statute for ever throughout your generations" (Leviticus 10:9, RSV).

In this connection it is significant that in the days of ancient Israel, when a man made a special dedication of his life to God, he took a pledge of total abstinence. You will find the record in the sixth chapter of the book of Numbers, verses 1-3.

"And the Lord said to Moses, Say to the people of Israel, When either a man or a woman makes a special vow, the vow of a Nazirite, to separate himself to the Lord, he shall separate himself from wine and strong drink" (RSV).

In the days of Jeremiah there was a family known as the Rechabites, who had adopted this program of total abstinence.

As a test of their fidelity the prophet set before them "pitchers full of wine, and cups" and told them to drink. They refused, the leader saying, "We will drink no wine, for Jonadab the son of Rechab, our father, commanded us, 'You shall not drink wine, neither you nor your sons for ever. . . .' We have obeyed the voice of . . . our father, in all that he commanded us, to drink no wine all our days, ourselves, our wives, our sons, or our daughters" (Jeremiah 35:5-8, RSV).

Because of their noble stand Jeremiah said to them, "Thus says the Lord of hosts, the God of Israel: Because you have obeyed the command of Jonadab your father, and kept all his precepts, and done all that he commanded you, therefore thus says the Lord of hosts, the God of Israel: Jonadab the son of Rechab shall never lack a man to stand before me" (verses 18, 19).

Thus while your Bible tells about the baleful results of alcohol, it also reveals that all down the centuries there have been those who have refused to be deceived by it. And it makes very clear where God stands on the matter.

Turning to the New Testament, we find that the apostle Paul had a great deal to say about unwise drinking.

"Let us conduct ourselves becomingly as in the day," he wrote to the Romans, "not in reveling and drunkenness" (Romans 13:13, RSV).

To the Ephesians he sent a warning not to "get drunk with wine, for that is debauchery" (Ephesians 5:18, RSV).

As for the Galatians, they were told that drunkenness would keep them out of heaven. "Now the works of the flesh are plain: immorality, impurity, licentiousness, idolatry, sorcery, enmity, strife, jealousy, anger, selfishness, dissension, party spirit, envy, *drunkenness*, carousing, and the like. I warn you, as I warned you before, that those who do such things shall not inherit the kingdom of God" (Galatians 5:19-21, RSV).

That this was no idle threat is evident from a statement in his first letter to the Corinthians. "Do you not know that the unrighteous will not inherit the kingdom of God?" he said to them. "Be not deceived; neither the immoral, nor idolaters, nor adulterers, nor homosexuals, nor thieves, nor the greedy, *nor drunkards,* nor robbers will inherit the kingdom of God" (1 Corinthians 6:9, 10, RSV).

Some people say that drunkenness—or alcoholism, to use the modern word—is a disease, but your Bible disagrees. It says plainly that it is a sin, classing all who allow themselves to get drunk with the worst of criminals.

Jesus put Himself on record on this point. When explaining one of His parables to His disciples, He pictured an unfaithful servant who began to "beat the menservants and the maidservants, and to eat and drink and *get drunk.*" At long last, said Jesus, a day of reckoning will come. The master of the servant will return "on a day when he does not expect him and at an hour he does not know, and will punish him, and put him with the unfaithful" (Luke 12:45, 46, RSV).

Speaking specifically to those who shall be living just prior to His second advent, He warned, "Take heed to yourselves lest your hearts be weighed down with *dissipation* and *drunkenness* and cares of this life, and that day come upon you suddenly like a snare" (Luke 21:34, RSV).

From all these passages of Scripture it is clear that the consumption of alcohol is a most serious matter in the eyes of God. And no wonder! It does so much both to the person who drinks it and to others who are affected by his foolish and often criminal actions.

In some states 60 percent of all fatal automobile accidents involve beverage alcohol. Millions of people in America are arrested each year on charges of drunkenness, drunken driving, and similar offenses.

For several years I polled the wardens of America's largest prisons. Again and again, before drug abuse became so common, they reported that from 70 to 90 percent of their inmates were incarcerated because of alcohol-related crimes.

Of the 110 million Americans who drink, at least 11 million are alcoholics. Problem drinkers are increasing at the rate of 630,000 a year.

In Britain more than 500 deaths and 25,000 injuries a year are caused by drinking drivers or pedestrians, according to the *British Medical Journal.*

In France, 17,626 persons died in one year because of cirrhosis of the liver. Another 4,452 died of alcoholic psychosis.

So the story of tragedy and sorrow caused by alcohol could be traced clear around the world.

How right was Robert Ingersoll when he said of strong drink: "It cuts down youth in its vigor . . . It fills the jails, supplies almshouses, and demands asylums. It engenders controversies, fosters quarrels, cherishes riots. It crowds penitentiaries and furnishes victims for scaffolds. . . . It is the sum of all villainies, the father of all crimes, the mother of all abominations. It is the devil's best friend and God's worst enemy."

With this dynamic denunciation all the latest discoveries of medical science are in full agreement.

Says Dr. Haven Emerson: "Alcohol is a depressant, a habit-forming narcotic drug, . . . a protoplasmic poison.

"Alcohol causes disease. Alcohol causes deaths from acute and chronic poisoning. Alcohol reduces resistance to infections, such as pneumonia.

"Alcohol reduces endurance, accuracy, and rapidity of muscular reaction of all kinds even when used in such small amounts as to show effects inappreciable subjectively by the user.

"Alcohol decreases expectancy of life. Alcohol reduces the chance of survival of offspring. Alcohol deteriorates emotional and nervous control as expressed in unreliable judgment and self-control."

All of which is true, the whiskey and beer advertisements notwithstanding. Thousands of doctors, judges, sports champions, and other public figures have testified that alcohol in any form should never be introduced into the human body.

To the dedicated Christian, the person who loves God with all his heart and soul and mind and strength, this can mean but one thing—total abstinence.

Said Paul, "So, whether you eat or drink, or whatever you do, do all to the glory of God" (1 Corinthians 10:31, RSV). And how could anyone glorify God by partaking of a poison that brings untold harm to the person who drinks it and incalculable sorrow and suffering to millions of others?

To glorify God in our bodies, we must avoid the use of any beverage likely to do it damage, including not only whiskey, wine, and beer, but other drinks containing harmful amounts of caffeine and similar alkaloids.

In this matter, as in all others, the motivating force should be love. When we love God sincerely we shall want to glorify Him in every way we can. When we love our neighbor as ourselves, we shall gladly desist from any practice that might harm him or set him a bad example.

Such love as this is "the fruit of the Spirit" (Galatians 5:22). When God comes into the heart by His Holy Spirit, He brings all the warmth, beauty, and purity of His love. Like sunlight shining through a prism it will reveal itself in the radiant hues of "joy, peace, patience, kindness, goodness, faithfulness, gentleness, self-control" (verses 22, 23, RSV).

Herein lies the secret of the temperate life, the life of "self-control," that does not have to be propped up by false stimulants. It is lived by the indwelling power of the Spirit of God, producing those heavenly graces that are a foretaste of the enduring joys of the kingdom eternal.

WHAT ABOUT
SMOKING AND DRUGS?

PERHAPS as you were reading the chapter entitled "Unwise Drinking" the thought occurred to you, What about tobacco and drugs? If a true Christian should avoid the use of alcohol, should he not also avoid these other narcotics? This is an important question that deserves careful study in the light of the latest scientific discoveries and the principles your Bible sets forth.

If you hope to find a text that says "Thou shalt not smoke," you will be disappointed. Tobacco is not mentioned anywhere from Genesis to Revelation and for the very good reason that its use is of comparatively recent origin. It was not known in Bible times. In fact, Western Europe never heard of it until Christopher Columbus brought back seeds from the West Indies in 1492. Nevertheless, the great principles of healthful living are so clearly enunciated in the Holy Scriptures that no one need be in any doubt as to what his attitude should be toward this habit.

In this connection it is good to read the apostle Paul's inspiring challenge to Christians of the first century A.D. You will find it in the twelfth chapter of his letter to the Romans: "I appeal to you therefore, brethren, by the mercies of God, to present your bodies as a living sacrifice, holy and acceptable to God, which is your spiritual worship. Do not be conformed to this world but be transformed by the renewal of your mind, that you may prove what is the will of God, what is good and acceptable and perfect" (verses 1, 2, RSV).

There is a definite suggestion here that every individual is accountable to God for the condition of his body. Having been created by God in the beginning and redeemed by Him at Calvary, he belongs to Him by a dual tie. Consequently, he is not free to do as he pleases without reference to God's desires. He cannot with impunity debase, defile, or destroy his body if for no other reason than that God has a prior claim to it. God expects it to be presented to Him as a "living sacrifice," unmarred by self-indulgence.

The sacredness of the body was also emphasized by the apostle in his first letter to the Corinthians: "Do you not know that your body is a temple of the Holy Spirit within you, which you have from God? You are not your own; you were bought with a price. So glorify God in your body" (1 Corinthians 6:19, 20, RSV).

This is in full harmony with the teachings of Jesus who said, "If a man loves me, he will keep my word, and my Father will love him, and we will come to him and make our home with him" (John 14:23, RSV).

Thus the body of the consecrated Christian is a dwelling place of God through the Holy Spirit. It is God's home, God's temple. Consequently its purity, health, and well-being are to be guarded as a sacred trust.

It is in the light of this great truth that all questions concerning eating, drinking, smoking, and the like should be considered. Every habit should be brought to the bar of conscience and asked, Is it helpful or harmful? Will it increase or decrease health and efficiency? Will it glorify or defile God's temple?

Thus confronted, smoking could not possibly be sustained. Modern science has demonstrated beyond the shadow of a doubt that it is one of the most dangerous habits anyone could acquire. In recent years evidence has piled on evidence that it is one of the major destroyers of health. When all the facts are assembled it may well be said that while liquor has slain its thousands, tobacco has killed its tens of thousands.

Dr. Leroy E. Burney, former surgeon general of the United States, shook the country in 1958 with his carefully worded statement in the *Congressional Record*: "Many independent studies have confirmed beyond reasonable doubt that there is a high degree of statistical association between lung cancer and heavy and prolonged cigarette smoking. . . . While there are naturally differences of opinion in interpreting the data on lung cancer and cigarette smoking, the Public Health Service feels the weight of evidence is increasingly pointing in one direction—that excessive smoking is one of the causative factors in lung cancer."

A more recent surgeon general, with a great deal more research to substantiate him, was more outspoken. Asked how he rated smoking as a health problem, Dr. C. Everett Koop was emphatic. "There is no hesitancy in my answer," he said. "Smoking is the number one public health problem in the United States today. Because of smoking, 350,000 people die prematurely every year—from cancer (of various organs, not just the lungs), from heart disease, from peripheral vascular disease (such as stroke), and from chronic obstructive lung disease. Roughly a thousand people a day die from smoking tobacco. It's as though a little better than two 747s filled with people crashed every day all year" (*Vibrant Life*, November/December 1985).

Since Dr. Koop made that statement, the number of deaths attributable to smoking in the United States has leaped to 450,000 annually.

Figures from Britain run a close parallel. With approximately 56 million inhabitants—roughly one fourth of the U.S.—Britain currently counts some 100,000 tobacco deaths annually (*Family Life*, Autumn 1990).

Compared to the number who die from smoking, the frightening number killed each year by AIDS is almost trivial.

Asked if he gave up smoking to avoid lung cancer, one California physician, chairman of the board of his city's hospital, replied that it wasn't fear of lung cancer that led him to stop, bad as that might be. "Lung cancer is fatal," he agreed, "but it's comparatively quick."

What he quit to avoid, he said, was emphysema. He didn't want to spend "year after year in the condition I've seen so many patients, continuously wheezing and coughing, forever straining in vain to get a satisfying breath."

In his book *Conditional Reflex Therapy,* Andrew Salter affirms that "the heavy smoker pays with 34.6 minutes of life for each cigarette he smokes. The pack-a-day smoker pays with 11.5 hours for each pack he smokes."

Harry Dinkman, in *Risk Appraisal,* published by the National Underwriter Company, says, "Habitual smokers have 62 percent higher incidence of gas on the stomach, 65 percent higher incidence of colds, 76 percent higher incidence of nervousness, 100 percent higher incidence of heartburn, 140 percent higher incidence of labored breathing after exertion, 167 percent higher incidence of nose and throat irritation, and 300 percent higher incidence of cough."

Dr. William J. Mayo, of the Mayo Clinic, Rochester, Minnesota, made the statement: "I do not smoke, and I do not approve of smoking. If you will notice, you will see that the practice of smoking is going out among the ablest surgeons, the men at the top. No surgeon can afford to smoke."

One of the most impressive studies concerning the effects of tobacco was conducted by the Sloan-Kettering Institute for Cancer Research. Basis of the research was 564 Seventh-day Adventists, chosen because they do not smoke or drink. Their records were compared with those of 8,128 members of other religious groups, all patients in Adventist hospitals. The results, presented to the California Medical Association in session, showed that among Seventh-day Adventists lung cancer is only one tenth as common as among the general population. Only three fifths as many suffer heart attacks, and those who do are at a much more advanced age.

The only case of lung cancer found among the Adventist patients occurred in a man who had smoked a pack of cigarettes a day for 25 years before joining the church.

Some have suggested that switching to *smokeless* tobacco would avoid the dangers of smoking. They propose a return to chewing tobacco and snuff. But research shows this to be a move in the wrong direction. Snuff may be even more addictive than cigarettes. And chewers face the very real possibility that their gums will pull back from their teeth; that white, leathery patches will develop on gums and cheeks and become malignant; that their face will become paralyzed; and that lip ulcers won't heal. A joint study by the National Cancer Institute and the University of North Carolina concludes that chewing multiplies the normal risk of death by cancer fifty times *(Listen* June, 1989).

Among the worst effects of smoking is its influence on young people. Scientific observers increasingly agree that most smokers begin as children experimenting with cigarettes Dad or Mother has left where the children can reach them. Many alcoholics begin by sipping wine from the family refrigerator. When the initial thrills wear off, these children look for something stronger — and they're off on the slippery road to drug addiction.

Glue and paint thinner are easy to come by. Sniffing the fumes brings aggressive behavior with a rapid heartbeat that in some cases has led to cardiac arrest. More often, there is loss of consciousness and fatal suffocation. In less severe cases there is injury to nerves, liver, and kidneys and permanent brain damage. But to begin with there is a rush of pleasurable feeling, and the children want it again. Soon they are looking for something stronger. Still in junior high, they are ready to be victimized by pot pushers — and worse.

Enter marijuana, a far more sinister enemy than some have supposed. In *Schools Without Drugs,* William J. Bennett, formerly director of the National Drug Control Policy, authorized this description of the effects of drugs in general and marijuana in particular: "Drug use impairs memory, alertness, and achievement. Drugs erode the capacity of students to perform in school, to think and act responsibly. . . . When a student clouds his mind with drugs, he may become a lifelong casualty. Research tells us that students who use marijuana regularly are twice as likely as their classmates to average Ds and Fs, and we know that dropouts are twice as likely to be frequent drug users as graduates."

Bennett might have added gang violence, prostitution, unwanted pregnancies, abortion, and prison records. With so much against them, what can these youth do but fail? Many commit suicide. Others reach for stronger drugs, cocaine and crack. The evils of these drugs is so much in the news that little need be added here.

With so much evidence to prove the harmfulness of tobacco and drugs it is surely high time for all sensible, reasonable men and women to give up these costly, health-destroying habits. And for all who love God and desire to present their bodies "a living sacrifice, holy and acceptable to God," this becomes an urgent imperative. No one who regards his body as the temple of the Holy Spirit could deliberately destroy it with harmful substances. Certainly he won't want to influence children and youth to do so.

But how to break the habit?

Medical authorities have made these suggestions:

When you decide to stop, stop. Do it at once. Make a complete break.

Destroy every evidence of the habit, including cigarettes, cigars, ashtrays, lighters, and all drug paraphernalia.

Get professional counseling. There are many local therapists to help you overcome smoking. The Seventh-day Adventists have helped tens of thousands with their Five-Day Plan to Stop Smoking, now known as Breathe-Free. They'll help you, too, if you ask. Or join a self-help group like Narcotics Anonymous or Cocaine Anonymous.

More effective still is earnest prayer for divine help. Tell God about your desire and your resolve. Open the door of your heart heavenward, and the Holy Spirit, flowing in, will bring you both strength and victory.

DIVINE HEALING

YOUR Bible is full of assurances of the healing power of God. "I am the Lord that healeth thee," He said to Israel in the wilderness (Exodus 15:26).

This glorious truth finds an echo in the Psalms, where David has left on record these gracious words of thanksgiving: "Bless the Lord, O my soul; and all that is within me, bless his holy name! Bless the Lord, O my soul, and forget not all his benefits, who forgives all your iniquity, *who heals all your diseases*" (Psalm 103:1-3, RSV).

Equally lovely is this passage found in Psalm 41:1-3: "Blessed is he who considers the poor! The Lord delivers him in the day of trouble; the Lord protects him and keeps him alive. . . . The Lord sustains him on his sickbed; *in his illness thou healest all his infirmities*" (RSV).

The more you think of this, the more reasonable it appears. For who else knows more about the human body than the One who created it in the beginning? Who else is so familiar with its built-in recuperative powers? Who else understands so perfectly the mysterious processes by which broken bones knit, severed nerves unite, ugly wounds close, great bruises disappear, and flowing blood coagulates?

All these marvels are evidence of infinite wisdom. They bear the hallmark of Heaven. Christian surgeons, beholding the intricate mechanism of the eye and the ear, the amazing arrangement of the brain cells, the elaborate details of the nervous and digestive systems, the ingenuity of the blood factory in the marrow of the bones, exclaim with reverence, "This is the finger of God!"

And because our bodies are the work of God, the product of His mind and His fingers, we can take new courage in times of sickness, turning to Him as to one who knows best what is needed for our recovery.

This faith will be strengthened as we note what God did when He came to live among men in the person of Jesus Christ. From the very beginning of His ministry Jesus healed the sick. Your Bible says that "he went about all Galilee, . . . *healing every disease* and every infirmity among the people" (Matthew 4:23, RSV). No symptoms baffled Him. Instantly He perceived both cause and cure.

Was a man dumb? Jesus loosed his vocal chords.

Was a man deaf? Jesus opened his ears.

Was a man blind? Jesus cleared his retina.

Was a man mad? Jesus calmed his mind.

Was a man paralyzed? Jesus reenergized his muscles.

Did a man have leprosy? Jesus caused a tide of clean new blood to renew the wasted tissues.

Miracles they were indeed, made possible by the power of God and His detailed knowledge of the human body. He knew what to do.

Centuries before He had said, "I am the Lord, your healer"; now He demonstrated the fact in person.

"When the even was come, they brought unto him many that were possessed with devils: and he cast out the spirits with his word, and *healed all that were sick* that it might be fulfilled which was spoken by Esaias the prophet, saying, Himself took our infirmities, and bare our sicknesses" (Matthew 8:16, 17).

To the twelve apostles Jesus confided the secret of healing. He taught them what to do for the sick, for He wanted them to continue His beneficent work after He returned to heaven.

"And when he had called unto him his twelve disciples, he gave them power against unclean spirits, to cast them out, and to *heal all manner of sickness and all manner of disease*" (Matthew 10:1).

Luke, himself a doctor, recorded this occasion thus: "He called his twelve disciples together, and gave them power and authority over all devils, and to *cure diseases*. And he sent them to preach the kingdom of God, and to *heal the sick*" (Luke 9:1, 2).

A little later Jesus widened the circle of His helpers, imparting to 70 disciples the same beautiful healing ministry. "Whenever you enter a town and they receive you," He instructed them, "eat what is set before you; *heal the sick* in it and say to them, 'The kingdom of God has come near to you' " (Luke 10:8, 9, RSV).

To Jesus, preaching without healing was an imperfect presentation of God's love. He knew that many would never appreciate the deep spiritual truths of His kingdom while their minds were dulled by sickness and their bodies racked with pain.

So the disciples went forth to do His bidding and discovered that their Master's "prescription" worked. They were happy beyond words at the good they were able to accomplish.

"And the seventy returned again with joy, saying, Lord, even the devils are subject unto us through thy name" (Luke 10:17).

Just before His ascension Jesus still further extended the possibilities of good by this means. "These signs shall follow them that believe," He said. "In my name shall they cast out devils; they shall speak with new tongues; they shall take up serpents; and if they drink any deadly thing, it shall not hurt them; *they shall lay hands on the sick, and they shall recover*" (Mark 16:17, 18).

Taking Jesus at His word, the disciples "went forth, and preached every where, the Lord working with them, and confirming the word with signs following" (verse 20).

After Pentecost amazing power flowed through them for the help and healing of a needy world. And the miracles of healing were not confined to a few isolated instances such as the sudden restoration of the lame man at the Temple gate (Acts 3:1-8), the paralytic Aeneas at Lydda (Acts 9:34), and the poor cripple at Lystra who had been lame from birth (Acts 14:8-10). Thousands were helped to a better and happier life.

On occasion there flowed through the Christian workers a positive flood tide of healing mercy, as during Paul's two-year sojourn in Ephesus. Your Bible says: "And God did extraordinary miracles by the hands of Paul, so that handkerchiefs or aprons were carried away from his body to the sick, and diseases left them and the evil spirits came out of them" (Acts 19:11, 12, RSV).

For three months after being shipwrecked on Malta, Paul carried on a wonderful healing ministry. Not only did he heal the father of Publius, "the chief man of the island," but many others also. "When this had taken place," the record says, "the rest of the people on the island who had diseases also came and were cured" (Acts 28:7-9, RSV).

That the apostle had no thought that he had a monopoly on this power is clear from his first letter to the Corinthians, in which he discussed the gifts of the Spirit. With his usual generosity and breadth of vision he wrote: "Now there are varieties of gifts, but the same Spirit; and there are varieties of service, but the same Lord. . . . To each is given the manifestation of the Spirit for the common good. To one is given through the Spirit the utterance of wisdom, and to another the utterance of knowledge according to the same Spirit, to another faith by the same Spirit, to another *gifts of healing* by the one Spirit, to another the working of miracles" (1 Corinthians 12:4-10, RSV).

Seeing that all these gifts of God are to remain with His people "until we all attain to the unity of the faith" (Ephesians 4:13, RSV), it is but reasonable to assume that they are available now, including the "gifts of healing." And they are. Without doubt many of the marvelous advances in medical science, which have proved of such incalculable blessing to mankind in these latter days, have resulted from the enlightenment by the Holy Spirit of godly doctors, nurses, dietitians, research chemists, and others who have dedicated their lives to the service and uplift of their fellowmen.

In addition, when all human efforts fail, and the best of medical science is at a loss to know how to proceed, God still steps in to heal miraculously when it seems best to Him to do so. This does not mean, of course, that everybody who is sick can expect to be healed. Nevertheless, it is most definitely true that the great God of love who once said, "I am the Lord, your healer," still stands ready to relieve the suffering and heal the sick in His own time and way.

If you are sick, you can tell Him privately of your needs or, if the matter is serious, you can follow the procedure outlined in the fifth chapter of the book of James:

"Is any one among you suffering? Let him pray. . . . Is any among you sick? Let him call for the elders of the church, and let them pray over him, anointing him with oil in the name of the Lord; and the prayer of faith will save the sick man, and the Lord will raise him up" (verses 13-15, RSV).

Presumably there are some conditions attached. One could not expect God to act miraculously in a case where the patient had not made a full surrender of his life to Him. One could hardly ask God for deliverance from lung cancer while still secretly planning to continue smoking. Nor could one hope to be cured of cirrhosis of the liver while hiding a bottle of whiskey under the bed.

Divine healing is possible today. If you need it, you may have it if God sees it is for your present and eternal good. But it will come only as a result of earnest prayer, unquestioning faith, full surrender, and a total resignation to His will.

As true today as ever are His words to ancient Israel: "It shall come to pass, if ye hearken to these judgments, and keep, and do them, that the Lord thy God . . . will love thee, and bless thee. . . . And the Lord will take away from thee all sickness."

WHY SOME PRAYERS ARE NOT ANSWERED

A S YOU continue to read your Bible, many questions are bound to arise in your mind. And no wonder; for truth is so limitless that no one can hope to compass it in any brief period of time.

Occasionally you may stumble on an answer accidentally, but usually it has to be searched for with diligence. Sometimes you may see it as a flash of light from heaven, but more often you will find it only after careful study and earnest prayer. Possibly you will need help from your pastor or a reliable Bible correspondence course.

In a book of this size it would be impossible to consider all the problems that might occur to a wide diversity of readers. Consideration will be given, however, to a few that most frequently arise.

One such question concerns answered prayer. Perhaps you have asked it yourself. If God is a God of love, why doesn't He answer all my prayers?

As noted in previous chapters, there is no doubt about God's *willingness* to answer. "Call unto me, and I will answer," He says (Jeremiah 33:3). Again: "Ask, and it shall be given you; seek, and ye shall find; knock, and it shall be opened unto you: for every one that asketh receiveth; and he that seeketh findeth; and to him that knocketh it shall be opened" (Matthew 7:7, 8).

Nor is there any doubt about God's *ability* to answer. He is "able to do exceeding abundantly above all that we ask or think" (Ephesians 3:20).

Nevertheless it is clearly evident, from everybody's experience, that some prayers are not answered. Why? Are any conditions attached to prayer? There are indeed. Here are seven:

1. *You must have faith.* "Whatever you ask in prayer, you will receive, *if you have faith*" (Matthew 21:22, RSV). You must believe that God is able to do what you ask Him to do. "Without faith it is impossible to please him. For whoever would draw near to God must believe that he exists and that he rewards those who seek him" (Hebrews 11:6, RSV).

2. *You must be thankful.* "Have no anxiety about anything, but in everything by prayer and supplication *with thanksgiving* let your requests be made known to God" (Philippians 4:6, RSV). "Thanksgiving" connotes a worshipful state of mind, which is as important as believing in God's power to help.

3. *You must be at one with God.* Says Jesus, *"If you abide in me, and my words abide in you, ask whatever you will, and it shall be done for you"* (John 15:7, RSV). This has the same meaning as Psalm 34:15: "The eyes of the Lord are upon the righteous, and his ears are open unto their cry." Identification with God's righteous purposes is essential.

4. *You must be resigned to His will.* "And this is the confidence which we have in him, that if we ask anything *according to his will* he hears us" (1 John 5:14, RSV). Jesus set the supreme example in Gethsemane when He prayed, "O my Father, if it be possible, let this cup pass from me; nevertheless not as I will, but as thou wilt. . . . Thy will be done" (Matthew 26:39-42).

As it is God's will that ultimately will be done, it is but wise and reasonable to yield to His will before you pray.

5. *You must be patient.* Says David: "I waited *patiently* for the Lord; and he inclined unto me, and heard my cry" (Psalm 40:1). Again, "Wait on the Lord: be of good courage, and he shall strengthen thine heart: wait, I say, on the Lord" (Psalm 27:14).

If all your prayers were answered immediately under the urgency

172

of your pleading, you would probably be sadly disillusioned. Human vision is so limited that it is always wisest to wait for God to answer as and when His wisdom may deem best.

6. *You must cherish no sinful desire.* Says the psalmist, *"If I regard iniquity* in my heart, the Lord will not hear me" (Psalm 66:18). This does not mean that a person has to be perfect before he can pray. Over and over again God invites sinners to call upon Him. But it does mean that unless you are sorry for your sins and are willing to be free from every evil thought, word, and deed, your prayers will not be effective.

As Isaiah says: "Behold, the Lord's hand is not shortened, that it cannot save; neither his ear heavy, that it cannot hear: but *your iniquities have separated between you and your God,* and your sins have hid his face from you, that he will not hear" (Isaiah 59:1, 2).

Sin separates man from God. Like dirt in an electrical connection, it stops the flow of power.

When the disciples were confronted by a man with a lunatic son they found themselves powerless. Wondering why, they asked Jesus to explain, not realizing that their failure was because of their own petty, quarrelsome thoughts as to who should be greatest in the kingdom of heaven. See Luke 9:38-44. God does not work miracles in such an atmosphere.

Nor does He answer prayers of a purely selfish nature. Says James: "You ask and do not receive, because you ask wrongly, to spend it on your passions" (James 4:3, RSV). A prayer for a new Cadillac or to win $100,000 on a TV program will not have a very high priority in the courts of heaven.

7. *You must pray in the name of Jesus.* "Whatever you ask *in my name,* I will do it, that the Father may be glorified in the Son; if you ask anything in my name, I will do it" (John 14:13, 14, RSV).

This means much more, of course, than merely saying "in Jesus' name" or "for Christ's sake" at the end of a prayer. It suggests a desire to glorify God by asking only those things that are pleasing to Him and will be helpful to His cause. As Samuel Chadwick once said: "To pray in the name of Christ is to pray as one who is at one with

173

Christ, whose mind is the mind of Christ, whose desires are the desires of Christ, and whose purpose is at one with that of Christ" *(The Path of Prayer,* p. 52).

Here, then, are seven conditions for successful praying. Follow them, and your prayer experience will take on new richness and beauty. Answers will begin to come. God will surprise you with the swiftness and greatness of His responses.

Should there still be delay for reasons you cannot perceive or understand, hold on to His arm of love. Keep on praying.

Remember Paul's experience. After being struck down on the Damascus road by a light "brighter than the sun," he suffered severely from a "thorn in the flesh" from which he often sought deliverance. "Three times I besought the Lord about this, that it should leave me," he says (2 Corinthians 12:8, RSV). But it didn't leave him. Instead he was given this message to sustain his spirit: "My grace is sufficient for you, for my power is made perfect in weakness" (verse 9).

For some reason known only to God, it was best for Paul to bear this trial. So his oft-repeated prayer was not granted.

It could happen this way with you. If so, do not lose heart. Hold fast your faith in God. Say with Jeremiah: "The steadfast love of the Lord never ceases, his mercies never come to an end; they are new every morning; great is thy faithfulness. 'The Lord is my portion,' says my soul, 'therefore I will hope in him' " (Lamentations 3:22-24, RSV).

Beyond all question, His grace is sufficient for you.

WHY SO MUCH SUFFERING?

IF GOD is good, if He is love, why is there so much suffering in the world? This is an old question, as old as pain, sickness, accident, and loss. People have been asking it for thousands of years and will go on asking it till the end of time.

Probably no completely satisfying answer will be available until God makes all things plain in His kingdom, but your Bible offers several helpful suggestions.

You will find the first reference to suffering in Genesis 3:16, where God reveals to Eve the consequences of her disobedience: "I will greatly multiply thy sorrow and thy conception; in sorrow shalt thou bring forth children." From this it might be deduced, and rightly so, that all suffering springs from that initial act of wrongdoing. Yet that is not the whole story. Just as there are many types of suffering, so there are many reasons for it.

1. *Some suffering is a result of ignoring basic law.* This is true both in the spiritual and physical realms, for through all creation runs the law of cause and effect: "Whatsoever a man soweth, that shall he also reap" (Galatians 6:7). If you break the laws of the land, you expect—if caught—to suffer punishment. If you break the laws of health, you know you will get sick. If you break the moral law, the consequences are just as certain. "For he that soweth to his flesh

175

shall of the flesh reap corruption; but he that soweth to the Spirit shall of the Spirit reap life everlasting" (verse 8).

2. *Some suffering is the result of accident or natural disaster.* Three times Jesus asserted that trouble often comes upon innocent people. When He was told about some Galileans whom Pilate had unjustly killed, He said, "Do you think that these Galileans were worse sinners than all the other Galileans, because they suffered thus? I tell you, No; but unless you repent you will all likewise perish" (Luke 13:2, 3, RSV).

Then He mentioned 18 persons upon whom a tower in Siloam fell, killing them all. "Do you think that they were worse offenders than all the others who dwelt in Jerusalem?" He asked. "I tell you, No; but unless you repent you will all likewise perish" (verses 4, 5).

On another occasion, as He passed a blind man along the way, His disciples asked, "Master, who did sin, this man, or his parents, that he was born blind?" Jesus answered, "Neither hath this man sinned, nor his parents" (John 9:2, 3).

In each case Jesus strongly repudiated the thought that the calamity happened as a result of the individual's sin. Usually when earthquakes, tidal waves, explosions, airplane accidents, and the like occur, the majority of sufferers have no responsibility whatever for the disaster.

3. *Some suffering results from power in the hands of evil men.* Says the prophet Habakkuk: "Thou art of purer eyes than to behold evil, and canst not look on iniquity: wherefore lookest thou upon them that deal treacherously, and holdest thy tongue *when the wicked devoureth the man that is more righteous than he?*" (Habakkuk 1:13).

One of the facts of life most difficult to understand is "the prosperity of the wicked" (Psalm 73:3). "They are not in trouble as other men," says David; "neither are they plagued like other men. . . . Their eyes stand out with fatness; they have more than heart could wish. They are corrupt, and speak wickedly concerning oppression; they speak loftily. . . . Behold, these are the ungodly, who prosper in the world" (verses 5-12).

176

This is a perfect picture of the dictators and racketeers who elbow their way to power in politics and other phases of organized society regardless of the consequences to others.

4. *Some suffering is a result of God's remedial judgments.* Just as a parent punishes his child to keep him in the right way, so God sometimes permits hardship and sorrow to come to His children in order to turn them from an evil course. "He doth not afflict willingly nor grieve the children of men" (Lamentations 3:33), but sometimes some correction becomes necessary. Should this ever happen to you, "know then in your heart that, as a man disciplines his son, so the Lord your God disciplines you" (Deuteronomy 8:5, RSV).

There is always a good reason for God's judgments. Comparing the correction of parents with that of the Lord, the writer to the Hebrews says: "For they verily for a few days chastened us after their own pleasure; but he for our profit, *that we might be partakers of his holiness*" (Hebrews 12:10).

In your Bible you will find several examples of sinners brought back to God through affliction.

When Jonah refused God's call to go to Nineveh and fled on a ship bound for Tarshish, he was thrown overboard and swallowed by a great fish. "Then Jonah prayed unto the Lord his God out of the fish's belly, and said, I cried by *reason of mine affliction,* unto the Lord, and he heard me" (Jonah 2:1, 2).

King Manasseh was carried captive to Babylon because of his fearful wickedness. But *"when he was in affliction,* he besought the Lord his God, and humbled himself greatly before the God of his fathers, and prayed unto him: and he was intreated of him, and heard his supplication, and brought him again to Jerusalem into his kingdom. Then Manasseh knew that the Lord he was God" (2 Chronicles 33:12, 13).

Nebuchadnezzar, king of Babylon, defied God and lost his reason for seven years.

Later he testified: "At the end of the days I Nebuchadnezzar lifted up mine eyes unto heaven, and mine understanding returned unto me, and I blessed the most High, and I praised and honored him that liveth for ever, whose dominion is an everlasting dominion, and his kingdom is from generation to generation" (Daniel 4:34).

Several times in the Old Testament God is portrayed as a refiner sitting by a furnace skimming off the impurities of His people. See Malachi 3:3; Job 23:10. Through Isaiah He says, "Behold, I have refined thee, but not with silver; I have chosen thee in the furnace of affliction" (Isaiah 48:10). Later in the same chapter He adds: "I am the Lord thy God which teacheth thee to profit, which leadeth thee by the way that thou shouldest go. O that thou hadst hearkened to my commandments! then had thy peace been as a river, and thy righteousness as the waves of the sea" (verses 17, 18).

Most of Israel's troubles could have been averted by obedience and right living, but when through disobedience affliction became necessary it was sent for their profit to lead them in the way that they should go.

5. *Some suffering is the result of dedication to Jesus Christ.* From Jesus Himself we have this warning: "If they have persecuted me, they will also persecute you" (John 15:20). This certainly came true in the life of the apostle Paul who, time after time, was imprisoned and beaten because of his fearless witness for his Lord.

Out of this full experience of suffering he assured Timothy: "All that will live godly in Christ Jesus shall suffer persecution" (2 Timothy 3:12). When he returned to Lystra, where he was once stoned, he told the members, "We must through much tribulation enter into the kingdom of God" (Acts 14:22).

So there are several causes of suffering, and sometimes it is difficult to classify correctly one's personal troubles. However, if you see to it that, whatever their cause, they drive you *toward* God rather than *away* from Him, the ultimate result is bound to be beneficial.

If you think that your affliction is the result of disobedience to some basic law, ask God to help you remedy the defect.

If you know it comes from an accident for which you are in no way responsible, pray for patience to bear it, wisdom to understand it, and love to forgive those who caused it. See Job 1:21; James 1:3; 5:11.

If what you endure is the result of the plottings of evil men, pray that God may turn them from their wicked ways; "rejoicing in hope; patient in tribulation; continuing instant in prayer" (Romans 12:12).

If you believe your troubles are a divine discipline, search your heart for the reason why God is displeased with you. Then plead for forgiveness and pledge Him your eternal devotion. See Hebrews 12:11; 1 Peter 5:10.

If you are enduring persecution for Christ's sake, "Rejoice, and be exceeding glad: for great is your reward in heaven" (Matthew 5:12). Remember, "If we suffer, we shall also reign with him" (2 Timothy 2:12).

Without doubt all of us need more of the glorious fortitude Paul revealed when he said, "None of these things move me" (Acts 20:24).

"Therefore," he told the Corinthians, "I take pleasure in infirmities, . . . in persecutions, in distress for Christ's sake: for when I am weak, then am I strong" (2 Corinthians 12:10).

For him and for all who endure to the end a glorious reward is awaiting. "Blessed is the man that endureth temptation: for when he is tried, he shall receive the crown of life, which the Lord hath promised to them that love him" (James 1:12).

HOW DID EVIL BEGIN?

WHEN God had completed His work of creation, your Bible says that He "saw every thing that he had made, and, behold, it was very good" (Genesis 1:31). But if at that moment everything was "very good," whence came the deceptive serpent described in chapter three? In other words, how did evil begin?

Obviously it did not begin with Adam, for Eve was the first to partake of the forbidden fruit. Yet Eve made her fatal mistake upon the urging of the serpent, which would seem to make this creature the prime cause of the tragedy of sin.

Attention is therefore focused upon this strange being that not only had access to the Garden of Eden and could talk to Eve in language she could understand, but was, at that early moment in the story of our world, already in open rebellion against the Creator. What was it? Or more correctly, who was it?

Clear light on this question is to be found in the twentieth chapter of the book of Revelation, where John says, "I saw an angel come down from heaven, having the key of the bottomless pit and a great chain in his hand. And he laid hold on *the dragon, that old serpent, which is the Devil, and Satan*" (verses 1, 2).

So the *serpent, Satan,* and *Devil* are synonymous terms. They refer to the same individual.

Thus it was not merely a talking snake that deceived Eve, but the mastermind of evil, using the serpent as a medium through which to contact the beautiful mother of the human race. Confirmation of this fact is found in 1 John 3:8: "He who commits sin is of the devil; for *the devil has sinned from the beginning*" (RSV).

A similar statement was made by Jesus in His denunciation of the Pharisees. "You are of your father the devil," He said, "and your will is to do your father's desires. *He was a murderer from the beginning*, and has nothing to do with the truth, because there is no truth in him. When he lies, he speaks according to his own nature, for *he is a liar and the father of lies*" (John 8:44, RSV).

This latter charge tallies exactly with the Genesis story, for almost the first words the serpent uttered were false. God said, "Thou shalt surely die" (Genesis 2:17), and the serpent said, "Ye shall not surely die." Not only was this the first lie, but, because of its consequences, it was the greatest lie ever told.

But the Bible has more to say about this serpent, Satan, or the devil. If you will turn again to the book of Revelation, you will learn exactly what happened:

"And there was war in heaven: Michael and his angels fought against the dragon; and the dragon fought and his angels, and prevailed not; neither was their place found any more in heaven. And the great dragon was cast out, that old serpent, called the Devil and Satan, which deceiveth the whole world; he was cast out into the earth, and his angels were cast out with him" (Revelation 12:7-9).

At first thought it may seem incredible to you that there could ever have been such a stupendous upheaval in the abode of eternal peace. Yet this is what your Bible states. And the more you study the subject the more you will come to realize that it is one of the most vital revelations to be found in the Book.

Obviously a rebellion on such a scale—involving one third of the entire angelic host (verse 4)—did not happen suddenly. It must have taken time to develop. And it must have begun in somebody's mind, possibly in the form of injured pride, and so spread from angel to angel throughout God's fair domain.

And that is exactly what did happen. The story is told in detail by two of Israel's greatest prophets.

Look now at the fourteenth chapter of Isaiah and read this remarkable passage: "How art thou fallen from heaven, O Lucifer, son of the morning! how are thou cut down to the ground, which didst weaken the nations! For thou hast said in thine heart, I will ascend into heaven, I will exalt my throne above the stars of God: I will sit also upon the mount of the congregation, in the sides of the north: I will ascend above the heights of the clouds, I will be like the most High" (verses 12-14).

Here Satan is called Lucifer, meaning the "daystar" or "son of the dawn," which affords a valuable glimpse into his past. Clearly he was once one of the most gifted of God's creatures, next in glory to the Son of God Himself. And here no doubt was the first cause of his pride and jealousy.

At some awful but unrecorded moment in the history of the universe there entered the mind of this beautiful angel the foolish and most perilous thought, Why am I of less account than God's Son? Why is His glory greater than mine? Why is His association with the Father closer than mine?

As he brooded upon fancied injustices there developed the first concept of rebellion. It was but a step from this to a plot to exalt himself "above the stars of God." "I will ascend above the heights of the clouds," he said to himself, "I will make myself like the Most High" (RSV).

Further light is thrown on this epochal occurrence in the book of Ezekiel, where Lucifer, or Satan, is referred to under the title of "the king of Tyrus."

"Thus saith the Lord God; Thou sealest up the sum, full of wisdom, and perfect in beauty.

"Thou hast been in Eden the garden of God; every precious stone was thy covering, the sardius, topaz, and the diamond, the beryl, the onyx, and the jasper, the sapphire, the emerald, and the carbuncle, and gold: the workmanship of thy tabrets and of thy pipes was prepared in thee in the day that thou wast created.

"Thou art the anointed cherub that covereth; and I have set thee so: thou wast upon the holy mountain of God; thou hast walked up and down in the midst of the stones of fire.

"Thou wast perfect in thy ways from the day that thou wast created, *till iniquity was found in thee"* (Ezekiel 28:12-15).

What a picture this gives us of Lucifer before he sinned! What a magnificent creature he must have been, glistening with all the colors of the rainbow as he stood close to the throne of God!

Yet even though he was so greatly privileged and so richly endowed he was not satisfied. Pride led him on to envy, jealousy, hatred, rebellion, and finally to ruin. Banished from heaven, he came to this earth, where he thought he could hurt God most by leading astray the innocent creatures recently created here.

But why, you ask, did not God destroy him there and then?

This involves both God's nature and character and His whole marvelous plan of redemption.

Of course, He *could* have killed the devil instantly with a word. But had He done so, He would have lent support to Lucifer's jealous charges that He was an autocratic tyrant, not the great lover He claimed to be. In order to convince the watching millions of the universe that Lucifer was wrong, it was essential that the consequences of his rebellion should be seen and recognized. It was equally essential that God should reveal throughout this incident, however protracted, that He is indeed love, personified and eternal.

Once this truth is perceived, the whole Bible becomes illuminated with a great light from heaven. The pieces of life's seeming jigsaw suddenly fall into place. Not only does the origin of evil become plain, but so also does the fall of man and God's immense concern for his recovery. Best of all, the cross of Christ glows with a new radiance as it is seen to be God's crowning answer to Satan's false accusations. Calvary appears as the ultimate evidence both of God's infinite love and the devil's infinite wickedness.

HOW WILL EVIL END?

THERE is so much wickedness in the world today, so much violence and corruption, so much drunkenness and debauchery, so much crime of every description, that some people think it will never end. Evil, they fear, has taken too strong a hold on the human race ever to be eradicated.

Yet one of the most glorious truths your Bible reveals is that someday, in God's good time, all evil will come to an end. Someday "there shall be no more curse" (Revelation 22:3) and no more "utter destruction" (Zechariah 14:11). The "former things"—all the mean, ugly, hateful things—"shall not be remembered, nor come into mind" (Isaiah 65:17).

This was one of the chief reasons why Jesus came to this world. "For this purpose the Son of God was manifested, that *he might destroy the works of the devil*" (1 John 3:8).

But He is not going to destroy just "the works of the devil," but the devil himself!

"Forasmuch then as the children are partakers of flesh and blood, he also himself likewise took part of the same; that through death he might destroy him that had the power of death, that is, the devil" (Hebrews 2:14).

Again and again this fact is stated in the Scriptures. You find it first mentioned in the third chapter of Genesis, where God says to the serpent, "I will put enmity between thee and the woman, and between thy seed and her seed; *it shall bruise thy head,* and thou shalt bruise his heel" (Genesis 3:15).

Thus, right at the beginning of the struggle between good and evil, its final outcome was revealed. The serpent's head would be bruised. The devil would be utterly defeated.

In the second psalm occurs this remarkable prophetic passage: "I will declare the decree: the Lord hath said unto me, Thou art my Son; this day have I begotten thee. Ask of me and I shall give thee the heathen for thine inheritance, and the uttermost parts of the earth for thy possession. Thou shalt break them with a rod of iron; thou shalt dash them in pieces like a potter's vessel" (Psalm 2:7-9).

Other verses in the Psalms are equally definite as to what is going to happen to those who turn their backs on God and ally themselves with His archenemy, the devil.

"For evildoers shall be cut off. . . . For yet a little while, and the wicked shall not be: yea, thou shalt diligently consider his place, and it shall not be" (Psalm 37:9, 10).

Solomon expresses his conviction thus: "The wicked shall be cut off from the earth, and the transgressors shall be rooted out of it" (Proverbs 2:22).

The prophet Malachi is even more definite on this matter. He says: "For, behold, the day cometh, that shall burn as an oven; and all the proud, yea, and all that do wickedly, shall be stubble: and the day that cometh shall burn them up, saith the Lord of hosts, that it shall leave them *neither root nor branch*" (Malachi 4:1).

Notice what John the Baptist says as he tells his listeners about the coming of the Messiah: "I indeed baptize you with water unto repentance: but he that cometh after me is mightier than I, . . . whose fan is in his hand, and he will throughly purge his floor, and gather his wheat into the garner; but he will *burn up the chaff with unquenchable fire*" (Matthew 3:11, 12).

Explaining the parable of the wheat and the tares to His

disciples, Jesus makes very clear what the fate of the obstinately wicked shall be.

"He that soweth the good seed is the Son of man," He says; "the field is the world; the good seed are the children of the kingdom; but the tares are the children of the wicked one; the enemy that sowed them is the devil; the harvest is the end of the world; and the reapers are the angels. As therefore the tares are gathered and burned in the fire; so shall it be in the end of this world. The Son of man shall send forth his angels, and they shall gather out of his kingdom all things that offend, and them which do iniquity; and shall cast them *into a furnace of fire*" (Matthew 13:37-42).

In harmony with this the apostle Peter declares that "the heavens and the earth, which are now, by the same word are kept in store, reserved unto fire against the day of judgment and perdition of ungodly men" (2 Peter 3:7).

If there is delay in bringing about the end of evil, he adds, it will not be a result of God's indifference, but because of His long-suffering love. "The Lord is not slack concerning his promise, as some men count slackness," he says; "but is longsuffering to us-ward, not willing that any should perish, but that all should come to repentance" (verse 9).

Eventually, however, God's purpose will be accomplished. The devil and all his works will be brought to nought. "The day of the Lord will come as a thief in the night, in the which the heavens shall pass away with a great noise, and the elements shall melt with fervent heat, the earth also and the works that are therein shall be burned up" (verse 10).

In the book of Revelation the apostle John gives the final touch of certainty to all this.

First, he tells how "the beast" and the "false prophet" will be "cast alive into a lake of fire" (Revelation 19:20). Then he pictures the ultimate fate of Satan and all the hosts of evil.

Led by the prince of darkness himself, these wicked multitudes will compass "the camp of the saints about, and the beloved city," whereupon fire will come down "from God out of heaven" and devour them. "And the devil that deceived them" will be cast into "the lake of fire" (Revelation 20:9, 10).

Thus your Bible is absolutely clear and positive that evil will come to an end—not by the conversion of Satan and his followers, but by their total elimination from the universe. God will remove their blighting influence once for all.

Perhaps you have been puzzled by the term "everlasting fire," which occurs in Matthew 18:8 and 25:41, but it is the *effect* of the fire, not the fire itself, that continues forever. Thus Sodom and Gomorrha suffered "the vengeance of eternal fire" (Jude 7), though the Dead Sea now covers the site where these cities once stood.

Likewise when Jesus said that the wicked will be cast into "hell" (Greek, *gehenna)* "where their worm dieth not, and the fire is not quenched" (Mark 9:48), He used the illustration of a city dump to describe the ultimate fate of those who reject God's mercy. Both fire and worms will continue their cleansing task until it is completed.

All connected with the great rebellion against the good government of God, whether in the beginning or now, whether angels or men, will ultimately vanish as "the smoke out of the chimney." They will be so completely consumed that there shall be left "neither root nor branch."

In the light of these facts new meaning glows in the glorious words: "God so loved the world, that he gave his only begotten Son, that whosoever believeth in him *should not perish,* but have everlasting life" (John 3:16).

God is love. He does not want anyone to perish. He yearns to give life, not death. "Have I any pleasure in the death of the wicked, says the Lord God, and not rather that he should turn from his way and live?" (Ezekiel 18:23, RSV). So He offers this way of escape.

It is still open. He continues to wait in long-suffering compassion for men and women to turn to Him. But He will not wait forever. He cannot and will not permit evil to continue throughout eternity. Someday He will cleanse His universe from every trace of it. And out of that fiery judgment will come "new heavens and a new earth" in which only righteousness shall dwell (2 Peter 3:13).

WHAT HAPPENS
WHEN SOMEONE DIES?

EVERY time a death occurs, this question arises in somebody's mind. Indeed, it has been asked again and again down the centuries since Eve gazed with sorrowing eyes on the body of her beloved Abel.

Perhaps you have looked upon the cold, still face of someone near and dear to you and wondered what has really happened to him.

Is he dead or not? Maybe there is something about him still alive somewhere. Maybe his spirit is in heaven, making the angels smile. Maybe—perish the thought!—he is groaning in purgatory or hell.

Here again your Bible is a wonderful help. So clear is its teaching on this subject that you need never worry about it again.

Look first at Genesis 2:7, which tells how man was made: "The Lord God formed man of the dust of the ground, and breathed into his nostrils the breath of life; and man became a living soul."

Notice that man was made of two parts: the dust of the ground and the breath of life. Together they formed "a living soul." God did not put a soul into Adam's body. He merely breathed into it. Then both together—body and breath—became a "living soul."

In full harmony is David's statement concerning what happens at death: "His breath goeth forth, he returneth to his earth; in that very day his thoughts perish" (Psalm 146:4).

188

In other words, when the breath goes forth, when a person stops breathing, all consciousness ceases and the body returns to dust. Such is death.

But does not the Bible teach that man has an immortal soul? No, it does not. Only once in all the Holy Scriptures is the word "immortal" used, and that is in 1 Timothy 1:17, where it is applied to God: "Now unto the King eternal, immortal, invisible, the only wise God, be honour and glory for ever and ever."

In his first letter to Timothy the apostle Paul refers to God as "the blessed and only Potentate, the King of kings, and Lord of lords; *who only hath immortality*" (1 Timothy 6:15, 16).

To the Corinthian Christians he makes abundantly clear when they may expect to become immortal. "The trumpet shall sound, and the dead shall be raised incorruptible, and we shall be changed. For this corruptible must put on incorruption, and this mortal must put on immortality" (1 Corinthians 15:52, 53).

If man is going to "put on" immortality at the last trump, he surely does not have it now. Indeed, the suggestion that man already has an immortal soul makes nonsense of the Scriptures.

Where then did this idea arise? In the Garden of Eden. It grew out of the first lie ever told. As you will recall, God told Adam that if he sinned he would surely die. Then Satan, in the form of a serpent, contradicted Him.

"Yea," he sneered, "hath God said, Ye shall not eat of every tree of the garden? . . . *Ye shall not surely die:* for God doth know that in the day ye eat thereof, then your eyes shall be opened, and ye shall be as gods, knowing good and evil" (Genesis 3:1-5).

From that day to this the devil has been circulating this falsehood under all manner of guises. Indeed, it has become the core of all false religions and the source of man's worst and most groundless fears.

But if man does not possess an "immortal soul," what does happen to him when he dies? Your Bible is very clear on this point too. It says: *"The dead know not any thing,* neither have they any more a reward; for the memory of them is forgotten. Also their love,

189

and their hatred, and their envy, is now perished; neither have they any more a portion for ever in any thing that is done under the sun. . . . There is *no work, nor device, nor knowledge, nor wisdom, in the grave,* whither thou goest" (Ecclesiastes 9:5-10).

Other passages are equally definite. Isaiah 38:18 says: "The grave cannot praise thee, death can not celebrate thee: they that go down into the pit *cannot hope for thy truth.*"

So there is no possibility of a second chance after death. Nor is there any scriptural basis for the idea that the dead immediately join the heavenly choir.

In the long, sad story of man's existence on earth there have been but two exceptions to the process of dying—Elijah and Enoch. Elijah was taken to heaven in a "chariot of fire," and Enoch "was translated that he should not see death" (Hebrews 11:5).

No one else has gone to heaven immediately upon the end of his sojourn here. Even David, whom God said was "a man after mine own heart," is still sleeping in his tomb.

"Men and brethren," the apostle Peter says, "let me freely speak unto you of the patriarch David, that he is both dead and buried, and his sepulchre is with us unto this day. . . . *David is not ascended into the heavens*" (Acts 2:29-34).

What has Jesus to say about this? With characteristic tenderness He says that death is like sleep. When someone tells Him that Lazarus is dead He says, "Our friend Lazarus has fallen asleep, but I go to awake him out of sleep" (John 11:11, RSV).

This concept, so beautiful in its simplicity, is wonderfully comforting. For it means that the dead are not languishing in some dread purgatory, or enduring hideous agonies in a blazing hell, or even watching anxiously from heaven the trials and sufferings of their loved ones on earth. They are asleep, awaiting in quiet, unconscious rest whatever God may have in store for them.

Thank God, the sleep of death is not eternal. For all who have loved and served Him faithfully there will be a great and glorious awakening.

SHALL WE MEET OUR LOVED ONES AGAIN?

"I F A man die," asks the patriarch Job, "shall he live again?" (Job 14:14).

How many have asked the same question down the tear-stained centuries! Every mother who has kissed her child in last farewell, every child who has sobbed out his loneliness at the loss of a beloved parent, has wondered whether a day of reunion would ever dawn. Welling up within each sorrowful heart has been the hope that death is not the end, that somehow, sometime, there will be life beyond the tomb.

"All the days of my appointed time will I wait," Job says, "till my change come. Thou shalt call, and I will answer thee: thou wilt have a desire to the work of thine hands" (verses 14, 15).

He is sure that the God who made him, and fashioned his character as a potter molds clay with his fingers, will not forget him. No matter how many years shall pass, God will still remember him and want him in His kingdom.

This same heartfelt conviction prompts him to utter these precious, ever-memorable words: "I know that my redeemer liveth, and that he shall stand at the latter day upon the earth: and though after my skin worms destroy this body, yet in my flesh shall I see God; whom I shall see for myself, and mine eyes shall behold, and not another; though my reins be consumed within me" (Job 19:25-27).

In the New Testament we find Jesus radiating confidence in life after death, and who could know the truth of it better than He? "The hour is coming, and now is," He says, "when the dead shall hear the voice of the Son of God: and they that hear shall live. For as the Father hath life in himself; so hath he given to the Son to have life in himself. . . . Marvel not at this: for the hour is coming, in the which all that are in the graves shall hear his voice, and shall come forth; they that have done good, unto the resurrection of life; and they that have done evil, unto the resurrection of damnation" (John 5:25-29).

"This is the will of him that sent me," He assures His disciples, "that every one which seeth the Son, and believeth on him, may have everlasting life: and *I will raise him up at the last day*" (John 6:40).

As if to demonstrate His ability to keep His promise, He raised many from the dead then and there, including Jairus' daughter (Matthew 9:25), the son of the widow of Nain (Luke 7:14), and Lazarus (John 11:43).

As people saw the dead come back to life they were astonished, saying, "God hath visited his people." They were right. He had. Here was the King of love and life in action, doing what He most wanted to do, healing the sick, the lame, the deaf, the blind, and most wonderful of all, raising the dead to life.

Gloriously He was fulfilling the prophecy of Isaiah: "The Spirit of the Lord God is upon me; because the Lord hath anointed me to preach good tidings unto the meek; . . . to bind up the broken-hearted, to proclaim liberty to the captives, and the opening of the prison to them that are bound" (Isaiah 61:1).

He had the keys of the prison of death and He used them marvelously "to comfort all that mourn; to appoint unto them that mourn in Zion, to give unto them beauty for ashes, the oil of joy for mourning, the garment of praise for the spirit of heaviness" (verses 2, 3).

All this was but a foretaste of something far greater to happen in the future—at that great "last day" when His wondrous voice will shatter the tombs of earth and bring forth all the righteous dead.

By rising from the dead Himself He gave surest evidence of His power over death and the ultimate resurrection of all who believe in Him.

"If in this life only we have hope in Christ," writes the apostle Paul, "we are of all men most miserable. But now is Christ risen from the dead, and become the firstfruits of them that slept.

"For since by man came death, by man came also the resurrection of the dead. For as in Adam all die, *even so in Christ shall all be made alive.*

"But every man in his own order: Christ the firstfruits; afterward they that are Christ's at his coming" (1 Corinthians 15:19-23).

There were some in Corinth who could not bring themselves to believe in life after death. They mocked at the idea of a resurrection.

They couldn't see how, if a man disintegrated completely at death, he could ever be put together again.

Paul answers them thus:

"Some man will say, How are the dead raised up? and with what body do they come? Thou fool, that which thou sowest is not quickened, except it die: and that which thou sowest, thou sowest not that body that shall be, but bare grain, it may chance of wheat, or of some other grain: but God giveth it a body as it hath pleased him, and to every seed his own body. . . .

"So also is the resurrection of the dead. It is sown in corruption; it is raised in incorruption: it is sown in dishonour; it is raised in power: it is sown a natural body; it is raised a spiritual body" (verses 35-44).

Then he moves into his grand peroration in which, under divine inspiration, he reveals the nature and certainty of the coming restoration to life of the saints of God:

"Behold, I shew you a mystery; We shall not all sleep, but we shall all be changed, in a moment, in the twinkling of an eye, at the last trump: for the trumpet shall sound, and the dead shall be raised incorruptible, and we shall be changed. For this corruptible must put on incorruption, and this mortal must put on immortality.

"So when this corruptible shall have put on incorruption, and

193

this mortal shall have put on immortality, then shall be brought to pass the saying that is written, Death is swallowed up in victory.

"O death, where is thy sting? O grave, where is thy victory?" (verses 51-55).

Amid all the harshness and cruelty of the Roman world, when life was cheap and death meant little—save to loved ones left behind—this glorious vista of endless life beyond the tomb brought unspeakable cheer to the believers. Here too was clear intimation that God preserves a perfect pattern of every individual and has the power to cause each one to live again.

As for Paul, he talked of it constantly, bidding every believer look for "that blessed hope, and the glorious appearing of the great God and our Saviour Jesus Christ" (Titus 2:13). For in that glad day the mighty miracle would be wrought and the faithful be taken to their eternal home.

"I would not have you to be ignorant, brethren, concerning them which are asleep," he writes to the Thessalonians, "that ye sorrow not, even as others which have no hope. For if we believe that Jesus died and rose again, even so them also which sleep in Jesus will God bring with him.

"For this we say unto you by the word of the Lord, that we which are alive and remain unto the coming of the Lord shall not prevent [go before] them which are asleep.

"For the Lord himself shall descend from heaven with a shout, with the voice of the archangel, and the trump of God: and the dead in Christ shall rise first:

"Then we which are alive and remain shall be caught up *together* with them in the clouds, to meet the Lord in the air: and so shall we ever be with the Lord. Wherefore comfort one another with these words" (1 Thessalonians 4:13-18).

Here indeed is rich comfort for the sorrowing; for not only do Paul's words provide added assurance that Christ will keep His promise and come again to raise the dead; it affords an added glimpse of how it will happen.

The righteous dead will be raised and the righteous living will be translated, and so together they will be caught up to meet the Lord in the air.

Together! Parents and children, brothers and sisters, friends and loved ones. All who have been separated by the cruel hand of death. Raised or translated, they will go together into the kingdom of God.

And because God says "together," we may be sure that we shall know each other there. Why not? What would be the point of being "together" if all were strangers?

Thus has God planned in tender love for the happiness of His people in the great hereafter.

It would not be right, however, to obscure the sad fact that this glorious privilege of happy reunion is not for all. All *could* enjoy it; God wills it to everyone without exception; but only those who accept His offer of salvation through Jesus Christ can hope to receive the rich blessings He has promised.

As for the rest, they will be resurrected, but not at the same time or to the same beautiful experience. See John 5:29. Their resurrection will come a thousand years later, and it will be but to meet God in the final judgment (Revelation 20:5, 12).

"Blessed and holy is he that hath part in the first resurrection: on such the second death hath no power" (verse 6).

Toward this glad goal all who love life and long for reunion with their loved ones should now set their hearts and hands, while time remains and God's mercy lingers.

WHICH IS GOD'S DAY?

HERE is another problem that troubles many people today. Deep down in their hearts they feel that they should keep one day of the week as a holy day, but because of changing times and customs, they are not sure which day, if any, is God's day.

Adding to their dilemma is the popular five-day workweek, which opens up all manner of alluring recreational possibilities, including fishing trips, boating expeditions, and attendance at sporting events. Friday night to Monday morning has become for millions a period of frenzied preparation for a trip—and clearing up after it—with no time whatever for even a brief interlude of worship.

Many of those who still go to church on Sunday seem to be of the opinion that this pious exercise completes their spiritual obligations for the day. This is evident from the large numbers who combine their churchgoing with shopping. Who has not noticed the well-dressed crowds in the supermarkets just before or just after churchtime as the "faithful" seek to save both time and gas by uniting the two activities?

Another source of perplexity arises from the fact that thousands of people of all religious faiths are now beginning to keep Saturday, the seventh day of the week, as a holy day, working on Sunday, the first day. Are they right or wrong?

No wonder many genuine Christians are troubled! Maybe you are too. Perhaps you are saying to yourself, I wish God would make plain just what He wants me to do.

If so, your worries may end now. You will find your answer, clear as day, in your Bible.

The Sabbath is the second oldest of all the institutions known to man. It was inaugurated by God Himself a few moments after He married Adam and Eve in the Garden of Eden.

For these two wonderful people their first sunset ushered in the first Sabbath, and their first sunrise marked the first Sabbath morning.

"On the seventh day God ended his work which he had made; and he rested on the seventh day from all his work which he had made. And God blessed the seventh day and sanctified it" (Genesis 2:2, 3).

Notice which day He blessed. It was the *seventh* day. Not the first, the fourth, or the sixth, but the seventh. This particular day He sanctified or set apart for holy use.

From this moment on, all who loved God worshiped Him on this holy day. Week after week, as the seventh day returned, they remembered Him, communed with Him, praised Him.

Down the centuries, as a result of the increasing inroads of sin, many forgot the Sabbath. But God did not forget it, nor did He change His day.

When He brought Israel out of Egypt He reminded them in spectacular fashion of its vital importance.

For 40 years He fed them in the wilderness with manna, which appeared miraculously only six days a week. A double portion came on the sixth day, but none on the seventh. See Exodus 16:26.

This went on for some 2,000 weeks! So if any Israelite had any doubt when he left Egypt as to which was God's day, it was most certainly removed by the end of this experience.

While the manna was still falling, God declared His will for Israel and all mankind in His Ten Commandments. And in the heart of this sacred law He said, "Remember the sabbath day, to keep it holy. Six days shalt thou labour, and do all thy work; but the *seventh* day is the sabbath of the Lord thy God" (Exodus 20:8-10).

From this time on every Israelite knew perfectly well which day was the right day. It was the seventh day and none other. They did not always keep it as they should, but they were without excuse as to what God required of them.

As the years rolled by, whenever Israel drifted into apostasy godly leaders called them back to the paths of righteousness, including observance of the holy Sabbath on the seventh day of the week.

About 700 B.C. the prophet Isaiah urged them to cease using God's holy day for their own pleasure. See Isaiah 58:13.

Two centuries or so later Nehemiah reminded the people who had returned to Jerusalem after the Babylonian captivity that God had spoken to them from Mount Sinai and given them "right judgments, and true laws, good statutes and commandments" and made known to them the "holy Sabbath" (Nehemiah 9:13, 14). He went further. He gave orders that the city gates should be shut each Sabbath evening to keep the traders out (Nehemiah 13:19).

Thus down to the middle of the fifth century B.C., while there was much forgetfulness of the Sabbath, and much wrong use of it, there was no doubt in anybody's mind as to which day it was.

Nor was there any question on this point when Jesus came. He found Himself in the midst of extremely strict Sabbathkeepers. The religious leaders were so particular about the day that they wouldn't even lift a finger to help the sick. When they saw a man actually carrying his bed on the Sabbath they acted as though he had committed the unpardonable sin.

But while their attitude toward the Sabbath was wrong, they were right about the day. It was still the seventh day of the weekly cycle that God had established in the beginning. If it had not been, Jesus would surely have told them.

And what was His personal relationship to this day, which, as a matter of fact, He had Himself instituted as an everlasting memorial of Creation? See Psalm 135:13.

He observed it as a holy day. Luke tells us that at the beginning of His ministry in Galilee, "he came to Nazareth, where he had been brought up: and, *as his custom was,* he went into the synagogue on the sabbath day, and stood up for to read" (Luke 4:16).

Nobody was surprised to see Him there. It was perfectly normal for Him to be present and take part in the service. He had been going to this synagogue since childhood. No doubt He had walked there with His mother hundreds of times. He must have known the way there so well that He could have found it in the dark. Equally well He knew the right day to go.

It is inconceivable that Jesus could have made a mistake over which was the proper day. On one occasion He said to the Pharisees, "The Son of man is Lord also of the sabbath" (Mark 2:28). By this He declared His authorship of it, His full knowledge of its meaning and purpose, and the correctness of the day to be observed.

From this it is clear that despite all the turbulence of 4,000 years of history, and all the trials and tribulations of the Hebrews in Egypt, in the wilderness, in Palestine and in Babylon, the true seventh-day Sabbath was miraculously preserved until Jesus came to place the benediction of His own example upon it. Sometimes obscured but never wholly lost, it was now confirmed by the Lord of the Sabbath Himself.

But did not Jesus change the day? No. Your Bible says not a word about any such change. What Jesus did do was to restore to this holy day its original meaning and intent.

"One sabbath he was going through the grainfield; and as they made their way his disciples began to pluck ears of grain. And the Pharisees said to him, 'Look, why are they doing what is not lawful on the sabbath?' And he said to them, 'Have you never read what David did, when he was in need and was hungry, he and those who were with him: how he entered the house of God, when Abiathar was high priest, and ate the bread of the Presence, which is not lawful for any but the priests to eat, and also gave it to those who were with him?' And he said to them, 'The sabbath was made for man, not man for the sabbath' " (Mark 2:23-27, RSV).

By so saying He did not minimize the importance of the Sabbath. Rather, He magnified it. The Sabbath was made for man—man's happiness, welfare, uplift, inspiration. The better the holy day was observed, the more good would man get out of it. To make it a day of penance and legalistic observance would be to miss its purpose altogether.

"Again he entered the synagogue, and a man was there who had a withered hand. And they watched him to see whether he would heal him on the sabbath, so that they might accuse him. And he said to the man who had the withered hand, 'Come here.' And he said to them, 'Is it lawful on the sabbath to do good or to do harm, to save life or to kill?' But they were silent. And he looked around at them with anger, grieved at their hardness of heart, and said to the man, 'Stretch out your hand.' He stretched it out, and his hand was restored" (Mark 3:1-5, RSV).

It was on this same occasion, Matthew tells us, that He asked the Pharisees, "What man of you, if he has one sheep and it falls into a pit on the sabbath, will not lay hold of it and lift it out? Of how much more value is a man than a sheep! So *it is lawful to do good on the sabbath*" (Matthew 12:11, 12, RSV).

Again and again during His brief sojourn among men He reemphasized this principle by precept and example. Many of His greatest miracles of healing were performed on the Sabbath. By every possible means He showed the people how the God of love wanted His day to be observed. But He never changed the day.

"Think not that I have come to abolish the law and the prophets," He said to His disciples; "I have not come to abolish them but to fulfill them. For truly, I say to you, till heaven and earth pass away, not an iota, not a dot, will pass from the law until all is accomplished. Whoever then relaxes one of the least of these commandments and teaches men so, shall be called least in the kingdom of heaven; but he who does them and teaches them shall be called great in the kingdom of heaven" (Matthew 5:17-19, RSV).

So Jesus did not abolish the fourth commandment, or "relax" it, or change it. And if *He* did not change it, who else could?

But perhaps He told His disciples to make a change after His death? No. On the contrary, your Bible states that even while He was in Joseph's tomb the women who planned to embalm His body "rested the sabbath day according to the commandment" (Luke 23:56).

But didn't the disciples gather together the next day to welcome Him after His resurrection and so start a new Sabbath? No. They gathered together, but it was "for fear of the Jews" (John 20:19). When Jesus appeared to them, they were "terrified and affrighted" (Luke 24:37). It took them quite a while to believe that He had actually risen from the dead.

Three other texts (Matthew 28:1; Luke 24:1; John 20:1) refer to the first day of the week in connection with Jesus' resurrection, but none suggests it was a new Sabbath. As to the two other first-day texts to be found in your Bible (1 Corinthians 16:1, 2; Acts 20:6, 7), the first refers to setting aside a gift for the poor at one's "own house" (Vulgate); and the second to a meeting that must have been held on Saturday night as time was reckoned in Paul's day.

How about later? Perhaps the first council of the Christian church changed the day? No. The report of this council is given in Acts 15, but it contains not a word on the subject. If any delegate had proposed anything so momentous as altering the Sabbath from the seventh to some other day, the matter would surely have been mentioned.

Paul was present at that meeting, and it is certain that he did not learn of any such proposal. When he arrived at Philippi the record says, "On the sabbath we went out of the city by a river side, where prayer was wont to be made: and we sat down, and spake unto the women which resorted thither" (Acts 16:13).

The next chapter tells how, when Paul came to Thessalonica, "as his manner was" he went into the synagogue "and three sabbath days reasoned with them out of the scriptures" (Acts 17:2). While his enemies declared that he "turned the world upside down" (verse 6), nobody accused him of attempting to change the Sabbath.

What about the other apostles? Did they advocate such a change? Again there is no mention of any such suggestion. True, the apostle John says, "I was in the Spirit on the Lord's day" (Revelation 1:10), but which is the Lord's day? It must be the seventh day, for the Lord calls it "my holy day" (Isaiah 58:13) and declares that He is "Lord also of the sabbath" (Mark 2:28).

If you still have lingering doubts on this matter, take a concordance and look up every reference to the Sabbath, the seventh day, the Lord's day, the first day, and kindred subjects. It may take you some time, but the study will be well worth it. It will settle your mind once and for all as to what your Bible says—and does not say—on this vital question. And it will help you to decide what you should do about it.

For in all your searching you will not find a single text that even suggests that God ever planned any change in His day, nor one that indicates He ever made such a change. Consequently you will be brought face to face with the simple and unassailable fact that the seventh day is still "the sabbath of the Lord thy God."

What about calendar changes? Perhaps they muddled things up so that no one can tell which is the right seventh day any more? No. While there have been changes in the calendar, there has been none in the sequence of the days of the week. Both Julius Caesar and Pope Gregory XIII revised the calendar, but neither of them changed the weekly cycle. The seventh day of the week is still the same as it was when Christ was on earth, and no one needs to go farther back than that.

So if you feel in your heart that you should keep one day a week holy and you are not quite sure what to do, here is your answer—right in your Bible. But when you decide to follow God's leading and keep His day, don't mix church and supermarket, or give God one hour and yourself 23. Let it be entirely His day, from sunset to sunset (Leviticus 23:32; Mark 1:32). Keep it altogether as a holy day when, free from all unnecessary labor, you think of spiritual things. Let it be a day of prayer, praise, and Bible study.

And do not do this to fulfill a legal requirement, but as an act of adoring love. Spend the day with God because you love Him and He loves you. Then it will be indeed the happiest day of the week, and the promised Sabbath blessings will be yours (Isaiah 58:13, 14).

HOW CAN ONE KNOW
THE TRUE CHURCH?

ACCORDING to the *1990 Yearbook of American and Canadian Churches* there are more than 200 different religious bodies in North America alone. Most of these are nominally Christian, varying in belief from "left" to "right," from extreme liberal to extreme conservative.

Some are large organizations with millions of members, while many are small splinter groups with comparatively few adherents. All, however, have one point in common. Each group believes that it is the chief—if not the exclusive—repository of truth and therefore has a duty under God to continue its separate witness. Some openly claim to be the true church of Jesus Christ, with a prior claim upon God's favor.

Because of such a confusing situation, it is no wonder that many, both within and without these organizations, are asking, Which, if any, is the true church? Maybe you have asked this question yourself.

Sometimes it is said that the true church is invisible, being made up of people of all denominations who love the Lord in sincerity and try to serve Him the best they know how. There may be some truth in this. Nevertheless, there is no good reason that the true church should not be visible. As your Bible makes clear, the time will come when good people everywhere will detach themselves from their present affiliations and identify themselves with the body that most closely conforms to God's ideals in this present evil world. See Revelation 18:4.

Suppose someday you should look for such a body; what should you expect to find? What should it teach? What should be its standards?

Here again your Bible can be a lamp to your feet and a light to your path. Within its pages you will find all the specifications necessary for easy identification.

1. *It will radiate the love of God.* Says Jesus: "By this all men will know that you are my disciples, if you have love for one another" (John 13:35, RSV). Love is paramount. Any group that is critical, censorious, and legalistic could not possibly be the true church. "He who does not love does not know God," says the apostle John, "for God is love" (1 John 4:8, RSV). "Beloved," he adds, "let us love one another; for love is of God, and he who loves is born of God and loves God" (verse 7). Again, in verse 16, he says, "God is love, and he who abides in love abides in God, and God abides in him."

In his great chapter on love the apostle Paul suggests that though a group claim to have apostles, prophets, teachers, and even miracle workers, if it does not manifest love, it is no more than a "noisy gong or a clanging cymbal." See 1 Corinthians 12:28-13:1, RSV.

In other words, love, expressed in kindness, graciousness, tolerance, and compassion, is the most conspicuous sign of the true church.

2. *It will exalt Jesus Christ as the Son of God.* Once when Jesus was talking with His disciples He asked them to tell Him who they thought He was. "Simon Peter answered and said, Thou art the Christ, the Son of the living God." Jesus replied, "Thou art Peter, and upon this rock I will build my church; and the gates of hell shall not prevail against it" (Matthew 16:16, 18).

"Upon this rock" Christ builds His church. Not upon Peter, of course, but upon Peter's glorious affirmation of the divinity of Christ. Belief in this great truth is fundamental. As Paul says: "If thou shalt confess with thy mouth the Lord Jesus, and shalt believe in thine heart that God hath raised him from the dead, thou shalt be saved" (Romans 10:9).

"Neither is there salvation in any other," says Peter: "for there is none other name under heaven given among men, whereby we must be saved" (Acts 4:12).

Declares John: "Whosoever shall confess that Jesus is the Son of God, God dwelleth in him, and he in God" (1 John 4:15). And what is true of the individual is true also of a religious group. Unless it exalts Jesus Christ as the Son of God and confesses His divinity before men, it is not and cannot be the true church. See Matthew 10:32, 33.

3. *It will honor the Bible as the Word of God.* In his second letter to Timothy, the apostle Paul says: "All scripture is inspired by God and profitable for teaching, for reproof, for correction, and for training in righteousness, that the man of God may be complete, equipped for every good work" (2 Timothy 3:16, 17, RSV).

Bidding farewell to the Christians in Ephesus, he says: "I commend you to God and to the word of his grace, which is able to build you up and to give you the inheritance among all those who are sanctified" (Acts 20:32, RSV).

Likewise he tells the Romans: "For whatever was written in former days was written for our instruction, that by steadfastness and by the encouragement of the scriptures we might have hope" (Romans 15:4, RSV).

Peter says that the Word of God "liveth and abideth forever" (1 Peter 1:23), and that the "holy men of God" who wrote it spoke "as they were moved by the Holy Ghost" (2 Peter 1:21).

Such was the attitude of the early Christians to the Holy Scriptures. They revered them as the inspired word of God. So will the true church today.

4. *It will regard the Ten Commandments as the holy law of God.* "By this we may be sure that we know him," says the apostle John, "if we keep his commandments. He who says 'I know him' but disobeys his commandments is a liar, and the truth is not in him; but whoever keeps his word, in him truly love for God is perfected. By this we may be sure that we are in him: he who says he abides in him

ought to walk in the same way in which he walked" (1 John 2:3-6, RSV).

So if we "know him" and if we are "in him" we will keep His commandments and walk as He walked.

How did Jesus walk? Unquestionably in the way of the Ten Commandments. "I have kept my Father's commandments," He says, "and abide in his love" (John 15:10). Again: "Think not that I am come to destroy the law or the prophets: I am not come to destroy, but to fulfil" (Matthew 5:17).

One great purpose of His first advent was to "magnify the law, and make it honourable" (Isaiah 42:21), and such will be the purpose of His true church in every age. Indeed, it is said of His people in the last days of earth's history: "Here are they that keep the commandments of God, and the faith of Jesus" (Revelation 14:12).

5. *It will observe the seventh day as God's Sabbath.* It is inconceivable that God's true church could keep any other day than *His* day. And His day, as your Bible so clearly points out, is the seventh day.

Observance of the seventh day is, in fact, an outstanding sign of the true church. "It is a sign," God says, "between me and you throughout your generations; that ye may know that I am the Lord that doth sanctify you" (Exodus 31:13).

This is repeated in Ezekiel 20:12: "I gave them my sabbaths, to be a sign between me and them, that they might know that I am the Lord that sanctify them."

So the true Sabbath is not only a memorial of Creation but also of sanctification. It was designed to remind God's people of His power to create and redeem. Consequently, it is a most fitting sign of His true church in every age, throughout all generations.

6. *It will practice the biblical method of baptism.* This follows very simply from the command of Jesus to His disciples: "Go ye therefore, and teach all nations, baptizing them in the name of the Father, and of the Son, and of the Holy Ghost" (Matthew 28:19).

Baptism in Bible times was not by sprinkling, but by immersion. You will find an example of this in Acts 8:38, where Philip and the

Ethiopian eunuch "went down both into the water" and later came up "out of the water." And there was good reason for this method, as Paul points out in his letter to the Romans.

"Know ye not," he says, "that so many of us as were baptized into Jesus Christ were baptized into his death? Therefore we are buried with him by baptism into death: that like as Christ was raised up from the dead by the glory of the Father, even so we also should walk in newness of life" (Romans 6:3, 4).

By allowing himself to be lowered under the water a new member of the church signified his willingness to die to his old life of sin. By rising out of the water he declared his determination to live a new life in Christ.

It was a fitting introduction to the true church, and its valuable meaning has not changed with the passing years.

7. *It will celebrate the Lord's Supper in simplicity.* Says the apostle Paul to the Corinthians: "I have received of the Lord that which also I delivered unto you, That the Lord Jesus the same night in which he was betrayed took bread: and when he had given thanks, he brake it, and said, Take, eat: this is my body, which is broken for you: this do in remembrance of me.

"After the same manner also he took the cup, when he had supped, saying, This cup is the new testament in my blood; this do ye, as oft as ye drink it, in remembrance of me. For as often as ye eat this bread and drink this cup, *ye do shew the Lord's death till he come*" (1 Corinthians 11:23-26).

Here is something the true church will do till the end of time. No grand and pompous ceremony is called for, but the reverent partaking of bread and wine in memory of the sufferings and sacrifice of its Founder.

How simple was the first such service is revealed in Matthew 26:20-30, Luke 22:7-20, and Mark 14:17-25, and John adds the sweet story of how, in preparation for the solemn ceremony, Jesus humbly knelt and washed His disciples' feet. "If I then, your Lord and Master, have washed your feet," He says, "ye also ought to wash one another's feet. For *I have given you an example, that ye should do as*

I have done to you. . . . If ye know these things, happy are ye if ye do them" (John 13:14-17).

The true church will be found following Jesus' bidding and example.

8. *It will possess the gifts of the Spirit.* When the Holy Spirit came upon the early church He brought "diversities of gifts" (1 Corinthians 12:4). To one was given "the word of wisdom; to another the word of knowledge by the same Spirit; to another faith by the same Spirit; to another the gifts of healing by the same Spirit; to another the working of miracles; to another prophecy; to another discerning of spirits; to another divers kinds of tongues; to another the interpretation of tongues" (verses 8-11).

Each of these gifts was for the help and blessing of the church. Those receiving them were to work together in harmony for the edification of the entire membership, with no exaltation of one above another.

Repeating this information to the Ephesians, Paul says: "He gave some, apostles; and some, prophets; and some, evangelists; and some, pastors and teachers; for the perfecting of the saints, for the work of the ministry, for the edifying of the body of Christ, till we all come in the unity of the faith, and of the knowledge of the Son of God, unto a perfect man, unto the measure of the stature of the fulness of Christ" (Ephesians 4:11-13).

In view of the fact that these gifts are to remain with the church until it attains "the stature of the fulness of Christ," it is reasonable to assume that some, if not all of them, are still available to the true church. Where they are most in evidence, that church is likely to be found.

9. *It will be modest in appearance, gentle in spirit.* It would be hard to associate the church of the humble Galilean with lavish display, ornate ceremonies, and wasteful extravagance. Such things are completely out of harmony with His life of humble, holy, selfless service for others.

Says the apostle Peter, remembering the precious days by Galilee, "As he which hath called you is holy, so be ye holy in all manner of conversation." Then he bids women not to overdress, but rather to put on "the ornament of a meek and quiet spirit, which is in the sight of God of great price." To men he says, "Love as brethren, be pitiful, be courteous: not rendering evil for evil, or railing for railing" (1 Peter 3:1-9).

This is the sort of church God wants today. Its members will manifest the same beautiful spirit both in their private lives and corporate activities.

10. *It will be clean-living, upright, and noble, eager to help in all good works.* The grace of God, says the apostle Paul, teaches us that "denying ungodliness and worldly lusts, we should live soberly, righteously, and godly, in this present world," if for no other reason than that Jesus "gave himself for us, that he might redeem us from all iniquity, and purify unto himself a peculiar people, zealous of good works" (Titus 2:12, 14).

Likewise Peter describes the followers of Jesus as "a chosen generation, a royal priesthood, an holy nation, a peculiar people."

"As strangers and pilgrims," he exhorts them, "abstain from fleshly lusts, which war against the soul; having your conversation honest among the Gentiles: that . . . they may by your good works, which they shall behold, glorify God in the day of visitation" (1 Peter 2:11, 12).

Ever seeking by divine grace to emulate the perfect example of their beloved Master, members of the true church will be conspicuous for their upright and noble lives and their eagerness to help the needy. When disaster strikes, be it fire, flood, or famine, they will be first in line to serve their fellow men.

11. *It will look eagerly for Christ's return.* This outreach to others will be an outgrowth of a firm belief in the personal return of Jesus. The church that is "zealous for good deeds" will look with longing for the fulfillment of the blessed hope, "the appearing of the glory of our great God and Saviour Jesus Christ" (Titus 2:13, RSV).

It will cherish the Master's promise, "If I go . . . , I will come again" (John 14:1-3).

It will be ever on the alert for the promised signs of His return (Luke 21:25-27).

It will heed His solemn warning to "watch" with increasing vigilance as it sees the day approaching (Matthew 24:42), while its constant prayer will be "Even so, come, Lord Jesus" (Revelation 22:20).

Belief in Christ's second advent is indeed one of the most vital marks of the true church.

12. *It will have a world program.* It cannot help it. Ringing in its ears will be the Master's command: "Go ye into all the world, and preach the gospel to every creature" (Mark 16:15). Nor will it ever forget His prediction: "This gospel of the kingdom shall be preached in all the world for a witness unto all nations; and then shall the end come" (Matthew 24:14).

In the light of these great passages of Scripture, the true church will not confine its activities to one locality, or one country, or even one continent. Its eyes will roam over the whole wide world. Its vision and compassion will reach to "every nation, and kindred, and tongue, and people" (Revelation 14:6).

With a mission program that encircles the globe, its members will dedicate themselves and their all to completing the proclamation of "the everlasting gospel" in order that their beloved Lord may soon return in glory. Fearlessly, daringly, confidently, they will cry "with a loud voice" to all mankind, "Fear God, and give glory to him, for the hour of his judgment is come: and worship him that made heaven, and earth, and the sea, and the fountains of waters" (verse 7).

If you should ever hear this message, look at its messengers and their manner of life. Examine their credentials in the light of your Bible. See whether they fit in with the twelve identifying marks set forth in this chapter. If they do, let your heart leap with joy. You may well have discovered God's true church, the spiritual home you have been seeking.

PROPHECIES THAT CAME TRUE

ONE of the most thrilling discoveries you will make as you study your Bible is the way it unveils the future. Its knowledge of things to come is the strongest proof of its divine inspiration.

Ability to read the future is not a human attribute. You and I can reason from cause to effect, but we can never be quite sure our deductions are right. News commentators boast of their correct forecasts, but never mention their erroneous guesses. Even the weatherman, aided by the latest scientific equipment, rarely ventures to predict more than a day or two ahead.

In contrast, God claims to know the future as perfectly as He knows the past.

"I am the Lord," He says: "that is my name: and my glory will I not give to another, neither my praise to graven images. Behold, the former things are come to pass, and new things do I declare: *before they spring forth I tell you of them*" (Isaiah 42:8, 9).

Again: "Remember the former things of old: for I am God, and there is none else; I am God, and there is none like me, *Declaring the end from the beginning,* and from ancient times the things that are not yet done, saying, My counsel shall stand, and I will do all my pleasure" (Isaiah 46:9, 10).

"Produce your cause," He challenges all false gods and their equally false prophets. "Bring forth your strong reasons. . . . Let them bring them forth, and shew us what shall happen: let them shew the former things, what they be, that we may consider them, and know the latter end of them; or declare us things for to come. Shew the things that are to come hereafter, that we may know that ye are gods" (Isaiah 41:21-23).

Thus with utter confidence God declares His knowledge of the future. But are such claims justified? What proofs are there in support of them?

Many. Your Bible is full of them.

Notice first the case of Noah and the Flood.

To the patriarch, God said, "The end of all flesh is come before me; for the earth is filled with violence through them; and, behold, I will destroy them with the earth. Make thee an ark of gopher wood" (Genesis 6:13, 14).

Later, when the ark was completed, He said, "For yet seven days, and I will cause it to rain upon the earth forty days and forty nights; and every living substance that I have made will I destroy from off the face of the earth" (Genesis 7:4).

Even so it happened, as the rest of the chapter records. "The flood came, and destroyed them all" (Luke 17:27). And in the book of Hebrews we read: "By faith Noah, being warned of God *of things not seen as yet,* moved with fear, prepared an ark to the saving of his house" (Hebrews 11:7).

Notice next Nahum's prophecy concerning the ancient city of Nineveh. At the height of its power and prestige he wrote: "Woe to the bloody city! It is all full of lies and robbery. . . . Behold, I am against thee, saith the Lord of hosts. . . . And I will cast abominable filth upon thee, and make thee vile, and will set thee as a gazing-stock. And it shall come to pass, that all they that look upon thee shall flee from thee, and say, Nineveh is laid waste: who will bemoan her?" (Nahum 3:1-7).

At the time Nahum spoke it must have seemed to those who listened that his words could never come true. Nineveh was so strong, so utterly invincible. How could so mighty a city ever become "empty, and void, and waste" (Nahum 2:10)?

Yet that is exactly what took place. Within 50 years Nineveh was overwhelmed by the Babylonians and from that moment began to fade from history.

In the seventh century A.D. a battle was fought between the Romans and the Persians on the very site where Nineveh had once stood. Describing the terrain, the historian Edward Gibbon wrote: "Eastward of the Tigris, at the end of the bridge of Mosul, the great Nineveh had formerly been erected: *the city, and even the ruins of the city, had long since disappeared;* the vacant space afforded a spacious field for the operations of the two armies" *(The History of the Decline and Fall of the Roman Empire,* chap. 46, par. 24; italics supplied).

Concerning Babylon, the prophet Jeremiah wrote: "Declare ye among the nations, . . . Babylon is taken" (Jeremiah 50:2). "For, lo, I will raise and cause to come up against Babylon an assembly of great nations from the north country: and they shall set themselves in array against her" (verse 9). "How is the hammer of the whole earth cut asunder and broken! how is Babylon become a desolation among the nations!" (verse 23).

"And Babylon shall become heaps, a dwelling place for dragons, an astonishment, and an hissing, without an inhabitant" (Jeremiah 51:37).

That was about 595 B.C., when Babylon was at the pinnacle of its power, and Nebuchadnezzar, its greatest king, was virtually ruler of the world. At that time Jeremiah's words must have seemed utterly ridiculous, without a chance of fulfillment. Yet they were fulfilled.

Not immediately. Twenty, 40, 50 years passed. Jeremiah died. So did Nebuchadnezzar. But Babylon remained apparently as strong as ever.

Then came the year 539 B.C. Belshazzar was now king. One riotous night, while he was feasting with a thousand of his lords, there appeared the fingers of a man's hand writing on the palace wall. The message said, "God hath numbered thy kingdom and finished it. . . . Thou art weighed in the balances, and art found wanting. . . . Thy kingdom is divided, and given to the Medes and Persians" (Daniel 5:26-28).

Thus God had not forgotten the prediction He had led Jeremiah to make nearly 60 years before—nor the similar prophecy written by Isaiah almost 200 years earlier. See Isaiah 13:19-22. All along He had been watching Babylon, weighing her deeds with infinite precision in the balances of divine justice. Now the hour of her judgment had come. "In that night was Belshazzar the king of the Chaldeans slain. And Darius the Median took the kingdom" (Daniel 5:30, 31).

Not only did the city change rulers, however. As century succeeded century, it gradually fell into decay. Its massive walls were leveled and its proud palaces and temples destroyed. Finally, covered by the shifting sands of the desert, it became virtually a lost city, until rediscovered by archaeologists in recent times.

After exploring the site in 1845 and 1850 Austen Layard wrote: "Shapeless heaps of rubbish cover for many an acre the face of the land. . . . On all sides, fragments of glass, marble, pottery, and inscribed brick are mingled with that peculiar nitrous and blanched soil, which, bred from the remains of ancient habitations, checks or destroys vegetation, and renders the site of Babylon a naked and hideous waste. Owls start from the scanty thickets, and the foul jackal skulks through the furrows" (*Discoveries in the Ruins of Nineveh and Babylon* [1853], chap. 21, p. 484).

More recently explorers have uncovered many remarkable ruins of the famous city, each one confirming the accuracy of the divine prediction concerning its fall.

Now consider Ezekiel's prophecy concerning Tyre, that famous city on the eastern shore of the Mediterranean, which wielded such widespread influence in ancient times. Shortly after the destruction of Jerusalem by Nebuchadnezzar, when Tyre was congratulating herself on the additional prosperity that would now flow into her own coffers, Ezekiel wrote: "The word of the Lord came unto me, saying, Son of man, because that Tyrus hath said against Jerusalem, Aha, she is broken that was the gates of the people: she is turned unto me: I shall be replenished, now she is laid waste: therefore thus saith the Lord God; Behold, I am against thee, O Tyrus, and will cause many nations to come up against thee, as the sea causeth his waves to come up. And they shall destroy the walls of Tyrus, and break down her towers: *I will also scrape her dust from her, and make her like the top of a rock. It shall be a place for the spreading of nets in the midst of the sea.*" "Thou shalt be built no more" (Ezekiel 26:1-5, 14).

Probably nobody took much notice of the prophecy at the time, except to regard it as the mutterings of a madman. How could great Tyre ever suffer such indignities?

Not long after, however, Nebuchadnezzar arrived at the gates of the city. For 13 years he besieged it. So long and hard did his soldiers labor at the battering rams that "every shoulder was peeled" (Ezekiel 29:18). Finally that portion of the city on the mainland was captured, though Nebuchadnezzar was robbed of the main booty, which the people of Tyre removed to their island stronghold a half mile away.

To some it must have appeared that Ezekiel's prophecy had failed. True, part of Tyre had been destroyed, but it certainly had not been made as bare as the top of a rock.

More years passed. Ezekiel died. Generations of Tyrians passed away. Then, in 332 B.C., came Alexander the Great and demanded the city's surrender. The Tyrians refused, and one of the most notable sieges of history began. Once again the island fortress proved seemingly impregnable. At last, in desperation, Alexander decided upon an unusual course. Demolishing the mainland city, he threw the debris into the water, thus constructing a mole 200 feet wide out toward the sea-girt citadel, across which his army marched to victory.

Today the remains of this mole may still be seen. Moreover, fishermen from the village of Sur, which has grown up around the ancient site, spread their nets upon the bare rocks from which the soil of Tyre was scraped by the famous Grecian conqueror nearly 2,300 centuries ago.

Thus another Bible prophecy came to pass. And the accuracy with which its smallest details were fulfilled is remarkable indeed. How could any man, unless divinely inspired, have known that ancient Tyre would be so completely demolished?

Look now at some of the many predictions concerning the Jews. Deuteronomy 28 records all the blessings designed to reward obedience to God's commandments and also the curses that would result from disobedience. "The Lord shall cause thee to be smitten before thine enemies," God said. "Thou shalt go out one way against them, and flee seven ways before them: and *shalt be removed into all the kingdoms* of the earth."

"And thou shalt become an astonishment, a proverb, and a byword."

"And *the Lord shall scatter thee among all people, from the one end of the earth even unto the other.* . . .

"And among these nations shalt thou find no ease. . . . .

"And *thy life shall hang in doubt before thee; and thou shalt fear day and night,* and shalt have none assurance of thy life" (verses 25, 37, 64-66).

The awful sufferings of the children of Israel down the centuries even to our own time, in pogrom after pogrom, have proved the truth of this prediction. And even though many thousands have returned to Palestine, the great majority of Abraham's descendants are still scattered among all people "from one end of the earth to the other" (verse 64, RSV).

An interesting time prophecy concerning the Jews is to be found in Jeremiah 29:10.

As they were about to be carried captive to Babylon the Lord said through Jeremiah: "After seventy years be accomplished at Babylon I will visit you, and perform my good word toward you, in causing you to return to this place."

Years later the prophet Daniel ran across these words and wrote: "In the first year of Darius . . . I Daniel understood by books the number of the years, whereof the word of the Lord came to Jeremiah the prophet, that he would accomplish seventy years in the desolations of Jerusalem" (Daniel 9:1, 2).

As a result of this discovery he gave himself to prayer that he and his people might be worthy of God's promised intervention. Shortly thereafter a royal proclamation was issued, permitting the Jews to return to Jerusalem. Many thousands took advantage of the opportunity, and again prophecy was fulfilled. See Ezra 1:1-11.

Another prediction relating to Jerusalem was made by Christ. To His disciples, who had just pointed out to Him the solid architecture of the Temple, He said, "There shall not be left here one stone upon another, that shall not be thrown down" (Matthew 24:2).

It was a daring forecast and it shocked His listeners; but within 40 years it came true. In A.D. 70 the Roman armies under Titus captured the city and totally destroyed the Temple. In their mad search for hidden treasure they broke down every wall and even tore up the foundations. Finally they drove a plowshare over the debris.

Then began the long period of subjection that Christ predicted when He said, "Jerusalem shall be trodden down of the Gentiles, until the times of the Gentiles be fulfilled" (Luke 21:24). Century after century the city has been dominated first by one conqueror, then by another. It was trodden down by the Romans, the Muslims, the Turks, the Arabs. Today Gentiles challenge every move the Israelis make in Jerusalem, and a Muslim mosque stands upon the site of Solomon's Temple, constant reminders of the truth of Christ's words.

Well did H. L. Hastings write: "So long as Babylon is in heaps; so long as Nineveh lies empty, void, and waste; so long as Egypt is the basest of kingdoms; so long as Tyre is a place for the spreading of nets in the midst of the sea; so long as Israel is scattered among all nations; so long as Jerusalem is trodden underfoot of the Gentiles; so long as the great empires of the world march on in their predicted courses—so long we have proof that one Omniscient Mind dictated the predictions of that Book, and that 'prophecy came not in old time by the will of man' " *(Will the Old Book Stand?* p. 20).

Confirming, establishing, and irradiating all other prophecies, however, are those concerning Christ Himself. There are scores of them, scattered all through the Holy Scriptures. The place of His birth was foretold in Micah 5:2 and the mode of it in Isaiah 9:6. Isaiah 61:1-3 outlined the burden of His ministry, while His rejection and suffering were predicted in Isaiah 53:3-6. Events at the cross were foreshadowed in great detail in Psalm 22:16-18 and Isaiah 53:9.

"No miracle which He wrought so unmistakably set on Him the seal of God, as the convergence of the thousand lines of prophecy in Him, as in one burning focal point of dazzling glory. Every sacrifice presented, from the hour of Abel's altar fire down to the last Passover of the Passion Week, pointed as with flaming finger to Calvary's cross! Nay, all the centuries moved as in solemn procession to lay their tributes upon Golgotha" (Arthur T. Pierson, *Many Infallible Proofs,* p. 39).

As Peter said: "To him give all the prophets witness" (Acts 10:43). He was the Desire of all nations (Haggai 2:7); the Prince of Peace (Isaiah 9:6); the Lord our Righteousness (Jeremiah 23:6); the Mighty One of Jacob (Isaiah 60:16); our Redeemer (Job 19:25; Isaiah 59:20); the Chief Shepherd of the sheep (Zechariah 11:16; 1 Peter 5:4); and the Bright and Morning Star (Number 24:17; Revelation 22:16). The focal point of all prophecy, He stands forth above all others as the supreme character of history, the ruler of time and eternity.

And because these many remarkable predictions have been fulfilled with such extraordinary precision we may have complete confidence in all the revelations of Holy Scripture, saying with Peter: "We have also a more sure word of prophecy; whereunto ye do well that ye take heed, as unto a light that shineth in a dark place, until the day dawn, and the day star arise in your hearts" (2 Peter 1:19).

THE NEXT
WORLD EMPIRE

PERHAPS the most dramatic of all the prophecies to be found in your Bible is the one recorded in the second chapter of the book of Daniel. Not only is it presented in a most unusual setting—the throne room of ancient Babylon—but it traces the course of history from that day to this, and beyond. It describes the rise of five world empires, four of which are past, the other still to come.

If you are wondering whether the next world empire will be China or the United States or perhaps some Middle Eastern power, you will be fascinated by this prediction, which bears the stamp of divine authenticity.

To catch the full import of the story, go back in imagination to that far-off day when it all began in Nebuchadnezzar's bedroom.

It is morning. The young king has just awakened with a worried look upon his face. He has had a strange dream that he cannot recall. So he summons his counselors and demands that they help him. Some of these are astrologers, some magicians, some sorcerers—all claiming knowledge of the occult.

To this assembly of "the wise men of Babylon" Nebuchadnezzar brings his strange demand: "Tell me what I dreamed last night!"

None is able to do it. Some offer to interpret the dream, but insist that they must first know what it was.

At this the king is greatly angered. "If you cannot tell me my dream," he cries, "I will have you all put to death."

All are helpless and silent, whereupon the king, becoming "very furious," orders their execution.

As the royal patrols go through the city arresting the wise men of Babylon, they come upon Daniel, the young Hebrew captive, whose keen intellect and sterling character have already won him a place among this select group. He seeks an interview with the king, begging for time, and promising that the dream shall be recalled to him.

His request is granted, and Daniel and his friends seek God in earnest prayer.

Daniel is now shown in vision the selfsame dream that had so greatly impressed Nebuchadnezzar the night before. Shortly thereafter, ushered into the royal presence, he finds himself face-to-face with the greatest ruler of ancient times. The king is expecting him, skeptical no doubt as to the result of the interview, and perhaps regretting that his somewhat hasty decree has made it necessary that this fine young man should be put to death. Then the prophet speaks:

"The secret which the king hath demanded cannot the wise men, the astrologers, the magicians, the soothsayers, shew unto the king; but there is a God in heaven that revealeth secrets, and maketh known to the king Nebuchadnezzar *what shall be in the latter days*" (Daniel 2:27, 28).

The conviction in the young man's voice, born of certain knowledge, stirs the king.

One can almost see him leaning forward with eagerness to catch the next sentences.

"As for thee, O king, thy thoughts came into thy mind upon thy bed, what should come to pass hereafter: and he that revealeth secrets maketh known to thee what shall come to pass" (verse 29).

Daniel now proceeds to recount the dream.

"Thou, O king, sawest, and behold a great image. This great image, whose brightness was excellent, stood before thee; and the form thereof was terrible. This image's head was of fine gold, his breast and his arms of silver, his belly and his thighs of brass, his legs of iron, his feet part of iron and part of clay. Thou sawest till that a stone was cut out without hands, which smote the image upon his feet that were of iron and clay, and brake them to pieces. Then was the iron, the clay, the brass, the silver, and the gold, broken to pieces together, and became like the chaff of the summer threshingfloors; and the wind carried them away, that no place was found for them: and the stone that smote the image became a great mountain, and filled the whole earth" (verses 31-35).

It is the very dream the king had seen and forgotten! Every detail is perfectly drawn. Nothing is missing. His inmost thoughts have been read by another! This is miraculous!

Breathlessly Nebuchadnezzar waits for the promised interpretation.

"This is the dream," says Daniel; "and we will tell the interpretation thereof before the king.

"Thou, O king, art a king of kings: for the God of heaven hath given thee a kingdom, power, and strength, and glory. And wheresoever the children of men dwell, the beasts of the field and the fowls of the heaven hath he given into thine hand, and hath made thee ruler over them all. Thou art this head of gold" (verses 36-38).

A smile of satisfaction passes over the king's countenance, changing to a frown as the young man says:

"And after thee shall arise another kingdom inferior to thee, and another third kingdom of brass, which shall bear rule over all the earth. And the fourth kingdom shall be strong as iron. . . .

"And whereas thou sawest the feet and toes, part of potters' clay, and part of iron, the kingdom shall be divided; but there shall be in it of the strength of the iron, forasmuch as thou sawest the iron mixed with miry clay.

"And as the toes of the feet were part of iron, and part of clay, so the kingdom shall be partly strong, and partly broken.

"And whereas thou sawest iron mixed with miry clay, they shall mingle themselves with the seed of men: but they shall not cleave one to another, even as iron is not mixed with clay. And in the days of these kings shall the God of heaven set up a kingdom, which shall never be destroyed" (verses 39-44).

In these few prophetic words Daniel outlines the course of the empire for centuries to come. There will be, he asserts, four world powers; four, and no more. Then there will come a period of division and conflict, culminating in a divine intervention and the setting up of God's eternal kingdom.

What has been history's answer to his daring prediction?

As to the first world power, there can be no question. It was identified by the prophet when he said to Nebuchadnezzar, "Thou art this head of gold." This great king was the personification of the might of Babylon, the greatest empire of the ancient world, which enjoyed full sovereignty from about 605 B.C.—when the power of Assyria was broken—until its overthrow, less than 68 years later, by the combined forces of Media and Persia, described so vividly in the fifth chapter of the book of Daniel.

Persia thus became the second universal empire, enjoying its supremacy for some 200 years. Then, early in the fourth century B.C., came the rise of Greece and the swift conquests of Alexander the Great. With incredible courage this youthful commander hurled his limited forces across the Hellespont at the vast hosts of Darius, utterly defeating them at Granicus, Issus, and finally at the decisive Battle of Arbela, 331 B.C.

Greece continued her overlordship for another century and a half, although becoming ever more conscious of the growing might of her western neighbor. On June 22, 168 B.C., at the Battle of Pydna, Perseus, king of Macedonia, was completely crushed by the armies of Rome, and on this day "perished the empire of Alexander the Great, which had subdued and Hellenized the East, one hundred and forty-four years after his death" (Theodor Mommsen, *History of Rome,* book 3, chap. 10).

From this famous battle is also dated "the full establishment of the empire of Rome," the fourth universal empire of the prophecy, whose iron will was fastened upon the world for the next six centuries.

But though Rome, with her invincible might, crushed all

opposition and brought whole nations into slavery; though her standards waved triumphantly from the Persian Gulf to the isles of Britain, and from the Baltic Sea to North Africa; though her Caesars called themselves gods and demanded the subservience of all men everywhere; yet she too came to her end, even as the prophet had declared long years before. All through the fourth and fifth centuries A.D. the frontiers of the empire were harassed by barbarian tribes, which attacked with increasing boldness and frequency; and finally, in A.D. 476, the imperial city of Rome fell before the onslaught of Odoacer, king of the Heruli.

So the fourth, or iron, empire came to an end, to be succeeded not by another universal empire, but by a group of heterogeneous kingdoms established by her conquerors, a strange mixture of strength and weakness, of "iron" and "clay," which has remained to the present day.

Marvelous indeed was this revelation given through the prophet Daniel. Yet the wonder of it increases as one studies further into all its fascinating details. Notice again the specifications—clear, definite, and unmistakable—that the fourth kingdom was not to be immediately succeeded by another of similar extent and universal supremacy. Instead, it was to be divided.

This all-important fact was repeated and emphasized in three different and significant expressions:

"And whereas thou sawest the feet and toes, part of potters' clay, and part of iron, *the kingdom shall be divided;* but there shall be in it of the strength of the iron, forasmuch as thou sawest the iron mixed with miry clay.

"And as the toes of the feet were part of iron, and part of clay, so the kingdom shall be *partly strong, and partly brittle* [margin].

"And whereas thou sawest iron mixed with miry clay, they shall mingle themselves with the seed of men; but *they shall not cleave one to another,* even as iron is not mixed with clay" (Daniel 2:41-43).

It is one of the most interesting, and indeed one of the most momentous, facts of history, that when the Roman Empire, weakened by internal corruption, was overrun by invading tribes from the north and east, it was divided into 10 separate kingdoms. With the overthrow of the last of the emperors in A.D. 476, and the establishment of the Herulian kingdom in Italy, the fourth kingdom, which had been strong as iron and had broken in pieces and subdued all kingdoms, was now broken in pieces itself.

Out of the welter of that destruction arose 10 kingdoms with some degree of permanence—the Anglo-Saxons, the Franks, the Alemanni, the Lombards, the Ostrogoths, the Visigoths, the Burgundians, the Vandals, the Suevi, and the Heruli. These were forerunners and progenitors of the nations of modern Europe.

All through the 15 centuries that have elapsed since the breakup of the Roman Empire, despite the most desperate and determined efforts to bind these parts together into one great whole again, the task has been found impossible.

Boundaries have changed, of course, but the prophecy said nothing about boundaries, or about the depredations of one nation upon another. Some nations might expand and others shrink. The fragments of iron might penetrate into the frontiers of the helpless clay. But the clay would remain, defying the power of the iron to weld itself together again.

Seen in the light of history, illumined by the glow of a thousand battlefields, where men by millions have died in fearful carnage, the ancient pronouncement *"They shall not cleave one to another"* is one of the greatest prophetic utterances of all time.

It is remarkable how many schemes have been laid to unite the nations of Europe. Men have made treaties until almost every nation was pledged in some way to every other nation. Between May 19, 1920, and May 19, 1939, no fewer than 4,568 "treaties and international engagements" were submitted for registration with the League of Nations. They have tried intermarriage until every ruling dynasty became related to every other dynasty and it was considered unethical for one of royal blood to wed outside this charmed circle. Yet every plan has failed. Every bond, durable as it seemed when made, has snapped under the strain of seething human emotions. While there has been "the strength of the iron" in these plans, there

YOUR BIBLE AND YOU

has always appeared the disastrous weakness of the clay.

Again and again down the centuries, ambitious, purposeful men have arisen, determined at all costs to abolish the frontiers of the ever-quarrelsome states and to rule over one united kingdom. Resentful of the differences of custom and language, angered by aggravating trade barriers, they have sworn to sweep them away once and for all. Yet they have failed.

Sometimes they have come within sight of success. Just one more victory, or one more year of planning, and their ambition might have been achieved. But it was not to be. Every time, in some strange and unexpected way, they have been defeated.

As far back as the ninth century A.D., Charlemagne made his attempt to unite Europe. He even permitted himself to be crowned emperor at Rome. But the iron and the clay, which he tried to blend together, quickly fell apart after his death. As one historian has said: "His scepter was the bow of Ulysses, which could not be drawn by any weaker hand."

In the sixteenth century Charles V became ruler of most of Europe, and had visions of completing its conquest. It was said of him that "no monarch until Napoleon was so widely seen in Europe and in Africa." Yet in 1555, because of failing health, he was compelled to abdicate and sign away his vast possessions to others.

Little more than 100 years later, Louis XIV of France became the dominant figure on the Continent. He reached out in all directions for more and more authority, overrunning the Netherlands, laying waste the Palatinate, and exclaiming, "There are no longer any Pyrenees." Nevertheless, a combination of opposing forces finally brought his grandiose schemes tumbling about him like a castle of cards. By the Treaty of Utrecht in 1713, his dominions "were pared away on every side."

Then less than two centuries ago came Napoleon, perhaps the greatest of all these would-be lords of Europe and conquerors of the world. After being proclaimed emperor in 1804, he consolidated his hold upon the people of France. For eight fearful years he swept over nation after nation, crowning himself king of Italy, placing his brother

Louis on the throne of Holland and his brother Jerome on the throne of the new kingdom of Westphalia, which he created. He made his brother-in-law Murat sovereign of his newly established Grand Duchy of Berg, and gave his brother Joseph the throne of Spain. No other conqueror ever made such thorough preparation for the establishment and perpetuation of a united Europe. Nevertheless, even before his plans were completed, rumblings of the coming disintegration could be heard.

In 1805 the French fleet was defeated at Trafalgar. In 1812 came Napoleon's Russian expedition, his retreat from Moscow, his subsequent defeat at Leipzig in October 1813, followed by his final overthrow at Waterloo in 1815.

In 1914 a similar attempt at European domination was made by Kaiser Wilhelm, whose armies swept over Belgium, France, Italy, and the Balkans. Their shattering blows suggested for a while that the final triumph would be theirs. But they were disillusioned. Suddenly the course of events changed, and before one could fully appreciate the magnitude of what was taking place, it had all ended at Versailles and Doorn.

In 1939 Hitler sought to succeed where the kaiser had failed. With fleets of U-boats, tanks, planes, and rockets he came close to achieving his ambition. For many months only one little island blocked his path to total victory. Then the United States moved in, the situation was reversed, and before long Hitler was dead — a suicide.

Thus has it happened in the past and thus, if need be, it will happen again. No matter who the aggressor may be, how large his armies or how powerful his armaments, he is foredoomed to failure.

Events may for a time appear to go contrary to the prophecy, but, ultimately, anyone who attempts to dominate Europe will come to an untimely end. He may achieve temporary triumphs. He may even overrun most of the Continent. Yet along the trail of his conquests there will grow up forces that will eventually destroy him.

Some may ask, What about the European Economic Community? Based on friendship, not conquest, surely it will last. But no. The prophecy knows no exceptions. The common market may continue for a while, but sooner or later it will go the way of all the rest.

The kingdoms that grew out of the division of the old Roman Empire will remain until the end, for it is "in the days of *these* kings," or kingdoms, that the fifth and final empire will be set up. And this will not be a man-made kingdom, created by human might out of human suffering. Rather will it be the kingdom of God, based on righteousness, truth, and love. It will be "cut out . . . without hands" because it will be altogether a work of God, not of man. It will result from divine grace, divine love, and divine intervention.

Amazing prophecy! Like a mighty beacon it shines across the centuries, illuminating the greatest events of time with light from heaven. Glittering on the gold of Babylon, shimmering on the silver of Medo-Persia, shining on the Grecian brass and the iron of Rome, lighting up the struggles and conflicts of our modern world, it glows at last upon the face of the King of kings as He returns to the earth in glory.

For He is the stone that will strike the image and break in pieces "the iron, the brass, the clay, the silver, and the gold." And His is the kingdom that shall "consume all these kingdoms, and . . . shall stand for ever."

Well may we ask ourselves whether we are ready for this epochal change of leadership and government soon to take place. Have we given ourselves irrevocably to God for time and eternity? Are we planning to be His loyal and devoted subjects through the endless ages to come?

OUR DAY FORESEEN

IN THE wonderful book of Daniel, besides the great prophecy concerning the next world empire, you will find several other prophecies worthy of careful study.

One of the most impressive, having all manner of fascinating aspects for everyone alive today, is that which reads: "But thou, O Daniel, shut up the words, and seal the book, even to the time of the end; many shall run to and fro, and knowledge shall be increased" (Daniel 12:4).

Undoubtedly this has a first application to an increased understanding of the book of Daniel to take place in "the time of the end." But few will deny that it has a secondary and no less important reference to all the vast increase of knowledge in a general sense that enlightens the minds of men and makes it possible for them to understand God's Word.

And here a great light shines upon this precious passage of Scripture, for it is an indisputable fact that the past couple hundred years have witnessed greater progress in education than any other period in history.

Every country today boasts of its universities, colleges, and schools. Many have compulsory education for the young, a thing unheard of at the beginning of the nineteenth century. Everywhere, too, a tide of literature, in hundreds of languages, is pouring from innumerable printing presses and being welcomed by millions in tribes and nations that have become literate only within the past few decades.

Furthermore, scientists of all nations are searching out more and more of the secrets of nature. Specialists in electricity, electronics, and aerodynamics are bringing to light resources hidden for centuries. Archeologists are digging with renewed avidity among the remains of buried civilizations, producing new evidence to prove the accuracy of Bible history. Astronomers, with their great new telescopes, are peering farther and farther into the mysteries of the universe, revealing ever more clearly the power and majesty of the Creator.

But the increase of knowledge has not been merely theoretical. It has burst forth in innumerable inventions, which have transformed man's manner of living to a degree never seen before. In a few brief years a veritable avalanche of new ideas has swept us from the steam age to the electric age, to the atomic age and the space age and the computer age.

We live in an era of unprecedented material progress and wonders innumerable.

It is hard to believe that such extraordinary developments have taken place so swiftly; and harder still to realize what a different world it was only a hundred years or so ago. In the 1850s there were no airplanes, no cars, nor any machines operated by an internal combustion engine. There were no trucks, tractors, or tanks. There were no electric lights, nor any electrical appliances. Anyone with a humble gas jet in his home was regarded as a plutocrat. Railroads were just beginning to be popular, though many people were still afraid of them. The sailing ship was still sovereign of the seas, with a few primitive steamships making their appearance amid much public excitement. Some newspapers existed, but no telephone or telegraph system. Antiseptics and anesthetics were unknown and a visit to a hospital was a nightmare. Modern surgery, dentistry, and ophthalmology were in their infancy. Nobody had ever heard of antitoxins, insulin, or antibiotics, or even a clinical thermometer! Certainly not coronary bypasses and organ transplants!

The fact is that a century and a half ago the world was just beginning to emerge from the mental torpor in which it had languished for ages. It was like a butterfly issuing from a chrysalis in which it had been mysteriously imprisoned from time immemorial.

Prior to 1850, most people were still living in much the same way their forefathers had lived for thousands of years. They were still traveling from place to place by coach and on horseback; still using animals when plowing their fields; still living in houses without running water or bathrooms; still reading by candlelight; still doing most of their work by hand.

How far and fast have we come since then! Imagine what Abraham Lincoln and William Gladstone might say if they should come to life today and be introduced to a television or radio program or taken to see the launching of a satellite. Most probably they would say, We don't believe it! And you couldn't blame them. Some of these developments are so amazing as to be almost beyond explanation even by those who have grown up with them.

Yet all this does not give a complete picture of the wonders of this marvelous age in which we find ourselves. Concurrent with the increase of knowledge and invention there has come about a movement of people without precedent in history. Millions are constantly rushing hither and yon by plane, train, ship, and car, all the while calling for more and more speed so that they may travel ever farther and faster in a limited amount of time.

Jet-propelled planes carry passengers in excess of 600 miles per hour, while military aircraft crack the sound barrier so frequently that the public no longer notices the shattering sonic boom. Astronauts hurtle through space at multiplied thousands of miles per hour.

All this has been accompanied by a complete exploration of the globe. A century ago much of it was enveloped in mystery. Only the most daring spirits set sail for lands afar. How different is the situation now! As Jules Verne once wrote: "There are no more impassable deserts, no more unfathomable seas, no more inaccessible mountains." The poles, once so fearsome, are crossed daily by airline passengers on regularly scheduled flights. Tropical jungles, once considered impenetrable, have been explored on a scale no one would have dreamed possible in years gone by.

Earth, in fact, is too small for modern explorers. So many men have walked on the moon that most people have lost count. Spacecraft have pierced the cloud layers on Venus, sampled the soil of Mars, and plunged past Neptune and Pluto toward the outer reaches of space.

What does it all mean? Read the prophecy again: "But thou, O Daniel, shut up the words, and seal the book, *even to the time of the end:* many shall run to and fro, and knowledge shall be increased."

Surely this day—our day—is the one the prophet had in mind. It was to this century that the angel bade him look. And as we behold the fulfillment of these prophetic words on such a lavish scale we cannot help admitting that we are living in the time of the end, amid the crisis at history's close.

All the vast, spectacular changes of our day have come to pass in God's providence to fulfill an urgent divine purpose: that knowledge of the book of Daniel—indeed, of the whole Bible—should be mightily increased and its message of the coming kingdom of God be heralded swiftly to earth's remotest bounds.

CHRIST UNVEILS
THE FUTURE

THE most detailed information concerning things to come is to be found in the Gospels of Matthew, Mark, and Luke, where Christ's own revelation of the future is recorded.

This is most natural, for who could know more about the *end* of the world than He who created it in the *beginning* (Colossians 1:16, 17)? And who could see more clearly into the ages to come than He who is "from everlasting to everlasting," and to whom a thousand years "are but as yesterday when it is past, and as a watch in the night" (Psalm 90:2-4)? Nor should we forget that it was Christ who, by His Holy Spirit, inspired the words of Moses, Isaiah, Jeremiah, Daniel, and "all his holy prophets which have been since the world began" (Acts 3:21).

So it was with the unerring vision of omniscience that He unveiled the future to His listening disciples and told of "things which shall be hereafter" (Revelation 1:19). Full knowledge and clear understanding enabled Him to speak on this subject "as one having authority" (Matthew 7:29), and as "never man spake" (John 7:46).

The discussion arose as a result of His disturbing declaration that the Temple would be destroyed and not one stone of it be left upon another (Matthew 24:2).

This worried His disciples, as well it may have done, and as soon as possible they "came unto him privately, saying, Tell us, when shall these things be? and what shall be the sign of thy coming, and of the end of the world?" (verse 3).

They presumed that the destruction of the Temple would synchronize with the end of the world, for to them nothing less than some such supernatural upheaval could ever sweep away so stable and stately an edifice. Reading their thoughts, Jesus seized the opportunity to warn them of the long period of time that must elapse before the final scenes of history would take place.

So, seated on the Mount of Olives, looking down on old Jerusalem, the Master Prophet drew back the veil of the future before the eyes of His followers.

"Take heed that no man deceive you," He began, "for many shall come in my name, saying, I am Christ; and shall deceive many" (verses 4, 5).

He was concerned about the danger of deception and returned to it later, saying, "If any man shall say unto you, Lo, here is Christ, or there; believe it not. For there shall arise false Christs, and false prophets, and shall shew great signs and wonders; insomuch that, if it were possible, they shall deceive the very elect" (verses 23, 24).

But He was equally anxious that His disciples should not become discouraged as time passed without their hopes being realized. So He warned them: "Ye shall hear of wars and rumours of wars: see that ye be not troubled: for all these things must come to pass, but the end is not yet" (verse 6).

Thus He sought to extend their vision. Many tragic events would occur before His return. "For nation shall rise against nation, and kingdom against kingdom: and there shall be famines, and pestilences, and earthquakes, in divers places. All these are the beginning of sorrows" (verses 7, 8).

In these words He let them know that international strife would exist all down the ages—and how accurate was His forecast! Every generation has been cursed with wars; some small, some great, but always increasing in destructiveness through the years, and always followed in dreadful but regular sequence by famines, pestilences, and depressions.

Yet all these calamities would be but the beginning of sorrows. Far worse tragedies would come. There would be persecution, bitter and cruel in the extreme. "Then shall they deliver you up to be afflicted, and shall kill you: and ye shall be hated of all nations for my name's sake. And then shall many be offended, and shall betray one another, and shall hate one another" (verses 9, 10).

One can almost see the tense look of anxiety on the faces of the disciples as, with their Lord, they peered down the centuries and beheld the coming trials of the children of God. They saw them thrown to the lions, tortured on the rack, burned at the stake, buried alive, sawn asunder, abused, tormented, massacred. It was a fearful and frightening picture, and there must have been a silence full of pain as Jesus quietly and sorrowfully continued: "Then shall be great tribulation, such as was not since the beginning of the world to this time, no, nor ever shall be" (verse 21).

His mind was now far down the ages, past the savage cruelties perpetrated on the Albigenses and the Waldenses, past the worst horrors of the Inquisition. In the distant future He saw a respite coming for His afflicted followers. Persecution, He said, would decline, as it did following the great Reformation, the Renaissance, and the spread of a new concept of religious liberty and the rights of man.

At that time, said Jesus, "Immediately after the tribulation of those days shall the sun be darkened, and the moon shall not give her light" (verse 29).

Marvelously, just seven years after the dissolution of an organization that had been active in carrying on the persecutions of the Inquisition, a mysterious darkening of the sun occurred. On May 19, 1780, over a large area, the light of day suddenly faded into the blackness of midnight. This was the famous Dark Day, of which Noah Webster wrote in his dictionary: "So called on account of a remarkable darkness on that day extending over all New England. . . . Birds sang their evening songs, disappeared, and became silent; fowls went to roost; cattle sought the barnyard; and candles were lighted in the houses" (1869 edition).

This was the day described by the Boston *Independent Chronicle* on June 8, 1780, in the following graphic language: "During the whole time a sickly, melancholy gloom overcast the face of nature. Nor was the darkness of the night less uncommon and terrifying than that of the day; notwithstanding there was almost a full moon, no object was discernible, but by the help of some artificial light, which when seen from the neighboring houses and other places at a distance, appeared through a kind of Egyptian darkness, which seemed almost impervious to the rays. This unusual phenomenon excited the fears and apprehensions of many people. Some considered it as a portentous omen of the wrath of Heaven in vengeance denounced against the land, others as the immediate harbinger of the last day when 'the sun shall be darkened and the moon shall not give her light.' "

But the enthralled disciples, peering breathlessly into the future as they listened to the prophetic words falling from their Master's lips, soon found themselves gazing upon another amazing scene.

"And the stars shall fall from heaven," said Jesus, continuing the sequence of signs of His return.

The stars fall! How could this be? Not the fixed stars, of course, but the meteors that rush into our atmosphere and sometimes give the impression that the heavens are crashing earthward.

Obviously, a celestial phenomenon on a stupendous scale was to follow the darkening of the sun. And so it came to pass.

"On the night of November 12-13, 1833, a tempest of falling stars broke over the earth. North America bore the brunt of its pelting. From the Gulf of Mexico to Halifax, until daylight with some difficulty put an end to the display, the sky was scored in every direction with shining tracks and illuminated with majestic fireballs" (Agnes M. Clerke, *History of Astronomy in the Nineteenth Century,* p. 328).

"Though there was no moon," wrote one observer, "when we first beheld them [the meteors], their brilliancy was so great that we could, at times, read common-sized print without much difficulty, and the light which they afforded was much whiter than that of the moon, in the clearest and coldest night, when the ground is covered with snow. The air itself, the face of the earth, as far as we could behold it, all the surrounding objects, and the very countenances of men, wore the aspect and hue of death, occasioned by the continued, pallid glare of these countless meteors, which in all their grandeur flamed 'lawless through the sky.' There was a grand, peculiar, and indescribable gloom on all around, an awe-inspiring sublimity on all above. . . .

"There was scarcely a space in the firmament which was not filled at every instant with these falling stars, nor on it, could you in general perceive any particular difference in appearance; still at times they would shower down in groups—calling to mind the 'fig tree casting her untimely figs when shaken by a mighty wind' " (from a letter published in the *American Journal of Science and Arts,* vol. 25 [1834]: p. 382).

Following this, said Jesus, most serious and troubled conditions would prevail throughout the world. After the "signs in the sun, and in the moon, and in the stars" there would come "upon the earth distress of nations, with perplexity; the sea and the waves roaring; men's hearts failing them for fear, and for looking after those things which are coming on the earth" (Luke 21:25, 26).

How appropriate are these words of Jesus to this twentieth century, with its two world wars and their fearful aftermath!

The past few decades have seen the destruction of many of man's greatest works, the blighting of his dearest hopes, the quenching of his most cherished ambitions. Today we glimpse new terrors looming up in the form of global pollution, destruction of the ozone layer, depletion of natural resources, warming of the atmosphere, and overpopulation—to say nothing of spreading famine, nuclear bombs and intercontinental ballistic missiles, lethal gases, and AIDS. In consequence we see "men fainting with fear and with foreboding of what is coming on the world" (Luke 21:26, RSV).

Up to this point Christ's revelation of the future was gloomy indeed. But He did not stop there. All these tragic happenings, He said, would be signs of His return. But someday, in the midst of all the global chaos, confusion, and disintegration, the climax of history would burst upon mankind.

"Then shall they see the Son of man coming in a cloud with power and great glory" (Luke 21:27).

When hope and joy and peace have well-nigh perished from the earth, when all that is good and beautiful shall have been destroyed or brought into imminent jeopardy, when human endurance shall have reached the breaking point, then suddenly, gloriously, majestically, the heavens will part and Christ will come to the rescue.

No wonder He added the cheering words: "When these things begin to come to pass, then *look up,* and *lift up your heads;* for your redemption draweth nigh" (verse 28).

He was speaking not only to the disciples who were sitting with Him on the Mount of Olives, but to us also who live today when the greatest of the signs of His return are being fulfilled. It is a message full of hope for you.

Look up! For you shall see the sublimest sight of the ages, the grand deliverance that God has planned and promised "since the world began."

Look up! and remember that God still lives and loves; that His faithfulness still "reaches unto the clouds" (Psalm 36:5); that "as the heaven is high above the earth, so great is his mercy toward them that fear him" (Psalm 103:11).

Look up! Recall that the Most High still rules "in the kingdom of men" (Daniel 4:17) and that His resolute purpose is to cause truth to triumph and make righteousness cover the earth "as the waters cover the sea" (Habakkuk 2:14).

Look up! and see the Conqueror of Calvary sitting at the right hand of God, preparing to return for His own. For beyond question His day of glorious victory is at hand. It cannot be long delayed. It is "near, even at the doors" (Matthew 24:33).

SIGNS OF OUR TIMES

SO VITALLY important is the second coming of Christ to every human being in all the world that your Bible speaks of it over and over again. And the frequency with which this epochal event is mentioned suggests that God, who loves mankind so dearly, is anxious lest some be caught unprepared when it occurs.

"Take heed to yourselves," Jesus warns His disciples, "lest . . . your hearts be overcharged with surfeiting and drunkenness, and cares of this life, and so that day come upon you unawares. For as a snare shall it come on all them that dwell on the face of the whole earth. Watch ye therefore, and pray always, that ye may be accounted worthy to escape all these things that shall come to pass, and to stand before the Son of man" (Luke 21:34-36).

Dr. J. B. Phillips renders this passage thus: "Be on your guard—see to it that your minds are never clouded by dissipation or drunkenness or the worries of this life, or else that day may catch you like the springing of a trap—for it will come upon every inhabitant of the whole earth. You must be vigilant at all times, praying that you may be strong enough to come safely through all that is going to happen, and stand in the presence of the Son of Man."

This need for preparation for Christ's coming, of being ready to meet Him face-to-face, is the real purpose of all the signs set forth in

Matthew 24, Mark 13, and Luke 21, considered in the previous chapter. Jesus wants His followers to watch for them, to be on the alert for every indication of His return.

But these are not all the promised signs. Many more are to be found throughout the Scriptures.

Here is another portent given by the Lord Himself. It concerns the moral state of society in the last days: "As it was in the days of Noah, so will it be in the days of the Son of man. They ate, they drank, they married, they were given in marriage, until the day when Noah entered the ark, and the flood came and destroyed them all" (Luke 17:26, 27, RSV).

This prediction makes it impossible for anyone to mistake the approximate time of Christ's second coming. He has but to watch for a return of conditions similar to those that existed before the Flood. When they appear he will know that the end is *near*, even though he cannot tell the day nor the hour that it will occur (Matthew 24:36).

What state of affairs prevailed in those far-off days? What were people doing that caused God to bring upon them such a fearful judgment?

"They ate, they drank, they married," presumably to excess. But this was not all they did. For the full story of their self-indulgence and depravity one needs but turn to the sixth chapter of Genesis. Three main charges are made against the antediluvians:

1. "They took them wives of all which they chose" (verse 2). Evidently there was much divorce and remarriage in those days, and probably outright polygamy.

2. "And God saw that the wickedness of man was great in the earth, and that every imagination of the thoughts of his heart was only evil continually" (verse 5). This suggests a total degeneracy of mind and body through brazen disregard of God's commands.

3. "The earth also was corrupt before God, and the earth was filled with violence" (verse 11). Apparently all law and order broke down as vicious, sadistic criminals roamed abroad in reckless, ruthless abandon.

Are such conditions visible today? Have the days of Noah

returned? Your newspaper contains the answer.

Divorce statistics tell the sorry tale, with one marriage after another breaking up and the parties thereto marrying again and again with a frequency that can only be described as legalized polygamy.

Every great city is honeycombed with vice and prostitution. Millions loudly argue the merits of abortion with scarcely a whisper about the immorality of the act that produces so many unwanted pregnancies.

Crimes of violence mount year by year. Armed robbery, rape, and murder have become so common that in many localities decent citizens dare not go out on the streets at night.

A similar warning sign occurs in Paul's second letter to Timothy. "Understand this," he says, "that *in the last days* there will come times of stress. For men will be lovers of self, lovers of money, proud, arrogant, abusive, disobedient to their parents, ungrateful, unholy, inhuman, implacable, slanderers, profligates, fierce, haters of good, treacherous, reckless, swollen with conceit, lovers of pleasure rather than lovers of God, holding the form of religion but denying the power of it" (2 Timothy 3:1-5, RSV).

Does this description also fit our times? Indeed it does, with astonishing accuracy. True, there have always been selfish, money-loving, proud, and arrogant people. Every generation has been stained with similar sins. What makes the present situation different is the universality of all these vices. The whole world is involved in the moral collapse as "evil men and seducers . . . wax worse and worse, deceiving and being deceived" (2 Timothy 3:13).

The deplorable growth of teenage violence, of drug abuse and suicide, of homosexualism and AIDS, of political corruption in the highest offices, of lawlessness of every kind and description, is evidence enough that "the last days" have arrived.

James contributes another sign of special interest. It touches upon the capital and labor problem, so much to the fore at this time. "Come now, you rich," he writes, "weep and howl for the miseries that are coming upon you. Your riches have rotted and your garments are motheaten. . . . You have laid up treasure for *the last days*. Behold, the wages of the laborers who mowed your fields, which you

241

kept back by fraud, cry out; and the cries of the harvesters have reached the ears of the Lord of hosts. You have lived on the earth in luxury and in pleasure; you have fattened your hearts in a day of slaughter" (James 5:1-5, RSV).

The woes of the rich are all too apparent today, what with confiscatory taxes and bank failures. Direction and management have also become one long succession of headaches, beset as they are with hostile takeovers, the need to restructure, and innumerable restrictions and limitations. Labor too has entered a new phase, with its representatives often sitting on boards of directors.

Caught in the midst of this titanic social struggle, now moving to its climax, is the humble, inoffensive Christian worker, whose one desire is to live at peace with all men. For such James has this comforting word: "Be patient, therefore, brethren, until the coming of the Lord. Behold, the farmer waits for the precious fruit of the earth, being patient over it until it receives the early and the late rain. You also be patient. Establish your hearts, *for the coming of the Lord is at hand*" (verses 7, 8).

From the apostle Peter we have yet another sign, relating to intellectual matters in the time of the end.

"First of all you must understand this," he says, "that scoffers will come *in the last days* with scoffing, following their own passions and saying, 'Where is the promise of his coming? For ever since the fathers fell asleep, all things have continued as they were from the beginning of creation.' They deliberately ignore this fact, that by the word of God heavens existed long ago, and an earth formed out of water, and by means of water, through which the world that then existed was deluged with water and perished. But by the same word the heavens and earth that now exist have been stored up for fire, being kept until the day of judgment and destruction of ungodly men" (2 Peter 3:3-7, RSV).

It is not hard to find such scoffers today. Many are in the garb of preachers while busily engaged in finding reasons why Christ will never keep His promise to return. Others are on university and college faculties, zealously promoting the godless theory of evolution and mocking at the Bible record of Creation and the Flood.

But all their hollow arguments and fanciful guesses are but additional proofs that the Word of God is true and that the last days are indeed upon us.

One more sign should be mentioned here. This, like so many others, comes from the lips of Jesus and concerns the worldwide preaching of the gospel. "This gospel of the kingdom," He says, "shall be preached in all the world for a witness unto all nations; and *then shall the end come."* The only difficulty about this prediction is that no one could ever know precisely when the gospel has been fully proclaimed. Nevertheless, it is a most impressive fact that the Bible, in whole or in part, has now been translated into nearly 2,000 languages and is being printed and circulated by millions of copies every year. Christian books and periodicals based on the Bible are also enjoying a similar global distribution.

Furthermore, earnest ministers of the gospel are taking advantage of radio and television to contact constantly growing audiences in all parts of the world. Thus, despite the magnitude of the obstacles to be surmounted, the message of salvation is now literally flying "in the midst of heaven . . . unto them that dwell on the earth, and to every nation, and kindred, and tongue, and people" (Revelation 14:6).

Such are some of the signs of Christ's second coming to be found in your Bible. They are indeed signs of *our* times, for they are being strikingly fulfilled in events and conditions confronting us all today.

Considered separately each one is of vital significance, but viewed together, stacked one upon another as it were, they have a meaning that should shake the world to its foundations. Their message is of measureless importance, affecting everybody's future, including yours and mine. In clarion tones they cry to all mankind, "The coming of the Lord draweth nigh!" (James 5:8).

HISTORY'S GLORIOUS CLIMAX

L OOMING upon the horizon of every man, woman, and child in the world is this greatest event of all time, the return in majesty and power of Jesus Christ. It will be history's glorious climax, marking the end of the world as we know it now, with all its sin, suffering, and sorrow, and the beginning of a new era in which righteousness, peace, and happiness shall forever flourish.

What will it be like? Your Bible gives the answer. Lest any should be deceived by a counterfeit advent—which is not beyond the power and cunning of Satan to attempt (2 Corinthians 11:14)—a most specific description is given of it.

1. *It will be visible to the naked eye.* Says John: "Behold, he cometh with clouds; and *every eye shall see him*" (Revelation 1:7). Again, in his first letter, he says: "Beloved, now are we the sons of God, and it doth not yet appear what we shall be: but we know that, when he shall appear, we shall be like him; for *we shall see him as he is*" (1 John 3:2).

To make assurance doubly sure that there will be nothing secret about His advent, Jesus Himself says: "For as the lightning cometh out of the east, and shineth even unto the west; so shall also the coming of the Son of man be. . . . And then shall appear the sign of the Son of man in heaven; and then shall all the tribes of the earth mourn, and *they shall see* the Son of man coming in the clouds of heaven with power and great glory" (Matthew 24:27-30).

2. *It will be audible to the human ear.* Says Paul: "The Lord himself shall descend from heaven with a *shout,* with the *voice* of the archangel, and with the *trump* of God" (1 Thessalonians 4:16).

Again: "We shall not all sleep, but we shall all be changed, in a moment, in the twinkling of an eye, *at the last trump"* (1 Corinthians 15:51, 52).

Says Jesus: "He shall send his angels with *a great sound of a trumpet"* (Matthew 24:31).

So His coming will certainly not be silent!

3. *It will be a sublime and majestic pageant.* Says Jesus: "For the Son of man shall come in the glory of his Father with his angels" (Matthew 16:27).

Again: "The Son of man shall come in his glory, and all the holy angels with him" (Matthew 25:31; see chapter 26:64).

As best he can in human language John seeks to describe what he saw in vision. "I saw heaven opened," he writes, "and behold a white horse; and he that sat upon him was called Faithful and True, and in righteousness he doth judge and make war. His eyes were as a flame of fire, and on his head were many crowns. . . . And he was clothed with a vesture dipped in blood: and his name is called The Word of God.

"And the armies which were in heaven followed him upon white horses, clothed in fine linen, white and clean. And out of his mouth goeth a sharp sword, that with it he should smite the nations. . . .

"And he hath on his vesture and on his thigh a name written, King of kings, and Lord of lords" (Revelation 19:11-16).

This does not mean that there will be literal horses riding down the skies. John's striking symbolism merely suggests the splendor of the pageantry that will accompany the Man of Galilee as He returns in royal majesty.

4. *It will resemble the scene at His ascension.* You will recall that, following His last farewell to His disciples, "while they beheld,

he was taken up; and a cloud received him out of their sight" (Acts 1:9).

Then, "while they looked stedfastly toward heaven as he went up, behold, two men stood by them in white apparel; which also said, Ye men of Galilee, why stand ye gazing up into heaven? this same Jesus, which is taken up from you into heaven, *shall so come in like manner as ye have seen him go into heaven*" (verses 10, 11).

They saw and heard Him go; so He will be seen and heard when He returns.

He was received into a cloud; and with the clouds of heaven will He come back.

But most important of all it will be "this same Jesus" who will appear, not somebody else. He will be glorified, yet unchanged. Time will not have aged Him, nor the passing centuries altered His personality. His disciples will recognize Him instantly and Thomas will exclaim once more, "My Lord and my God!" (John 20:28, RSV).

The King of kings and Lord of lords will be the same Jesus who healed the sick and opened the eyes of the blind in Galilee; the same Jesus who cleansed the lepers and made the lame to walk; the same Jesus who spoke gently to the woman taken in adultery, who wiped away the mourner's tears, and who took little children upon His lap and loved them. He will be the same Jesus who died on Calvary's cross, rested in Joseph's tomb, and rose from the dead on the glorious resurrection morning. Most touching and convincing of all will be the print of the nails in His hands (John 20:27; Habakkuk 3:4).

What will happen on that day of days? Many things.

First, there will be stupendous seismic upheavals. Having beheld the mighty spectacle in vision, John says, "The heaven departed as a scroll when it is rolled together; and every mountain and island were moved out of their places" (Revelation 6:14). "And there was a great earthquake, such as was not since men were upon the earth, so mighty an earthquake and so great. . . . And every island fled away, and the mountains were not found" (Revelation 16:18-20).

Second, the righteous dead will be raised to life. "The dead in

Christ shall rise first" (1 Thessalonians 4:16). "All that are in the graves shall hear his voice, and shall come forth" (John 5:28, 29).

Third, the righteous living will be translated—as Enoch was in the dawn of history. "Then we which are alive and remain shall be caught up together with them in the clouds" (1 Thessalonians 4:17).

Fourth, the resurrected dead and the translated living will have immortality bestowed upon them by God as a reward for their loyal and unswerving devotion to Him. "For this corruptible must put on incorruption, and this mortal must put on immortality" (1 Corinthians 15:53). See Romans 2:6, 7.

Fifth, the wicked—those who have persistently rejected all offers of divine mercy—will be destroyed (Revelation 19:11-21).

John describes this awesome scene in these graphic words:

"And the kings of the earth, and the great men, and the rich men, and the chief captains, and the mighty men, and every bondman, and every free man, hid themselves in the dens and in the rocks of the mountains; and said to the mountains and rocks, Fall on us, and hide us from the face of him that sitteth on the throne, and from the wrath of the Lamb: for the great day of his wrath is come; and who shall be able to stand?" (Revelation 6:15-17).

Sixth, the righteous will welcome their returning Lord with abounding happiness, saying, "Lo, this is our God; we have waited for him, and he will save us: this is the Lord; we have waited for him, we will be glad and rejoice in his salvation" (Isaiah 25:9).

Seventh, all the righteous, both resurrected and translated, will begin their journey to their heavenly home. For in that day Jesus will fulfill the promise that He made to His disciples long ago: "In my Father's house are many mansions: if it were not so, I would have told you. I go to prepare a place for you. And if I go and prepare a place for you, I will come again, and receive you unto myself; that where I am, there ye may be also" (John 14:2, 3).

What a wonderful day that will be!

And it is a day in your future. You may share its glories and joys if you will.

YOUR ETERNAL HOME

BEYOND the second coming of Christ there stretches an endless vista of delight. All who love Him will discover the deep and wonderful meaning of immortality, the sheer bliss of knowing that life will go on and on forever, without fear of sickness or death.

What will this life be like? Will it be worth living? How and where will it be spent?

Once more your Bible has the answers. Within its hallowed pages you will find a detailed picture of your eternal home.

And it will not be a little pink cloud on which you will sit through all eternity strumming a golden harp! What a caricature of God's glorious plan is this widely held belief! What a travesty of His infinite wisdom and love! Your future will be infinitely more beautiful and satisfying than you have ever imagined.

The first millennium will be spent in heaven, where the saints will live and reign with Christ "a thousand years" (Revelation 20:4). While there they will have access to the books of record and so satisfy themselves why some loved ones are not among the saved and why God deals as He does with the wicked. See 1 Corinthians 6:3.

Then they will return to this earth to witness the moving scenes recorded in the closing chapters of the book of Revelation.

"And I John saw the holy city, new Jerusalem, coming down

from God out of heaven, prepared as a bride adorned for her husband" (Revelation 21:2).

As the majestic city settles upon the earth, the wicked dead will come to life. Satan—who has been "bound" for a thousand years by the fact that he has had no one to tempt—will resume his nefarious plotting, persuading the hosts of the doomed to compass "the camp of the saints about, and the beloved city" (Revelation 20:9).

But they will not capture it. Instead they will meet God. They will see Him upon His "great white throne" and stand in awe as "the books" are opened and final judgment is pronounced. At last, in sight of all the redeemed, all the angels, and every creature in the universe, the story of sin will come to a dramatic close as fire flashes from heaven and Satan and his followers are consumed. See verses 9-15.

Then will come to pass the apostle Peter's prediction concerning "the day of the Lord." "The elements shall melt with fervent heat, the earth also and the works that are therein shall be burned up" (2 Peter 3:10). Every trace of evil will be so completely removed that it will "not be remembered, nor come into mind" (Isaiah 65:17).

Out of the ashes of the old world God will make the new—"new heavens and a new earth, wherein dwelleth righteousness" (2 Peter 3:13). John tells us that he saw in vision "a new heaven and a new earth: for the first heaven and the first earth were passed away" (Revelation 21:1).

This new earth will be the everlasting home of the redeemed, fulfilling the prophecy of Jesus that the meek "shall inherit the earth" (Matthew 5:5). See Psalm 37:11.

Here will be your home through all the ages to come. Consider some of the things your Bible says about it.

1. It will be a *real* home. Not some ethereal, vaporous cloud where disembodied spirits roam, but a real home for real people. The resurrected saints will be as tangible as their risen Lord. "They shall build houses, and inhabit them; and they shall plant vineyards, and eat the fruit of them" (Isaiah 65:21). Not that they will always be building houses and planting vineyards, but they will have creative

minds and use their God-given talents in innumerable worthwhile activities.

2. It will be a *beautiful* home. There will be no vast badlands, no dreary deserts, no great wastes of water. Instead the whole globe will resemble Eden in its primeval loveliness. "The wilderness, and the solitary place shall be glad for them; and the desert shall rejoice; and blossom as the rose. It shall blossom abundantly, and rejoice even with joy and singing: the glory of Lebanon shall be given unto it, the excellency of Carmel and Sharon, they shall see the glory of the Lord, and the excellency of our God" (Isaiah 35:1, 2).

More beautiful than Yosemite, more marvelous than Yellowstone, more majestic than the snowcapped Rockies will be this wonderland of God's redeemed. It will surpass the gorgeous island scenery of western Canada, the lovely lochs of Scotland, the mountain-ringed lakes of Switzerland, the cliff-girt fiords of Scandinavia. Vistas of unimagined beauty will stretch in every direction, while upon the ears of the inhabitants will fall delightful harmonies, wafted on gentle winds from the angelic choir around God's throne.

3. It will be a *peaceful* home. It will never know war or strife of any kind. No rival powers will struggle for supremacy. There will be but one nation, one language, one King. "Then will I turn to the people a pure language, that they may all call upon the name of the Lord, to serve him with one consent" (Zephaniah 3:9). Every root of bitterness will have been purged away, with every cause of controversy. The golden rule will never be forgotten, and purest love will motivate every word and deed.

You won't need to lock your door at night, for there will be no burglars! Your home will have "neither bars nor gates" (Ezekiel 38:11). There would be no purpose in them. There will be no reason to fear anybody, or anything, at any time.

Nor will there be any quarrelsome neighbors, or people nursing petty grievances and jealousies. So complete will have been the transforming power of the Holy Spirit that the principles of Heaven will be enshrined in every heart. By beholding Jesus, everyone will have become changed into His likeness. His character will be theirs.

Even the animals will be at peace, and the life of the weakest will never be in danger. "The wolf and the lamb shall feed together, the lion shall eat straw like the ox. . . . They shall not hurt or destroy in all my holy mountain, says the Lord" (Isaiah 65:25, RSV).

4. It will be a *happy* home. Everybody will be satisfied with all that God has so bountifully provided. No word of grumbling or discontent will be heard.

Nobody will ever have to apologize, for there will be nothing to be sorry about, no unkind words to recall, no wounds to bind up. "The remnant of Israel shall not do iniquity, nor speak lies, neither shall a deceitful tongue be found in their mouth: for they shall feed and lie down, and none shall make them afraid" (Zephaniah 3:13).

There will be no sin or sinners, nor will anyone have a single evil thought. And because there will be no sin, there will be no death. So there will be no more partings, no more saying goodbye.

Families once broken by death, but reunited at the resurrection, will revel in joyous fellowship forever and ever. "And God shall wipe away all tears from their eyes; and there shall be no more death, neither sorrow, nor crying, neither shall there be any more pain: for the former things are passed away" (Revelation 21:4).

5. It will be a *healthy* home. "The inhabitant shall not say, I am sick" (Isaiah 33:24). Consequently there will be no hospitals or doctors. All who ever suffered from sickness or disease in the past will be completely restored. "The eyes of the blind shall be opened, and the ears of the deaf shall be unstopped. Then shall the lame man leap as an hart, and the tongue of the dumb sing" (Isaiah 35:5, 6).

Famines will be unknown, and nobody will ever go hungry. There will be plenty of food for all. "In the midst of the street of it, and on either side of the river, was there the tree of life, which bare twelve manner of fruits, and yielded her fruit every month: and the leaves of the tree were for the healing of the nations" (Revelation 22:2).

6. It will be a *glorious* home. When John saw the New Jerusalem coming down from heaven, he said it looked like a dazzling jewel, "having the glory of God: and her light was like unto a stone most

precious, even like a jasper stone, clear as crystal" (Revelation 21:11).

This wonderful city, the capital of the new earth, has gates of pearl, streets of gold, and foundations of precious stones. The very things the redeemed denied themselves in this life for Christ's sake "and the gospel's" will in God's providence become commonplace for them in the life to come.

Summing up the glories of the eternal home, the Lord says through the prophet Isaiah:

"I will make thee an eternal excellency, a joy of many generations. . . . Violence shall no more be heard in thy land, wasting nor destruction within thy borders; but thou shalt call thy walls Salvation, and thy gates Praise.

"The sun shall be no more thy light by day: neither for brightness shall the moon give light unto thee: but the Lord shall be unto thee an everlasting light, and thy God thy glory. . . . Thy people also shall be all righteous: they shall inherit the land for ever, the branch of my planting, the work of my hands, that I may be glorified" (Isaiah 60:15-21).

7. It will be *God's* home. "The throne of God and of the Lamb shall be in it" (Revelation 22:3). Transcending every other joy of the redeemed will be the continual presence of Jesus. And nothing in all the glory land will afford such enduring happiness as this. Golden streets, pearly gates, beautiful homes, exquisite scenery, would indeed afford little lasting satisfaction without this priceless privilege.

"Oh, heaven without my Saviour
Would be no heaven to me:
Dim were the walls of jasper,
Rayless the crystal sea.

But He *will* be there, for "they shall see his face" (verse 4). Beloved of all His people, He will "lead them unto living fountains of waters," studying with them the mysteries of the universe and helping them to perceive ever more clearly the length and breadth and height and depth of the wisdom and love of God.

"And the government shall be upon his shoulder: and his name shall be called Wonderful, Counsellor, The mighty God, The everlasting Father, The Prince of Peace. Of the increase of his government and peace there shall be no end, upon the throne of David, and upon his kingdom, to order it, and to establish it with judgment and with justice from henceforth even for ever" (Isaiah 9:6, 7).

Such is the heavenly home God has planned for His redeemed, the home that is waiting for you. He wants you to be there and share eternal happiness with Him.

He has prepared all this for you and offers it to you "without money and without price." Earnestly, tenderly, He asks you to accept it. Listen:

"The Spirit and the bride say, Come. And let him that heareth say, Come. And let him that is athirst come. And whosoever will, let him take the water of life freely" (Revelation 22:17).

Come! Come! Come! He pleads. He couldn't be more eager, more insistent.

Do not postpone your acceptance of His offer. Do not put it off till a more "convenient season." You may leave it too long. Even tomorrow may be too late.

Time is running out. All the promised signs of history's approaching climax have come to pass or are even now being fulfilled before our eyes. "The end of all things is at hand." Consequently, to every heart, with greater insistence than ever, comes the urgent admonition, "Seek the Lord while he may be found, call upon him while he is near" (Isaiah 55:6, RSV).

He is near you now. By His Spirit He is speaking to you as you read these lines. This moment above all others is your opportunity to seek Him and call upon Him and tell Him that you accept His gracious offer and want to spend eternity with Him. Tell Him that you love Him. Thank Him for all He has done for you and all He is planning for you in the future.

As He said to Israel of old so He says to you now, "To day if ye will hear his voice, harden not your heart" (Psalm 95:7, 8). Don't resist His pleading. Don't try to find excuses for not doing what your conscience tells you is right.

If you know there is something between you and God, ask Him to help you remove it. If there is some unwise friendship you should break, some habit you should give up, some restitution you should make, do it now! Today, while you hear His voice, while your heart is still tender, give yourself to Him without reserve. Bow your head at this moment and say, "Jesus, my Lord, I come. I yield my all to Thee. I would be Thine forever."

Say this, and mean it, and all life will be different for you. Great happiness will flood your soul. Heaven will be yours here and hereafter.

And your Bible, your precious Bible, which tells you all these wonderful things, will be your guide and stay each passing day till Jesus comes to take you home.

Experience happiness no problem can take away!

When problems weigh you down, where do you turn? Millions of people have found the answer in a relationship with Jesus Christ.

Happiness Digest shows how you too can experience His joy and guidance, and offers help in the calm assurance that God is in ultimate control and very much interested in your life.